HANDBOOK OF
MODERN TOURISM

HANDBOOK OF

MODERN TOURISM

Edited by

Praveen Sethi

ANMOL PUBLICATIONS PVT. LTD.

NEW DELHI - 110 002 (INDIA)

ANMOL PUBLICATIONS PVT. LTD.
4374/4B, Ansari Road, Daryaganj
New Delhi - 110 002
Ph.: 23261597, 23278000
Visit us at: www.anmolpublications.com

Handbook of Modern Tourism

ISBN 81-261-0437-6

PRINTED IN INDIA

Published by J.L. Kumar for Anmol Publications Pvt. Ltd., New Delhi - 110 002 and Printed at Mehra Offset Press, Delhi.

Contents

Preface

Travel is an ancient phenomenon. From the very earliest historical period, travel has had a fascination for man. Man has travelled from the very earliest times. Much of travel in the beginning was largely unconscious and rather a simple affair. The cumbersome procedures as we witness in travel today were not to be found in olden days.

In modern tourism sex tourism enjoys the vital role. World sex tourism has further institutionalised the exploitation of women within patriarchal societies although its more overt forms do appear to be on the decline. However, the reasons for this probably relate more to the threat of AIDS to the visitor rather than widespread concern for the sex worker or fundamental changes in gender and economic relations. Indeed, modern mass tourism and its accompanying images only serve to promote unequal gender relations in which women are subordinate to male interests. Tourism will continue to be a mainstay of the region's economies.

However, while tourism prostitution may decline, the intrinsic inequality of host-guest relationships in modern tourism can only continue to perpetuate the current scenario of gender relations tourism is sex tourism.

Editor

1

Development of Modern Tourism

Travel is an ancient phenomenon. From the very earliest historical period, travel has had a fascination for man. Man has travelled from the very earliest times. Much of travel in the beginning was largely unconscious and rather a simple affair. The cumbersome procedures as we witness in travel today were not to be found in olden days. No travel formalities existed. Travel in the distant past was not a thing of pleasure as is the case now. The traveller of the past was a merchant, a pilgrim, a scholar in search of ancient texts, and even a curious wayfarer looking forward to new and exciting experiences. Trade and commerce was however the strongest force in the ancient past; it made people travel to distant lands in order to seek fortunes. Gradually, opening of the new trade routes gave a big boost to travel. Travellers from distant lands started moving about in large numbers and visited many places for the purpose of commerce. With the opening of the trade routes travel became easier and rather more regulated.

At the market places, travellers made contacts with each other resulting in increased flow of trade and commerce. Trade relations matured into cultural relations and better understanding of each other's way or life. As civilization developed, conscious travel in order to explore and see the world began. There are many early references to this effect. The invention of money by the Sumerians (Babylonia) and development of trade and commerce beginning about 4,000 B.C. perhaps marks the beginning of the modern era of travel. Sumerians first grasped the idea of money and used it in their various business and commercial dealings. Many traders could pay for transportation as well as accommodation either with money or by the exchange of goods. Shulgi, the ruler of ancient Babylonia, claimed to have protected roads and built resthouses at various places for respectable wayfarers. The forerunners of modern day accommodation, these resthouses were the ideal places for halt for the travellers of those days.

Homer's Odyssey records the wanderlust of the ancient Greeks. The Phoenicians were probably the first real travellers in the modern sense as they travelled from place to place as traders. Early travel in the Orient particularly in India and in China was also largely based on trade and commerce. Travel to orient, particularly to India was undertaken by travellers from all over the ancient world. This was done for a variety of reasons--the most important among them being trade and commerce. India and China enjoyed the reputation of being countries of fabulous wealth. It is on record that long before the Christian era, travellers visited India in search of fortune. This trend continued and became more marked in course of time with Europeans heading towards the Indian shores for the sole purpose of trade and commerce. Not only did India attract a series of invaders starting with Alexander of Macedonia, but also great travellers like Vascoda-Gama. Many foreigners, Arabs and Europeans alike came io India to establish trading posts. The great explorer, Christopher Columbus set out to find a new route to India and in the process discovered the new world. India throughout had a great fascination for foreign travellers. Mark Twain described it as a fabulous world of "Splendour and rags, the one country under the sun with an imperishable interest, the one land that all men desire to see". Trade and commerce remained a strong force for many travellers to undertake long journeys to distant lands. This was followed by an urge to explore new lands and to seek new knowledge in ancient and distant lands. There are many references of great explorers who spent many formidable years of their lives in search of knowledge.

Even if we go back just the few hundred years to the third century A.D., since the first exploration of Alexander the Great, or only about 700 years since Marco Polo and their amazing explorations crossing many lands, we get fascinating accounts of these great persons. These great explorers can be credited with the distinction of perhaps being the pioneers who subsequently paved the way for modern travel. When Alexander the Great during his journeys reached India; he found well-maintained roads covered with shady trees. Along one royal highway, 1,920 kilometres long and about 19 metres wide people travelled in chariots, palanquins, bullock carts, on horses, camels and elephants. Young Marco Polo left Venice in the year 1271 with his father and uncle. They travelled through Persia and Afghanistan to the "roof of the world", the then unknown Pamir Plateau. After crossing the wind swept Gobi desert, he reached Kublai Khan's palace and remained in China for over twenty years. On his way back home, he stopped in Sumatra, Java, India, and Ceylon, The first medieval traveller to reach the orient was probably Benjamin of Tudela, a Jewish scholar who left Saragossa in the year 1160 A.D. He wrote a detailed account of his thirteen-year journey through Europe, Persia and India, giving information on the Jewish communities, and the geography of the various places he visited. Yet another famous traveller who recorded interesting accounts or this travel experiences was in Batutah. Ibn Batutah wrote a detailed diary of his travel experiences. He was born at

Tangier in 1304 A.D. In 1325 A.D., he left his home, and passing through various countries in Africa and West Asia, crossed the Sindhu in 1333 A.D, The travels took him as far as Indonesia and China. Out of a total of more than 17000 miles he covered more than 14,000 miles in course of his travels through India, Maldives and Ceylon.

There are also accounts of some European travellers who visited India during the period described above. The Francisco Friar, John of Monte Corrino visited India on his way to and back from China during the last decade of the thirteenth century. Mention may also be made here of the famous Portuguese Chronicle--the commentaries of the Great Alfonso D'Albuquerque. Later on in the sixteenth and seventeenth centuries many more European monks, travellers, and adventurers visited India and many other places in search or knowledge.

The expeditions of these great travellers returned with new ideas and also with fabulously rich treasures from rich and highly advanced civilizations of Asia and other areas of the world. The actual number or individuals who participated in various explorations as travellers in search of knowledge however represented only a small proportion of effluent of the total population. Travel was considered to be hard and not a thing of pleasure. The transport and communication systems as we know now were non-existant. The land migrations were done by foot and on horseback, elephant, camel and river craft in Europe, Asia and Africa, and the very limited exploration by rafts and primitive vessels moved by tides, oar and sail.

Pleasure travel

The concept of pleasure travel as it existed in the west can be associated with the Roman empire. Romans probably were the first pleasure travellers. Travel received a great stimulus from the good communication system and security of the Roman empire. There existed a fine network of roads and new roads were built increasingly wherever the Romans went. Travel literature was published extensively giving routes, the names of the major roads, distances between places and time required in travelling to them. The Romans were able to travel over a hundred or more miles in a day using relays of horses. They journeyed primarily to see famous temples in the Mediterranean areas particularly the monuments and the famous pyramids of Egypt. The Romans also travelled during holiday occasions, particularly the famous Olympic Games.

"Spas" and seaside resorts which developed during this period may be associated with pleasure travel. Medicinal baths and seaside resorts which later were named as "Spas" were very popular with the Romans. The inland 'Spa' had its origin in a belief in the efficacy of its mineral waters for medicinal purposes, either by drinking the water or by immersing in it. The patients using the spas would require certain diversions, and gradually, the Spa resorts added facilities for pleasure and entertainment to their medical facilities. The visitors now not only enjoyed the medicinal baths but also various forms of entertainments. Theatrical productions, athletic competitions, festivals and other forms of entertainment and amusements were often provided at the sites where spas were located. The spas had become extremely popular with travellers. Subsequent development of spas after their original use for recreational purposes by the Romans played big role in the development of pleasure travel in many countries in Europe. Development of various seaside resorts is also linked with it. In the later half of the eighteenth century, people started realising the possible curative effects of sea water. Sea bathing also became very popular and many believed that bathing in sea water was more beneficial than inland spas. The seaside resorts began to appear as an alternative to the original inland spa. By the year 1865, there were major seaside resorts in Britain, France and few more countries of Central Europe. This development was a result of demand for vacation travel. However, the use of these resorts was still confined to those with considerable means. Nevertheless, both the spas and the seaside resorts paved the way for the modem pleasure travel all over the world where millions of people visited various seaside resorts each year.

The fall of the Roman empire in the fifth century was a great setback for pleasure travel in Europe. During the Dark Ages only the very adventurous and brave persons would travel. A trip at this period in history was considered dangerous. No one would associate travel with pleasure, Also with the decay of the Roman empire cam, a sharp decline in trade and commerce. In the absence of a prosperous community with the incentive to travel for pleasure, travelling ceased to exist for its own sake.

Religion as a motivator

Travel for religious purposes assumed a significant importance during the Middle Ages. The practice of travelling for religious reasons, going on a pilgrimage for example, became a well established custom in many parts of the world. By the end of the Middle Ages large number of pilgrims were travelling to the main shrines in Europe, and travel again assumed an interesting character. However, travel was still dominated by religious motivations. Very little actual pleasure travel was undertaken. The adoption and spread of Christianity subsequently led to numerous pilgrims making their way to the Holy land. So deep and strong was the hold of faith that the ritual of pilgrimage flourished over the centuries. Religion was a great unifying force.

Pilgrimages strengthened religious bonds. It provided the impetus for a 'stay-at-home' agrarian society to break out of its narrow geographical confines. It also exposed people to new manners and customs, different kinds of food and modes of dress. It encouraged exchange of ideas and also fostered trade. It served as a powerful means of forging unity and understanding between people from widely different regions. The powerful influences of a crusading religion that slowly penetrated a foreign land, such as Christianity in Europe and later in America, and Buddhism, Islam, and Hinduism in Asia took place to permit an assimilation and perpetuation of very distinctive languages, literature, music, art, architecture, philosophy and forms of government. Religion thus played and continues to play a crucial part in travel.

The grand tour

The Renaissance marked the next important stage in the history of travel. The reappearance of tourism in Europe follows the Italian Renaissance and the development of a full scale urban systems and network of roads. By the end of the fifteenth century Italy itself became the object of attention. At this time Italy was Europe's economic and cultural leader. It was however totally disunited politically. Wars were fought on Italian soil. These wars played an important part in the dissemination of the Renaissance and the subsequent development of the 'grand tour'. Although in decline materially, Italy was still the intellectual capital of Europe. For the aristocracy and intelligentsia of northwest Europe it represented both the classical heritage and all the latest ideas and inventions. A growing number of young noblemen were being sent abroad to complete their education in France and Italy. The development of the Grand tour followed a shift in the focus of culture and of economic and political power. The wealthy and educated, of states whose position of dominance in the world was comparatively new, visited countries that had passed their peak of prestige but were still venerated for historical and cultural reasons. Thus Romans visited Greece and the eastern Mediterranean; the English, from the sixteenth century onwards, visited Italy. The Grand tourist respected the learning, antiquities and social refinements of the old world.

The eighteenth century is conventionally considered the golden age of the Grand Tour, especially the thirty years between 1763 and 1793. With the new wealth of the English bourgeoisie the number of tourists had multiplied. The Grand Tour was no longer an aristocratic preserve. It had been invaded by the bourgeoisie. During this period a great many poets, authors and intellectuals visited Italy and other countries nearby with a view to broaden their knowledge and learn new arts and crafts. The Grand tourists paved the way for the popular tourism of the nineteenth and twentieth centuries.

The introduction of annual holiday in Europe was another important landmark which encouraged many people to undertake travel in large numbers during the eighteenth century. The eighteenth century became the great age of travel. The annual holiday was the forerunner to the paid holiday which later was responsible for an extraordinary growth of tourism. The term holiday derived from holy days was associated with religious observances. In the present day it is used generally in a secular sense meaning a respite from the routine of daily workday life and a time for leisure, recreation and amusement. A feature of ancient Rome, public holidays were among the most enjoyable events. The most enjoyable public holiday was the 'Saturnalia'-- the feast of Saturn celebrated in December, when all classes indulged in feasting and frolic. Also in Europe certain days commemorating religious festivals and saint's days became holy days on which there was cessation from work. In the year 1552 in England an act was passed during the reign of Edward VI "for the keeping of holidays and fasting days". This act still continues to be on the Statute Book, Subsequently, public and semiofficial offices in England frequently closed on certain saint's days. There were however, no general public holidays until the time of the Industrial Revolution. The concept of modern annual paid holiday is very largely an outcome of the Industrial Revolution.

The Middle Ages by and large did not constitute a favourable period for the pursuit and development of tourism. The process of the development of imagination however was continued by the innumerable events, for the most part connected with wars. Discoveries and exploring expeditions, pilgrimages, wandering scholars and mercenary soldiers were the principal sources for information about the outside world. Nobles accompanied by their retinues visited the pivotal centres of religious and secular power, the education of young noblemen at foreign princely courts became a fashion which spread still further with these noblemen's educational travel, which naturally included the element of pleasure as well. The travels of friends and the trips of students during those days to the different university towns enriched the popular imagination. The beginning of the 18th century saw the setting in of the practice of going to watering-places which owed its renewal to a more liberal conception of life after the Roman bathing cult had fallen into oblivion with the fall of the Roman empire. The increase in population and the resultant divisions of the social classes increased the interest of people in the activities and doings of others. Thus it was quite natural that the rising bourgeoisie took over the living habits of the nobility. The advent of Enlightenment in the 18th century and with it the introduction of a Dew attitude towards Nature gave rise to romanticism and fancifulness. These in their turn influenced and transformed the attitude towards the distant and the strange. Hitherto, in popular understanding "foreign" had always been associated with danger and suffering. It was this emotional content of the term "foreign" which now underwent a complete transformation. The scientists who had initiated a new awareness were followed by poets and painters who widened further the orbit of the world of imagination and thus aroused desires, wishes and needs. The 19th and 20th centuries, with the growth of communications, the printing technique and last but not least through the multifarious dramatic events concerning mankind, enlarged the definition and conception of the world and increased the desire to see it. The distant and the strange showed a seductive quality, Social development made it possible for ever larger classes to corroborate their conceptions and ideas with actual experiences.

Industrial revolution and development of travel

The concept of modern tourism came into being in the second half of the nineteenth century hand in hand with the development of the industrialized societies of Western Europe and North America. Development of industrialized societies of Western Europe and North America can therefore be considered as responsible for growth of modern tourism. Though an accurate analysis of the history of tourism can be traced no further back than half a century, the scattered figures published from 1855 onwards, together with official statements, observations by various travel writers, and the various travel guides and other literature on sale at the time, point to the direct relationship between the birth of these societies and the expansion of tourist movements. Development of industrialized societies was a direct result of industrial revolution in the west. In its wake the industrial revolution brought in tremendous changes in society. With the impetus of the industrial revolution little more than a century ago, the tempo of the accelerated change took a big jump. As has been mentioned earlier, travel before the industrial revolution was mainly a matter of seeking knowledge, engaging in commerce and trade and undertaking pilgrimage. There is a little evidence of the extent and volume of private travel in the medieval period.

The industrial revolution was responsible for the change in the economic and social systems. It threw up great factory towns, big and small. The working class was in the beginning burdened by long working hours and poor working and living conditions. For a great number of people there was little relief from routine of putting in long hours of work in difficult conditions in the factory setup of those days. Sudden concentration of population in towns and cities created unhealthy social conditions. As the industrial momentum gathered and the cities and their populations increased at an enormous rate, the need for escape became even more acute The prosperous and well-to-do who could afford proceeded to various resorts. Industrialization also brought in an increase of material wealth and certain improvements in transport and communications during the second half of nineteenth and early twentieth century. The factors like increasing need to find relief from workday routine and the city dweller's yearning for physical adventure and comforts and pleasure and development of resorts and spas for health and relaxation produced a fertile ground for the development of pleasure traffic on a big scale. Many resorts owe their present day popularity to their original discovery by wealthy minorities during the Roman empire. The nineteenth century saw the development of large-scale pleasure zones at some considerable distance from the large cities and metropolitan centres of Central Europe. The French Riviera with Nice, Cannes and Monte Carlo were some of these pleasure zones. By the end of the century the Riviera was unmistakably the most popular pleasure zone. Its development only became possible when escape to the south had become a major feature of tourism in Europe. Many health resorts were developed to cater to the increasing needs of wealthy people. Until the 1920s it remained a winter resort area. The summer heat was considered not only intolerable in itself but a danger to health. As late as in the 1920s Cannes was trying to compete itself to the English health resorts with a view to attract the rich and respectable English clientele. In the late nineteenth century the Italian Riviera also began to be popular with the English and French. By the early twentieth century rich Americans started to appear in considerable numbers on the Riviera scene. The appearance of Americans on the Riviera was something of a new development as they were late comers on the European tourist scene. One of the reasons could be the distance involved. Only the rich Americans could visit Europe at that time. It was however only after the First World War that Americans were to emerge as pioneers of a new tourism.

Rail transport

Introduction of Railways, in the nineteenth century was yet another crucial landmark in the travel history. Passengers were first carried by rail in 1830 in England. The newly completed railway track between Liverpool and Manchester in England featured special provisions for carrying passengers in addition to freight. However the birth of organised rail travel came in the year 1841. A Baptist preacher of. Derbyshire was on his way to a temperance meeting in Leicester when he was inspired with the idea of engaging a special train to carry the friends of temperance society from Leicester to

Loughborough and back to attend a quarterly delegate meeting. The man behind this was Thomas Cook. He broached his idea to his friends. A few weeks later 570 passengers made the journey by the Midland Counties Railway at a specially reduced fare This venture was followed by various excursions to beauty spots. In the year 1843, 3,000 school children were taken on a trip from Leicester to Derby. From 1848 to 1863 Cook conducted circular tours of Scotland, with 5,000 tourists a season.

The success of the Liverpool and Manchester railway, opened in the year 1830, encouraged many other countries in Europe to open railway lines. Railway tracks were laid in France, Austria and in Switzerland. Across the Atlantic the tracks were laid in America. This revolution in transport technology produced an immediate expansion in European tourism. In the year 1881, the railways carried over 600 million passengers over lines operated by one hundred odd companies. The railways were now keen to stimulate travel and to improve the system. There was also now an element of competition and the various railway companies tried to make travel as comfortable as possible. In the early 1870s first class railway travel was introduced by art American, G.M. Pullman, who developed the Pullman coaches with their luxury furnishing and dining facilities. Long distance travel could now. be undertaken in comfort and with pleasure. The Pullman cars manufactured in America were imported by some railway companies in England and other countries in Europe. The cars which were very comfortable for long journeys were first introduced in America. The longer distances in America necessitated the ensuring of greater comfort for passengers. By the year 1872 the Pullman Company had 700 cars working over 30,000 miles of railway under contract with over 150 different companies. The introduction of railways thus vastly increased the opportunities for escape from the rigours of city life as a result or urbanisation. The railways can be considered as one the most powerful motives for mass travel in nineteenth as well as twentieth centuries. The railways carried and continue to carry millions of passengers all over the world majority of which are from large urban centres.

Sea transport

The shipping like the railways made significant contribution to travel during the nineteenth century. While railways were responsible for inland travel especially in Europe, the steamship crossed the boundaries and made strides in intercontinental travel. The shipping technology made a number of innovations in the nineteenth century. In America a number of sailing ships were built which were considered to be superior to those built in England or elsewhere. The English felt a great need for improved communications across the Atlantic with America for the purpose of trade and commerce and passenger transportation. As a result of this there were great strides in the development of deep-sea shipping. The history of the Cunard Steamship Company in England demonstrates important features in the growth of North Atlantic Shipping. A subsidy in the form of the award of mail contract represented a recurring theme in the development of passenger transportation. With the passage of time toward the last quarter of the nineteenth century, emigrant traffic became an important factor in North Atlantic travel. America was considered at that time the 'new world' full of opportunities and fortunes for people in Europe. A great number of people from the continent started going to America in search of fortune. First Great Britain and later Germany along with other countries became the principal generators of emigrants to the 'new world'. Many travelled as tourists to see the new world. Opening of the

Suez Canal in 1869 brought about the possibility of a much shortened route between West and East and in turn stimulated the introduction of better steamship carriage to the far-east.

Use of the ships in the cruising fashion for the charter and operation of cruises on a limited scale dates from the mid-nineteenth century. One of the earliest cruises perhaps was that described by Mark Twain in his first book, The Innocents Abroad, published in 1869. Cruising however did not play a significant part in the world of shipping until the beginning of the twentieth century. The period just before the First World War can be considered the heyday of liner passenger service. It was an era of large and comfortable fast ships operated by relatively small number of companies in various countries. The glamour of the deep-sea travel was however reserved for the wealthy Europeans and Americans. In the luxury liners, a big space reserved for the not too wealthy was used by the emigrant traffic. In fact the biggest volume of transatlantic passenger trade was the emigrant traffic. In the first half of the twentieth century, the descendants of those migrants must have formed a large part of the transatlantic tourist movement. Transport by water makes a significant contribution to the development of travel on land and by air. Scheduled liner transport, formerly much used for inter-continental travel has presently almost vanished. The expansion of international tourism has however led to an increasing use of ferry boats by tourists on short sea crossing. Tourist sea transport on the whole does not seem to have a promising future. Long distance sea travel may continue to contract, although there will always be a limited demand for sea cruising, since this leisure and attractive mode of travel has great appeal. In the recent past one of the most important developments in sea traffic has in fact been that of holiday sea cruises, especially in the Mediterranean and Caribbean and also in South-east Asia. By the turn of the twentieth century all the main characteristics of modern tourism were evident in embryo. Changes in mental attitudes towards pleasure seeking, the recognised value of travel for education, an increase in material wealth and improvements in transport, social prestige, the growing need to find relief from working routine--all these factors produced a fertile ground for the development of excursion traffic on a large-scale.

Upto the first quarter of the twentieth century tourism was essentially a luxury commodity within the reach of only a Privileged few having both plenty of free time and considerable purchasing power. Admittedly, such tourism had a charm all its own associated as it was with elegant luxurious hotels, such long distance trains as the 'Orient Express' and the blue riband transatlantic liners like the `Queen Mary'. Although all the main characteristics of modem tourism were evident by this time, only the privileged few managed to indulge in this luxury. It is also true that certain associations, which recruited members from among the embryonic middle and working classes, organised excursions, holiday camps, family rest and holiday homes, etc., but only very few people benefited from such activities at that time.

Paid holidays and mass tourism

The concept of mass tourism emerged along with the introduction of holiday with pay. It was in the last quarter of the nineteenth century that increasing attention was paid to the desirability of holiday with pay and at least of cheap holidays for working class people. This group had still largely failed to benefit from the new opportunities offered by travel by rail. During this period a few factories gave paid holidays to their workers in some countries in the West. The introduction of annual paid holiday is very largely of English origin and this had important repercussions on development of mass tourism. The annual paid holiday was established during the inter-War Years as a reality for a considerable part of the working population. By the year 1939, in U.K., some eleven million people were covered by the Holidays with Pay Act. Introduction of paid holiday had led to great mobility of the population, created new industries, resulted in the creation and growth of many towns of distinctive function and broadened the horizons of millions of people. In fact the introduction or paid holidays can truly be associated with development of modern mass tourism. In the year 1936, modern tourism really got under way when, at the instigation of its trade union representatives the International Labour Organisation (ILO) adopted the first convention that was to support serious movements to promote paid holidays and, in turn, tourism. That convention on paid holidays was an innovation well ahead of time, when only fourteen countries, mostly European, had enacted general legislation on paid holidays. Soon afterwards tourism experienced an extraordinary growth. Paid holidays are now established all over the world, and in most countries a minimum duration of one to three weeks is specified either by law or by collective agreements between the employer and the workers.

The right to paid holidays has universal recognition now. The trend is to grant longer holiday periods. The employers have realized that the paid holidays have not affected industrial production. The legal minimum in many countries at present is three weeks. Some countries have even gone beyond this and grant four weeks of paid holiday. Today it is recognised that in Western Europe the fifth week, even from the standpoint of output, may also be regarded as a productive investment. Sweden has recently enacted legislation introducing this additional week of paid holidays. Worldwide, more than 500 million wage-earners are entitled to paid holidays. Out of this number, roughly half are in Europe, little less than 30 per cent in the Americas, and the rest in Asia and the Pacific. Presently the wain potential for tourism markets is made up of wage-earners and their families. As a result of economic and social changes due to further industrialization the world over and the rationalization of the tertiary sector, the number of wage earners in the world is bound to grow at a much faster rate than before. This in turn will give wage-earners increasingly longer holidays. The concept of paid holidays which originated with the advent of industrialization in the West has given modern tourism a tremendous boost.

The First World War was responsible for temporary halt to tourist movements. There was considerable decline in tourist travel not only within Europe but also all over the world. However, soon after the war tourist travel quickly reached pre-War peak levels, and within three or four years, greatly exceeded them. The War also brought about many changes which were destined to influence the volume of tourism. The War was, for example responsible for breaking down international barriers and resulted in the fostering of an ideal, optimistic, peaceful internationalism-just the climate in which tourism was most likely to flourish. The Second World War marked a watershed. Before it, in the twenties and thirties, organised tourism was chiefly a matter of trains, boats or coaches. In the post-1945 era, such travel was increasingly by aeroplane, thus allowing the pleasure periphery to expand into new mass destinations like Spain, Greece, Bermuda, Cuba, Hawaii, etc. Each decade has seen a massive increase in the importance of aircraft in this process until today, when we are on the verge of truly global tourism.

Post-War era also saw a rise in the standard of living of the working and the middle classes in America and in certain European countries. Soon after the War the tourists began to appear in countries where tourism had been practically unknown a few years earlier. The early traveller had advanced from the scholar and the pilgrim of the past to the pleasure seeker of today. The major tourist countries enjoyed an unprecedented boom in the late twenties. In the year 1929 there were nearly one and a half million visitors to Switzerland, over one million visitors to Italy and about two million to Austria. Great Britain also received a considerable number of visitors.

Development of road and air transport specially the former is the major factor which was largely responsible for and continues to be so for the great spurt in modern tourism. Transport is the necessary precondition of travel. Travel is a matter or being somewhere else and to be elsewhere certainly implies use of transport. For the greater part of contemporary tourism, transport means airlines and the private cars. As a broad generalization it can be said that holidaymakers travelling away from home to a foreign country spend the major portion of their total holiday money n transport and travel. Travel costs form as much as about 40 per cent of the total holiday expenditure. This fact has been brought about by a number of studies. Tourist traffic as we know it today could not have developed without relatively inexpensive and efficient modes of transportation.

The War itself had direct repercussions on motor and air transport. It necessitated innovations in the fields of motor and air transport for the purpose of using them in the war. Subsequently, however, after the war was over these were utilized by people for travel and transport. Many roads andairports which were built for use during the war later helped the movement of great many people for the purpose of travel.

Road transport

Upto the beginning of the twentieth century, tourists travelled almost exclusively by rail and steamship. The invention of the new transport medium, travel by a private car and coach received its first great impetus in the ten years which preceded World War I. The entire shape of tourist industry was therefore transformed by the invention of this new transport medium. The growth of the private car may be identified as a major cause of the decline of the railways. In both USA and the United Kingdom, passenger rail traffic almost halved in the first ten years or so after the first World War. The motor car gradually came to be the alternative means of transport for both short and medium range journeys. Subsequently with the growth of a fine network of fast and superfast national and international highway systems, long journeys were also performed by motor car and motor coach.

The motor car has revolutionalised holiday habits. Although the first motor car had come into operation by the end of the 19th century, upto the time of the First World War their numbers were small. After the Second World War their numbers jumped manifold. It became increasingly important in the pursuit of leisure and tourism. The actual number of holiday makers travelling by road increased tremendously as more and more people took holidays away from home. The provision of the good motor roads and road services were important factors in the development of both domestic and international tourism. With the tremendous increase in the road traffic, improved roads and dual carriage ways were introduced after 1930. In 1930s the Germans pioneered the development of motorways with their autobahnen. Improvements in road transport facilities stimulated tourism in many European countries such as France, Spain and Germany. Mention may be made of great progress made in USA in building highways, expressways and superhighways. In many other countries of the world newer and faster roads were built which made, movement of traffic by road faster and comfortable.

Mobility can perhaps be considered as one of the major causes of the development of the motor transport. The motor car had provided the actual mobility so that people are no longer anchored to a particular holiday centre as they tended to be when they mostly travelled by train. Speed is yet another important factor which economises on time and therefore makes it possible for people with limited amount of time to travel to distant places. People with even one week of holiday considered it sufficient to travel. The gradual spread of the network of roads opened up many new areas and made many places hitherto not very accessible easy to get to. The railways on the other hand tended rather to concentrate and restrict movement to particular channels. Road transport made striking advances in subsequent years. Soon after 1950, when the difficulties and restrictions of the immediate postwar years had begun to straighten themselves out, there were rapid developments in transport; whereas the car ownership multiplied, the motor coach appeared in increasing numbers and the coach tour became popular. Greater use of motor car and coach is being made at present for the purpose of tourism. A great majority of people travel by the above modes in Europe. Increasing use of this mode of transport is being made in USA and Canada as also in other major tourist countries. The construction of motorways in many countries has made speedy travel over long distances by car and the coach easy and have made many remote places more accessible. The development of 'motorail', the carrying of cars and coaches over extended distances by train is making it passible for holiday makers to use their motor cars in holiday areas.

Though economic conditions in the recent years as a result of increasing fuel costs and the energy crisis, have not favoured travel by private motor car, road transport remains the mode most used by international visitors. The world economic crisis which brought about cutbacks in the use of transport facilities, did not however seriously impair the growth of road transport. In many countries of Europe increasing emphasis is being given to the construction of new roads. Several countries are continuing to build motorways and highways. In Czechoslovakia, 1,700 kilometres of motorways are due to be built by the year 1992. In Bulgaria work continues on the 1,100 kilometre long Sofia-Varna motorway. Poland was planning to bring its motorway network upto 4000 kilometres by 1991. France under the eighth plan is planning heavy investments for motorways in the Paris region during the next four years. In Italy the state is spending large amounts to strengthen existing motorways and also to build new ones. Elsewhere in many countries of the world new road systems are being built to cater to the increasing volume of road transport including tourist transport.

There are large scale highway programmes in the pipeline at present in different regions of the world. When completed, these will cater to the ever increasing demands of the tourists. Mention may be made of the following highway programmes.

(i) The Trans-Afr can Highway: This highway, 6,596 kilometres long will cross Kenya, Uganda, Zaire, the Central African Empire, Cameroon and Nigeria. Several feeder roads are also planned particularly in Gabon, Democratic Republic of Congo and Tanzania.

(ii) The Trans-West African Highway: This road will link

Dakar and Ndjamena running through Senegal, Mali, Upper Volta, Nigeria, Cameroon and Chad for a distance of 4,771 kilometres.

(iii) The Trans-East African Highway: The Trans-East African Highway will link Cairo in Egypt with Gaborone in Botswana, passing through Sudan, Ethiopia, Kenya, the United Republic of Tanzania and Zambia. The Trans-East African Highway will be little over 9000 kilometres long. There will be 20,000 kilometres of feeder roads.

(iv) The Trans Europe North-South Motorway: The Trans-Europe North-South Motorway is at the project stage. It will be a multi-lane motorway linking the Baltic Coast of Poland with the frontier of Iran and Syria. Branches will be extended to Italy, Yugoslavia and Greece. In addition to countries mentioned above, the project will also involve Austria, Bulgaria, Hungary, Romania and Turkey. Technical and financial assistance will be provided by United Nations Development Programme with the Economic Commission for Europe as executing agency.

(v) The Pan-American Highway: This highway, 23,000 kilometre's long, is now being built and will link Fairbanks in Alaska in the United States of America with Tierra del Fuege in Southern Chile.

(vi) The Asian Highway: The Asian Highway project, calling for a network of about 66,000 kilometres covering 15 countries, came into being as a result of the decision of the United Nations Economic and Social Commission for Asia and the Pacific (ESCAP) and the cooperation of Afghanistan, Bangladesh, Burma, Cambodia, India, Indonesia, Iran, Laos, Malaysia, Pakistan, the Republic of Viet-Nam, Singapore, Sri Lanka and Thailand. The target was to provide at least one through route from east to west connecting as many countries as possible with suitable links to other countries not falling along the routes. Through the efforts of the countries concerned, the target is being achieved, and it is now possible to travel throughout the whole countries concerned, with the exception of Burma. Greater emphasis is being placed on filling in the remaining gaps, upgrading substandard sections and improving the existing services over the Asian Highway network. Work on Eastern missing link on the Indian section of the Asian Highway routes connecting Iran and Singapore is nearing completion near Galgalia.

Air transport

The role of the air transport in the development of the international tourism is becoming increasingly important. Air transport has certainly been a key factor in the growth of international tourism, especially in respect of long distance and intercontinental travel. Although commercial travel took place before Second World War, air transport for the masses has essentially been a postwar phenomenon. The main period of growth was during the 1960s when overseas holiday became a symptomatic benefit of a society experiencing rising living standards.

In Europe, the years immediately after World War I witnessed the attempts to create commercial airlines. The war itself bad a direct bearing on the development of air transport in a similar way as had with motor transport. Certain commercial civil air services were inaugurated and developed in this period. Besides Europe, air transport however was developed in many other countries including in India during this period. Although international air travel was born at the end of World War I and slowly grew between the two wars, it was only at the end of World War II that it made a tremendous breakthrough. It emerged into a practical mode of transport over long distances only in the late 'forties when the aircraft industry in America applied the technical and manufacturing resources it had developed during the war.

The removal of wartime restrictions on international travel and the tremendous increase in speed, safety and comfort provided by the new aircrafts released the long pent-up wanderlust of the people the world over. In the year 1952 the two-class travel was introduced which was made possible by the larger capacity of the new aircrafts. The larger capacity of the new aircrafts resulted in lowering air fares. The steady fall in the real cost of flying has been chiefly productive in traffic across the Atlantic and within the USA, stimulated by the introduction of tourist fares in the year 1952. This period also saw the first postwar attempt to build a "package holiday" around air transport, the model for most of today's global tourism. The growing willingness of tourists to take to air travel during this period was responsible for the annual flood of North Americans across the Atlantic to Europe. This trend continues even today. Within Europe, there has been the spectacular explosion of the Mediterranean resorts.

The advent of the jet travel in 1958 was the most dramatic event which introduced an entirely new dimension of speed, comfort and efficiency to air transport and brought mass travel to its present level. Air travel from the year 1960 as a result of introduction of jets grew tremendously. The most decisive development during this period wag however the development of inclusive tours in which travellers are carried on charter flights at rates substantially below those of normal scheduled services. It only slowed down after 1973 as a result of the worldwide oil crises which resulted in widespread recession and galloping inflation. In spite of this, world air travel today is almost six times what it was in 1960.

The fact that in spite of rising fuel costs and inflation the industry was able to control successfully fare levels was due to economies of scale provided by the very big aircraft of today. The improved fuel efficiency of later models of jet engines and the ingenuity and marketing expertise of the airlines, travel agencies and tour operators are other factors. The latter is illustrated by the North Atlantic route--the golden route of tourist traffic, which saw the successive introduction of excursion fares in 1948, coach fares in 1952, family fares in 1955, economy class fares in 1958, affinity group fares in 1963, group inclusive tour fares in 1967, youth fares in 1972 and apex fares in 1975. As a result of these innovations in air travel, fares per seat mile declined in real terms, between 1963 and 1975.

Great advances have been made in air travel in the recent years, more particularly for overseas holiday making. Tourism in turn has had a significant impact on the aircraft industry and on the carriers. Factors like comfort, speed, and safety influence the tourists' choice of mode of transport. New wide-bodied jets such as Boeing 747, the Mc-Donnell-Douglas DC 10, the Air Bus A 300 and Lockheed Tristar L-1011 are all part of response to the requirements of the ever growing travel market. The technical brilliance of the supersonic aircraft like the Concorde and of the Tupolev 144 are the remarkable landmarks in the aviation history. The industry has a bright future in spite of the rising fuel costs and the inflation engulfing the entire world. As far as the long range international travel in the 'eighties is concerned, the large majority of the aircraft used will continue to be of the current wide-bodied generation. In order to achieve farther economy in running the aircraft to offset the increase in aviation fuel costs, the subsequent decade of the nineties may make substantial further advance in the form of still larger aircraft such as the double-deck 800-seater derivative of the Boeing 747. The skytrain concept which is the latest introduction in the aviation world has brought about a considerable reduction in Atlantic fares. Conceived by Fred Laker, the skytrain type of fares introduced during recent years on the Atlantic route and now proposed for the Pacific may be followed by many other routes in the eighties. This new application of the concept to long-distance international travel is likely to stimulate the growth of tourist traffic in the coming years. With a view to meet the competition of the skytrain fare, the standby and budget fares have recently been introduced by the schedule airlines on the Atlantic route. The future of the air transport is bright. Airlines will continue to play a vital role in the growth of international tourism for a long time to come.

Transport thus is a single key factor which has largely been responsible for the spurt in tourism especially the modern tourism. Tourist traffic as we know it today could not have developed without the development of various modes of transport from time to time. Early travel in the nineteenth century was dominated by the railway and the steamship. Upto the beginning of the twentieth century tourists travelled almost exclusively by rail internally and by steamship overseas. World War I witnessed the development of motor and air transport and in the years which preceded the world war private car and coach travel made much progress. However, the years between the two world wars, mainly witnessed the significant development of the private motor car and also of the bus and coach travel. Post-World War II period saw the great development of civil aviation. It was the aeroplane--the most glamorous of all modes of transport which came into its own in the 'fifties and gave international tourism a real shot in the arm. International tourism as we know it today has been largely shaped by air travel.

An interesting development lately is taking place in the field of transportation. The energy crisis since 1974 which resulted in widespread recession and galloping inflation have rather adversely affected travel by air and the private motor car--it is becoming increasingly expensive to travel by air and by the private car and coach.

The fuel consumption per passenger kilometre is two to four times more in autombiles and ten times more in aeroplanes as compared to trains. This factor of increase in oil prices is responsible for the remarkable achievement in recent years in the growth of faster and cheaper rail transport. Besides the cost factor, the railways, also have an advantage over the airlines in that the terminal stations are often located in the heart of the cities and the train timings are generally more convenient. To add to this the growing congestion on highways and airports has given a further impetus to the trend.

All the above factors coupled with advanced technology and increasing needs for mobility are leading to a renaissance of the rail transport. The railways which were pioneers in the growth and development of early mass travel and were relegated to a secondary place with the introduction of motor and air transport once again are assuming an important role. In almost all the European countries, the United States of America, Asia and elsewhere revolutionary ideas for achieving higher speeds and comfort are being conceived and put into practice.

The trend however was discernible before the world was affected by the energy crisis. It was in Europe when the designs for faster and comfortable trains were first formulated. In the year 1960 British Railways electrified its London-Manchester line, a very busy line, to achieve the speed of 160 kilometres per hour. The new high speed trains on this line reduced their running time by full one hour from the former three-hour forty minutes trip.

Passenger traffic almost doubled in five years. In West Germany, a new inter-city system introduced in 1971 provided rapid train service at two-hour intervals between every major city in the country and brought over 30 per cent more passengers in the first twelve months. Passengers were provided with extra conveniences like telephones, secretariat services, latest stock quotations and 'ala carte' dining-car service round the clock. Similarly in France, the 160 kilometres per hour turbine train service, which began in 1970 between Paris and Caen in northern France cut travel time by almost one-fifth. Passenger loads went up 25 per cent in the first year. High speed train services elsewhere in Europe connect Paris and Lyons in France, Rome and Milan in Italy and Moscow and Leningrad in U.S.S.R.

In the United States of America, the combination of rail-cruise and railbus offered by AMTRAK resulted in 1974 in a rise of 11.2 per cent over 1973 in the number of passenger kilometres performed.

Long distance trains running on the AMTRAK system between New York and San Francisco have been lately modernised. The AMTRAK is adding, new double-decked Pullman coaches gradually on the system with a view to encourage more rail travel. High speed train services now connect highly populated Washington-Baltimore Philadelphia-New-York-Boston 'Corridor' in the United States.

In Asia, it was Japan which took the epoch-making decision to use the latest technology and convert the rail line between Tokyo and Osaka, covering a distance of 515 kilometres into a high speed track. This ambitious project was completed in the year 1964. The super fast train known as Hikari Express--`bullet train,' travels on the new Tokaido line at a crashing speed of 210 kilometres per hour cutting the journey time to less than three hours againt six and a half hours taken earlier. Encouraged by the success of its bold venture, it went further and built the new Sanyo line, 565 kilometres in length on which trains travel even faster at a maximum speed of 260 kilometres per hour. Elsewhere in Asia, new and faster rail tracks are being introduced The number of passengers carried by rail have been increasing in Malaysia, Philippines and Thailand.

In India railways have made great strides in technology resulting in increased speed, comfort and carrying capacity Efforts were initiated as early as in the year 1964 to increase the speed of some trains to 120 kilometres per hour. The tests enabled the railway authorities to introduce the first high speed train, 'Rajdhani Express', between New Delhi and Calcutta. It was originally meant to run at a cruising speed of 120 kilometres per hour to cover a distance 1441 kilometres in 17 hours and 30 minutes.

A fully air-conditioned comfortable train now runs at 130 kilometres per hour reducing the running time to 16 hours and 20 minutes. The special coaches for the train have been manufactured in India. In the year 1972, another such train was introduced between New Delhi and Bombay at a speed of 120 kilometres per hour to cover a distance of 1384 kilometres in 16 hours and 50 minutes. Trials have already been successfully conducted over small sections on both these routes to run the trains at 160 kilometres per hour.

Taking advantage of improvements in track for the 'Rajdhani Express' trains, a number of other important trains on trunk routes were designed as super fast trains and the speeds were increased up to 110 kilometres per hour. A number of new high speed trains have been introduced linking large metropolitan cities with important tourist centres.

More and more railway systems in different parts of the world are experimenting with newer concepts. Research is going on to run the trains at even faster speeds. By 1981, it was estimated that a train traveller between Paris and Lyon in France will be able to cover the 460 kilometres distance in less than two hours, almost half the time required today. The passengers will then ride at 300 kilometres per hour in a sleek turbine powered train that, despite its 5,000 horsepower engines will be, smoother and more silent than an aeroplane.

In September 1981 a new high speed train owned by the state run S.N.C.F. Railroad Company shattered the 26 year old world record for rail speed by clocking 380 kph (236mph.). The record breaking time was achieved near the Central French City of Tonnerre during a test-run of the French manufactured T.G.V train. It broke the previous record of 331 kph (205 mph) that was set in 1955. The T.G.V train is scheduled to begin commercial operation in September 1981 between Paris and Lyon. Its commercial speed is expected to be 260 kph (161 mph) covering the 560-kilometre (287-mile) distance between Paris and Lyon in one hour and 48 minutes. The fastest train on earth capable of 236 mph., T.G.V, which stands for train a grande Vitesse (of great speed) was launched during the end of September, 1981. In the comfortable, sound proofed cars, the only noises were the quiet hiss of air conditioning, the strains of Chopin--and the popping of Champagne corks.

Also in the 1980s, a traveller between London and Glasgow was able to cover the distance of 644 kilometres. in three hours in an advanced Passenger Train (APT). Some experts even talk of potential speeds of 480 to 500 kilometres per hour on rails. The day is not very far off when trains will cruise at such speeds. The new technology aims at dispensing with conventional rails. It aims at providing an, air-cushion to replace the conventional run on a track. The projected aero-trains will not only be fast but also relatively sleek looking, noise free, low on pollution, and above all cause no wear and tear on the track because they never touch it. In Japan and France many such experiments have already been performed successfully.

2

Tourism Prostitution

Sex tourism is one of the most emotive and sensationalised issues in the study of tourism. Although it is prevalent in Western capitalist nations, sex tourism has generally come to be associated with 'Western', usually male, visits to the Third World. Otherwise known as tourism prostitution, sex tourism can be defined as tourism for which the main purpose or motivation is to consummate commercial sexual relations. Sex tourism has become substantial fare for Western media over the past decade, a factor which has fed into often sensationalist reports of tourism prostitution in Thailand or the Philippines. However, much of the recent attention given by commercial media to sex tourism has not arisen because of any new-found concern for the disempowering nature of tourism prostitution, rather it has emerged because of the spread of AIDS. Therefore, current concern with sex tourism does not reflect a discovery of relationship between gender issues and tourism development, but is instead often regarded as a health concern.

Sex tourism is a major component of International travel to South-east Asia and has been given both overt and covert encouragement by government as a source of foreign exchange. For example, the Philippine Women's Research Collective reported that sex tourism is the third largest source of foreign exchange for the Philippines,

Although exact figures are impossible to obtain, one estimate Suggests that 70-80 per cent of male tourists travelling from Japan, the United States, Australia, and Western Europe to Asia do so solely for purposes of sexual entertainment. While Gay's estimate is almost certainly on the high side, especially given contemporary concerns over AIDS, it is likely that 'sexual entertainment is a major motivating factor for many male travellers to the region.

The study of sex tourism is difficult because of a number of factors:

(a) the seeming blindness of many tourism researchers to actually acknowledge that a link exists between sex and the tourism industry, particularly in respect of sex as a motivating factor for travel and the sexual relationships between hosts and guests;
(b) the extreme difficulties to be had in conducting research on tourism prostitution, which is typically an illegal informal activity, often with substantial crime connections, and which may place both researcher and subject at risk from brothel owners, criminal gangs and syndicates, and police and politicians who wish to keep the subject hidden and away from public examination;
(c) the lack of common methodological and philosophical frameworks with which to explain the complex web of gender, productive, reproductive and social relations which surround sex tourism.

With few exceptions, there is an apparent blind spot or natural reticence among academics to acknowledge the relationship between tourism, and sex. Nevertheless, if an effective analysis of the proposition that tourism is as true of metropolitan tourist resorts of the first world as it is of the third world, then such studies are necessary. For example, despite claims by Mathieson and Wall that there is little evidence to Confirm or deny a positive link between prostitution and tourism there has been a long history of this relationship. Just as Miami has become synonymous with vice, the combination of sun, sea, sand and sex has become associated with tourism resorts in general. Tourist promotion often focuses on the more licentious attributes of the tourist and high lights the erotic dimensions of a tourist destination:

Tourism promotion in magazines and newspapers promises would-be vacationers more than sun, sea, and sand; they are also offered the fourth 's'— sex. Resorts are advertized tinder the labels of 'hedonism', 'ecstacism', and 'edenism'... One of the most successful advertizing campaigns actually failed to mention the location of the resort: 'the selling of the holiday experience itself and not the destination was the important factor. Most observers who have examined the motivations of tourists have overlooked the very explicit messages purveyed in tourist advertisements. Despite the self-confessed selling of hedonism by the tourist industry, it is interesting to note that several studies of tourist brochures and images have failed to identify the pervasive use of erotic images in promoting travel destinations. Furthermore, the 'red light' districts of many cities are tourist attractions which draw the sensation seeking tourist as participant or observer.

There is a substantial lack of systematic research on sex tourism. This is because of the often informal and illegal nature of tourism prostitution, and the general unwillingness of police, government authorities, and politicians to acknowledge its existence. Given the circumstances surrounding sex tourism it is therefore extremely difficult to measure the scale of sex tourism at any given location and obtain interviews with prostitutes and other sex industry workers and their customers.

Furthermore, Burley and Symanski suggest that widespread disdain for prostitutes inhibits researchers and hinders the reliability of accounts.

The analysis of sex toursim is also complicated by the several forms which tourism prostitution takes:

(a) casual prostitutes, who move in and out of the pursuit according to financial need. This may be regarded as incompletely commercialised and the nature of the relationship between partners is ambiguous;

(b) Prostitutes who operate through in termediaries and who visit tourists in their accommodation;

(c) sex workers who operate out of clubs and brothels, which are often regarded by authorities as a mechanism for the containment of prostitution;

(d) bonded prostitutes working in, brothels who have often been sold in order to pay debts or reduce loans. Bondedprostitution is a form of slavery in which the body of the prostitute is treated solely as a commodity to be bought and sold without the prostitute's consent.

In addition, it should be noted that prostitution is often patially, economically and socially differentiated between locals and tourists, a point that is often forgotten by many researchers who tend to blame all prostitution on tourism.

A major problem in studying sex tourism, as with any analysis of gender issues, are the considerable divergences in approaches towards feminist and gender studies. Most theoretical developments in the study of women and gender have emerged from the studies of women in the First World, not from Third World studies. Indeed, Barrett has described that a feminist theoretical framework remains fragmentary and contradictory.

Nevertheless, research into the nature of sexual politics and the interrelated structures of gender relations may shed some insights on sex tourism.

Sexual politics examines the links between sexuality and power. Gender and sexuality are socially constructed at both the personal level of individual consciousness and interpersonal relationships and the social structural level of social institutions. The control of sexuality through, for example, such mechanisms as formalised tourism prostitution, is a key component of domination. Sex tourism serves, to establish certain erotic images of Asian women in Western society which are then perpetuated within the social institutional structures of the destination. For example, Davidson reported a Frankfurt advertisement which stated, Asian women are without desire for emancipation, but full of warm sensuality and the softness of velvet'. More recently, Southeast Asian airlines such as Thai Airlines, Singapore Airlines and Cathay Pacific have portrayed 'submissive' Asian women in their promotional material, with Singapore Airlines running a campaign of 'Singapore Girl you're a great way to fly'. The control of sexuality harnesses erotic power for the needs of larger, hierarchical systems by controlling the body and hence the population. Therefore, there is a need to examine the processes by which power as domination occurs on the social structural level namely, the institutional structures of racism, sexism, and social class privilege and annexes the basic power of the erotic on the personal level.

Connell identified three interrelated structures of gender relations: first, the division of labour; second, power, particularly as connected to masculinity; and third, 'cathexis' 'the construction of emotionally charged social relations with objects in the real world'. The three structures contribute to the Institutionalisation of a 'gender order' which described the historically constructed pattern of power relations between men and women at the societal level. From this perspective, which relies heavily on notions of structuration, gender relations are stable to the extent that groups constituted in the network of gender relations have interests in the conditions for cyclical rather than divergent practice.

Gendered perspectives on sex tourism which place significant emphasis on the exercise of power in gender relations will have substantially different insights on the conditions which allow sex tourism to prosper. For example, the economic justification, provided for sex tourism in, Fiji in the early 1970s by Naibavu and Schutz argued that prostitution as a fully localised industry provided income for unskilled female workers for most of whom no other employment would be available. It required no foreign capital investment, but attracted significant foreign exchange with minimal leakage. By contrast, a gendered perspective views the acceptance of the inevitability of prostitution as being vested in the assumption that access to sexual relations is a male right, and that viewing prostitution as woman's choice reduces all women to the lowest and most contemptible status within male-dominated society.

Prostitution is both an indication of an unjust social order and an institution that economically exploits women. But when economic power is defined as the causal variable, the sex dimensions of power usually remain unidentified and unchallenged.

Any oversimplified utilitarian justification for prostitution may obscure the gender and class interests associated with tourism' prostitution, According to Thanh-Dam, prostitution is differentiated in response to the processes of 'capitalist development and conditioning labour relations, demand and supply'. In contrast, feminist researchers such as Hawkesworth and Rogers argue that prostitution is a direct result of the patriarchal structure of society. The reality for many of the women involved In the sex tourism industry lies somewhere in between. The roots of disempowerment are found not only in economic status and within the sphere of production but also in reproduction and social and cultural structures. As Connell and other writers on gender issues have indicated, the explanation for the exploitation of women through tourism prostitution ties in the interweaving of class relations and gender relations. The present chapter therefore draws upon empirical evidence and attempts to synthesise the interpretations and arguments used by authors working from different theoretical perspectives in arriving at an understanding of sex tourism in Southeast Asia.

Development of sex tourism in South-east Asia

The economic and social problems of Asian women tend to be viewed by Western feminists as stemming from the patriarchal nature of local Cultures. Yet there is not an un-differentiated Asian model of women and gender relations, although the state as a structure is dominated by patriarchal interests. Each region within Southeast Asia needs to be examined in terms of its own particular set of gender, class and social relations. However, certain generalisations about the role and position of women within Southeast Asia and the development of sex tourism can be made.

The growth of the newly industrialised economies within South-east Asia through the relocation of multinational export-processing manufacturing forms to the region has led to the highest rates of female employment in the Third World. In each country of South-east Asia women constitute at least 26 per cent of the labour force, and 36-45 per cent in the Philippines,

Laos, Burma and South Korea. The transfer of export-processing plants to Southeast Asia from Japan, North America and Europe has led to a demand for young, unmarried, relatively educated women who are assumed to have the manual dexterity and docility needed for the tedious, repetitive and monotonous work. 'The new%, international division of tabour has perpetuated existing gender disparities in wages, except in situations where labour market shortages have significantly improved the status of women in the workforce. Despite the high rates of female labour force participation,

> Women's 'status' in Southeast Asia is not necessarily 'better' than in regions where their involvement in remunerated work is lower, since many of the' activities engaging women are those which reinforce patriarchal power structures, such as prostitution and sexual services in Thailand and the Philippines.

Ong's argument that the new trade in the labour and bodies of Asian women is more rooted in corporate objectives of profit-maximisation than in the persistence of indigenous values, is only partially correct, 'The new international division of labour and the spread of consumerism to the Third World has had substantial impacts on gender, racial, and social relations in South east Asia, but rather than supplant indigenous values, it has built on them. Indeed, as noted above, it was the indigenous set of gender relations which helped to provide a female labour force for various multinational enterprises and which has assisted in the development of sex tourism. In spite of high rates of remunerated employment among women in east Asia, religious and cultural ideals emphasise that their primary responsibility is to home and family. Women who have fled rural poverty, only to be forced into prostitution by urban unemployment, are victims of a double standard. Brydon and Chant point to the fact that economic development has had an equally important role to play in reinforcing women's secondary status. When women move into the labour force their work is often of a highly exploitative nature, whether in a multinational-owned factory or brothel.

Sex tourism may be conceptualised as a series of linkages between a legally marginalised form of commoditisation within a national industry, dependent upon, but performing a dynamic function within, an international industry. The postwar development of the new international division of labour has meant radical restructuring of the economies of Southeast Asia through their closer integration within the global economy, The influx of rural women to Urban centres in order to support village families has encouraged the marginalisation of female participation in the labour market. In both the light manufacturing industries of the electronics revolution and in the sex industries, women have been integrated into the global economy. Indeed, Ong argued, that women who have lost jobs in the industrialised sector have been forced to seek work in hotels and brothels. However, the new international division of labour should be seen as only one stage in the development of sex tourism in east Asia.

In east Asia the institutionalisation of international sex tourism commenced with the prostitution associated with American and Japanese colonialism and militarisrn and has now become transformed through the internationalisation of the regional economy.

Prostitution is illegal in most South-east Asian countries, but laws regarding tourism prostitution is illegal in most South-east Asian countries, but laws regarding tourism prostitution are poorly enforced by authorities in the region's patriarchal societies. Prostitution in South-east Asia clearly existed before the arrival of tourists. One of the ironies of the current Japanese involvement in sex tourism is that the Japanese used to export their own prostitutes *Kara-Yuki San* to their colonies. *Kara-Yuki San* were bonded Japanese women who were sent abroad to serve as prostitutes in ports frequented by Japanese merchants and soldiers. However, since the 1920s when the Japanese government issued the Overseas Prostitution Prohibition Order, and with the prohibition of legal prostitution in Japan in 1958, women from the former colonies 'are now imported into Japan as prostitutes. In addition, the nature of sex tourism varies from country to country according to different gender, cultural and social factors. For instance, in a report on child prostitution Rogers states that in Thailand child prostitution is 90 per cent female, in Sri Lanka 90 per cent male, and in the Philippines, young boys account for 60 per cent of child prostitutes.

The evolution of sex tourism in Southeast Asia has generally gone through four distinct stages. The first stage is that of indigenous prostitution, in which women are already subject to concubinage and bonded prostitution within a patriarchal society which regards such sexual relations as acceptable and normal. The second stage is that of economic colonialism and militarisation in which prostitution is a formalised mechanism Of dominance and a means of meeting the sexual needs of occupation forces. For example, the American presence In Taiwan from the Korean War through to the end of' the Vietnam War provided a major stimulus for tourism prostitution centred on Shuang Cheng Street in 'Taipei. Similarly, until the closure of the bases, the 12,000 registered and 8,000 unregistered hostesses in Olongapo City provided the major source of sexual entertainment for the United States military personnel based at Subic Naval Base and Clark Air Force Base m the Philippines. In this stage both the indigenous and occupier's set of gender relations are used as a justification by government and occupying forces tor economic or military enforced prostitution thereby encouraging the dependency of host regions on the selling of sexual services as a means of income generation. The commoditisation sexual relations is marked in the third stage by the gradual substitution of overseas military forces by international tourists. For example, Australian criminal elements made substantial investments in the sex industry in Angeles City near Clark Air Force Base in the Philippines prior to it being closed, in order to offer sexual services to Australian tourists as well as American servicemen. Bacon reported that Australians now have a financial interest in more than 60 per cent of the 500 bars and 7,000 prostitutes around the base. At this third stage, sex tourism now becomes a formal mechanism by which authoritarian governments can further national economic goals.

The fourth, and current, stage for most of the nations of Southeast Asia is that of newly industrialised nation status. Despite the increased material standard of living for many areas, tourism prostitution is still widespread. The series of stages in the development of sex tourism have established and reinforced a network of gender conditions which may take many years to dismantle, particularly given their continued maintenance by patriarchal elite structures. The following overview of sex tourism in South Korea and Thailand indicates the four stages of development of sex tourism.

The term kisaeng originally referred to females who served a similar social function as the geisha in Japan. The word is now, however, synonymous with Japanese-oriented tourism prostitution in Korea. 'No less than 100,000' tourist service girls were estimated to be operating in South Korea in 1978, although this figure excluded the large number of unregistered sex workers,

Gay estimated that some 260,000 prostitutes were operating in South Korea, the majority of whom originated from economically marginal rural areas. Kisaeng girls were required to obtain identification cards from authorities in order to enter hotels. While at the government 'orientation programme' for sex workers, which was a prerequisite for issuance of the card, women were told that their carnal conversations with foreign tourists did not prostitute either themselves or the nation, but expressed their heroic patriotism. The orientation programme was regarded as similar to that given by the Japanese to the 100,000 Korean women who were forced to serve in the 'women's volunteer corps, as prostitutes to the ' Japanese troops during World War II. Indeed, the relationship between sex tourism and the use of 'comfort women' by the Japanese armed forces during World War II is now expressly made by Korean Chruch Women's groups. The South Korean Church women's Alliance adopted the 'comfort women issue, not so much as a major cause in its own right, but rather in the hope that it could be a vehicie to generate feelings against Japanese sex tours. According to Korea Church Women United:

> The only difference we can find... is the circumstances under which they are conducted —the one during the Japanese invasion days was in a war effort; the other, currently in a sovereign state.

Kisaeng sex tourism is dependent on the Japanese. Following the severing of Japanese diplomatic ties with Taiwan in 1973 there was a massive increase in Japanese tourism, predominantly male, to South Korea. *Kisaeng* sex tourism has taken three major forms:

(i) the establishment of kisaeng houses in the major urban areas geared towards tourists;

(ii) *kisaeng* act as companions to Japanese businessmen and travel with them during their visit to Korea. This role is regarded as an integral component of the conduct of Japanese business overseas and may be likened to a contemporary equivalent of the 'comfort women' role that Korean women were forced to take during World WarII;

(iii) kisaeng has been exported to Japan, with at least one report of 'musical talent' being sent to 50 Japanese kisaeng houses operating in Osaka.

The authoritarian nature of successive South Korean governments has played a major role in the commoditising of women through kisaeng tourism. Existing sets of gender relations, reinforced through periods of colonisation by the Japanese, have been consciously maintained by government policies which have exploited women's bodies for national economic gain. The 1988 Seoul Olympics saw South Korea put on a modern facade for the world but despite the promotion of cultural and natural attractions by the government *kisaeng* tourism is still a major factor in attracting Japanese male tourists to the country. Korean women's groups have attempted to draw attention to Japanese sex tourism in recent years, most successfully by highlighting the 'comfort women" issue. However, the Korean government appears at pains not to damage its economic relationship with Japan and provides little support for the women's movement. The continued maintenance of the authoritarian, patriarchal institutional structure by the present Korean elite can only continue to perpetuate the existing set of gender relations which allows kisaeng tourism to exist.

The tidal wave to modernize this land has brought along in its wake the spurring on of tourism a form of 'prostitution tourism' which is condoned and encouraged, for the sake of foreign exchange, by the powerful in our country. This depersonalization of the sex act and through it the dehumanization of Korean women, takes sex from being a soul-body relationship to one of a 'subject-object' relationship, in which the Subject is the man who buys and the Object is the woman who is sold. This deliberate action of earning foreign exchange by selling the flesh and souls of our women for sexual exploitation, is not only stripping the human dignity from Korean women, but is also an affront to all humanity.

Substantial debate has surrounded the indigenous gender relations of Thai society, several authors have argued that women have enjoyed relative equality, while others have noted that women have long been subordinated, with the patriarchal Buddhist culture maintaining both class divisions and exclusion from women from political power. Indeed, the importation of elements of elements Brahminical culture into Thai society has allowed concubinage polygamy to be legitimised and has created a ready-made framework within which sex tourism can be acceptable to government aid local elites.

The promotion of sexual service is an important element in the marketing of Thailand to tourists. It seems likely that in no other country has tourist motivation been so explicitly linked to sex. In 1957 there were 20,000 prostitutes, by 1964 400,000, and between 500,000 and a million in the early 1980s. Not all the prostitutes cater to sex tourists. Indeed, Cohen argued that the women working with farangs are in many ways the 'elite' among the prostitutes: they earn significantly more than those working with Thais, enjoy greater independence, and are rarely controlled by pimps or pushed into prostitution against their will. However, according to Richter, Cohen's empathetic and empirical approach describes the lifestyle of only a tiny minority of female prostitutes. Most have no such protective ambiguity. Furthermore, many Thai women become ' rented wives', somewhat similar to the kisaeng of Korea, who often return to tourist generating regions, particularly Germany, Holland, and Japan, where they may suffer linguistic and social isolation while often being forced to form sexual services.

The economically marginal rural areas of the northeast and northern provinces of Thailand have been the major source for child and female prostitutes, with many families and villages economically dependent on remittances from the prostitutes. The rapid and uneven development of Thailand has been closely viewed as integrating militarisation, tourism, and industrialisation as institutionalised systems of female exploitation. Phongpalchit has argued that the economic condition of northern Thailand stems from the hegemonic power of Britain and the United States which have encouraged export-oriented development on the Central Plain at the expense of the north. The northern provinces are structurally disadvantaged within, the Thai economy and iii the absence of alternative income sources, a vested interest and dependency upon continuation of the sex industry is created providing an assured supply of workers for the sex industry based in the nation's urban and industrial centres.

Until the end of the 1980s the Thai government placed great emphasis on sex tourism as a means to earn foreign exchange, to the extent that ministers often openly advocated tourism prostitution as means of Job creation. Successive Thai governments therefore continued to perpetuate existing gender relations and exploitation through support of the sex tourism industry. The last five years have seen public statements from Thai government control of sex tourism, but the reasons for this probably lie more within concerns for AIDS and the image of the country overseas than in any intrinsic changes in social attitudes.

In 1989 the Thai Public Health Ministry started campaigning against prostitution and the promotion of Thailand as a sex tour destination. The primary reason for the campaign was the recognition that sexually transmitted diseases such as AIDS could pose major problems for Thailand's rapidly growing tourism industry. A Ministry survey of AIDS indicated that about 3,000 prostitutes in Thailand were carrying the AIDS virus and a World Health Organisation report estimated that the number of infected people in Thailand was between 45,000 and 50,000, compared to an official figure of 14,000. In tourist centres such as Chiang Mai, tests have suggested that one of every two prostitutes in the region carries the virus. According to the Thai Deputy Public Health Minister, Suthas Ngernmuen

> Thailand's profitable tourist industry has been an inhibiting factor in promoting AIDS awareness... More than two-thirds of the overseas visitors entering Thailand art, single men, and medical officials avoided publicising the appalling AIDS statistics for fear of damaging the country's healthy tourist business... But it is long past time for the government to change Thailand's image as a sexual paradise.

We should promote tourism in more appropriate ways, and campaign more against AIDS. The Thai government has considered a number of options to the spread of AIDS, operating testing programmes for certain visitors, and distributing condoms in hotels and at the airport. Part of the AIDS programme includes rehabilitating and skilling prostitutes, while the Defence Ministry is providing an AIDS education programme for servicemen. The public Health Ministry has proposed the issuing of health cards brothel workers which would indicate the holder's personal background and the results of tests conducted for sexually transmitted diseases, including AIDS. The issue of three-monthly health cards is only an indirect measure of controlling AIDS and does relatively little to deter the sex tourist. Instead health cards may only further attract visitors to certain brothels or locations and may also allow the possibility of corruption in order to obtain cards which give workers in the sex industry clean bills of health. If the Thai government is to be serious about controlling AIDS a major emphasis has to be given to replacing Thailand's image as a sex tour destination and, more significantly, providing alternative economic and social support mechanisms for those who are forced to use prostitution as a means of employment. However, Thailand's tourism authorities are extremely sensitive to reports on the causes and consequences of the rising incidence of AIDS and other sexually transmitted diseases in Thailand. After a damning examination of the sex trade and the major role it plays in Thailand's tourism industry by the Far Eastern Economic Review, the Governor of the Tourism Authority of Thailand, Dharmnoon Prachuabmoh, attacked the Review and argued that any effective measures adopted by the Thai government to curb the spread of AIDS were acceptable, and that the welfare of the Thais, not the tourist dollar, was top priority.

The AIDS scare has already impacted on some Thai tourist destinations. Visitor arrivals by road from Malaysia were estimated to have dropped by over half during 1989 at the southern town of Hat Yai, renowned for its bars and massage parlours. Similarly, AIDS has tarnished the image of Pattava, and this, associated with environmental problems, is believed to have contributed to a sharp decline in the number of visitors to the resort area in the later 1980s.

In order to attract more female tourists and to counteract Thailand's image of sex tourism and AIDS, the chairman of the Tourism Authority of Thailand and a leading anti-AIDS campaigner, Minister Mechai Viravaidya, planned a Women's Visit Thailand year campaign in 1992. According to the Minister:

> We want women to come particularly from countries where some of their men have come here on sex tours... We want them to see A hat their men get up to and how they have exploited uneducated women and children. We want their women to come and see the good Thai women and encourage Thai women to stand up to the brutality and disrespect they have suffered. More action must come from Thai women themselves, otherwise the country will still be seen as the brothel of the world.

The Minister's stance led him to be criticised severely by some members of the tourism industry and accused of a conflict of roles. It is readily apparent that some sections of Thailand's tourism industry are still keen to promote sex tourism because of its financial benefits. However, the long-term health implications, through the spread of AIDS and other sexually transmitted diseases, and the social impacts of sex tourism are enormous and represent a potential time-bomb for Thailand's economic and social development. In order to confront the implications of sex tourism for Thai society and economy, the government must overcome official corruption and deep-rooted cultural attitudes towards sex and the role of women. Such a task will not be easy, but unless the government takes firm and decisive action, not only will the broader tourism industry be damaged, particularly that geared towards the family market, but the human base of Thai economic development will be undermined. However, as long as the gap between the city and the rural areas continues to widen, real living standards in the country remain low, and the preexisting set of gender relations continue to be maintained by successive military regimes, the women of the rural north will continue to furnish Thailand's sex industry with its raw material.

Sex tourism is an integral part of the tourism Industry of east Asia. It has developed for a number of reasons. The indigenous set of gender relations in many parts of east Asia providėd the ender base upon which sex tourism could thrive. However, the post-war militarisation of the region plus the integration of the area in the international economy has provided a further dynamic element in the Perpetuation of pre-existing gender and social relations, including institutionalised racism. The significance of economic marginality and racial inequality as a casual factor in Prostitution is witnessed in the origins of prostitutes. For example the majority of tourism prostitutes in Taiwan are not Han Chinese but instead come from the island's aboriginal population which is Polynesian-Malayan in origin and which live in marginal rural areas. Similarly, hospitality girls working in the ago-go bars in the tourist night-life belt of Ermita in the Philippines come mainly from low-income families in economically marginal rural areas. According to the Philippine Women's Research Collective many women expend almost a quarter of the total income to support family members in Manila or send remittances back to the home province, a situation which is replicated throughout the region.

The desire for economic development by many of the region's newly independent nation states has led to dependence on tourism as a source of foreign exchange. Indigenous gender relations have allowed many women to be sold as commodities in order to achieve this goal, whether it be through sex tourism, as cheap labour in multinational manufacturing enterprises, or as migrants. For example, following the campaign against sex tours by Japanese and Filipina women, number of Japanese tourists to Manila decreased while the proportion of

Fillpina women travelling to Japan increased. Economic relations both within the new international division of labour and between the First and Third Worlds has only exacurbated gender inequality. A direct analogy has been drawn between prostitution in the Third World and that in metropolitan resort centres where the women may be largely drawn from economically and socially disadvantaged sections of the population whose position illuminates forms of 'Internal colonialism commonly found in stratified, industrial societies.

The stability of the gender relations which allow the maintenance of sex tourism is a reflection of the interests of the groups which constitute the gender order. The insidious tourist first attitude of many governments of eastern Asia has actively promoted images of subservient women waiting on the needs of the tourist. To change this set of circumstances will therefore require fundamental change both within the host countries and in the international tourism industry.

East Asian sex tourism has further institutionalised the exploitation of women within patriarchal societies although its more overt forms do appear to be on the decline. However, the reasons for this probably relate more to the threat of AIDS to the visitor rather than widespread concern for the sex worker or fundamental changes in gender and economic relations. Indeed, modern mass tourism and its accompanying images only serve to promote unequal gender relations in which women are subordinate to male interests. Tourism will continue to be a mainstay of the region's economies. However, while tourism prostitution may decline, the intrinsic inequality of host-guest relationships in mass tourism can only continue to perpetuate the current set of gender relations tourism is sex tourism.

3

International Tourism and its Future

The practice of corporate strategy, strategic management or business policy is an integrative procedure, which attempts to draw together all aspects of the organization's decisions into a coherent whole. Although these decisions are often taken at different levels in the organization and, in practice, are often uncoordinated, corporate planning is the responsibility of top management. It is only top management who can have the strategic vision necessary to take decisions on a company-wide long-term basis. This explains the difference between strategy that has a long-term aim and tactics that represent shorter-term contingent decisions aimed at implementing partial elements of the overall strategy.

Any company faces a variety of corporate and environmental pressures. Those pressures that impact on objectives may be termed stakeholders. These stakeholders, who can influence the firm, include: shareholders, management, suppliers, customers, employees and governments. In addition, objectives must take into account environmental change and, in the actions of competitors. The outcome of the process 'of setting objectives will represent a balancing of these interest groups.

Shareholders

It is frequently stated that the only objective of the firm is to maximize profits. As a long-run objective it is essential for survival that the assets of the company in the broadest possible sense earn a rate of, return superior to that which they could earn elsewhere. However, to give operational content to this and to achieve a balance between' the very long-term and shorter-term objectives, it is essential to set sub-goals and to satisfy other stakeholders. This is the essence of the, managerial theories of the firm, which propose a trade-off between profits and management satisfaction. Despite this trade off, and others, it is essential that shareholders remain content to hold shares, which represent ownership of the firm. If shareholders become dissatisfied, then it is open to them to dispose of their shares and thus to precipitate a change in ownership, with possible serious consequences for policy, including a change of management. Indeed, it may be managers themselves who own the company or, in the case of 'management buy-outs', who acquire a company from its existing shareholders.

In many countries, institutional shareholders are very important. These may include financial institutions, banks and intra-group holding. Where the proportion of shares held by powerful outside bodies is large, the influence of such bodies will be significant.

Similarly, the key form of ownership in many countries is the private company. This may be a family group, a cluster of related families or even a single individual. The owner/manager/entrepreneur will be a uniquely powerful figure in deciding corporate strategy, and the boss's word is final may be a sufficient explanation of strategy in these cases. Because financial institutions and the corporate framework differ so much between countries, private ownership does not necessarily only apply to small companies. In Germany, for instance, the private company can be become very large before there is any necessity to consider, change to a publicly quoted company.

For all private companies, however, corporate strategy influenced by the necessity to raise capital. Ibis is particularly for, rapidly growing private companies. The approach of p companies to the capital market is fraught with difficulties. The key, problem is the need to raise capital without losing control. Often, the competitive advantage of smaller firms rests in the possession of unique skills, products, technology or ideas. This compounds the problems when it becomes necessary to raise capital to exploit the idea without giving the idea away! Under these pressures many family-owned or closely held companies are constrained to issue shares, thus relinquishing total control.

The pressure then to earn a good (short-term) rate of return to prevent shareholder disquiet, takeover or buy-out provides a constraint on policy. Any policy that ignores the influence of the capital market in this way is bound to run into problems. Private companies are more able to withstand these pressures because they are insulated to some degree from the immediacy of returns required by a publicly quoted company. Indeed, in the leisure, tourism and travel field, it is noticeable that the entrepreneur Richard Branson brought his Virgin group of companies back into private ownership after being publicly quoted, so that they could concentrate on long-term policies by the exclusion of short-term earnings. The shareholder profile is thus a key influence on objectives.

Managers

Managers are the most important decision-makers in a company. In many cases, they will not be owners of the firm but will be professionals implementing, in theory at least, the wishes of the owners. In practice, it is an increasing trend that managers are given share-holdings in the firm for which they work in order to secure their loyalty, ensure that they work on behalf of all shareholders and to reward them for performance. However, we can separate the pure motivations of managers from managers as shareholders.

Models of managerial discretion suggest that managerial remuneration and discretionary income may well be traded off against increasing the net worth of the company (as measured, for instance, by the share price). In addition prestige, particularly among peer groups, may also be important. This may lead, for instance, to a desire for growth for its own sake or to becoming international. The objectives will be paid for by trading off other benefits.

The issue of ownership versus control has been a long-standing one in the corporate literature. The relationship between owners and managers is thus vitally important in the formulation of objectives.

Suppliers

Suppliers will be dependent on the company through purchasing behaviour. They will have a vested interest in the company's success as a buyer of products or services. In situations where the company is reliant (even dependent) on its suppliers, then it is important to take their interests into account. Examples include hotels being dependent on catering supplies and the famous network of sub-contracting that characterizes Japanese business. There is, of course, a tendency for the large and powerful to take over the small in purchasing chains, and such internalization strategies are as, characteristic of the tourism industry as elsewhere. However, control in a chain of supply can be exercised without ownership, as the retailing firm Marks and Spencers; have shown. Excessive dependence on key suppliers may, however, bias strategy and objectives.

Customers

Companies that forget customers in any part of the process of corporate planning, including the formulation of objectives, are doomed to failure. It is a truism that companies cannot ignore the market. It is through the medium of management that the impact of customers is felt. A key role of managers is to predict market demand. In an industry as fragmented, volatile and seasonal as tourism, this becomes an even more major task. Moreover, as a tourism company is involved in face-to-face transactions with people, contacts are vital and feedback is likely to be immediate.

Employees

The goodwill of employees is a *sine qua non* of successful operation in which human contact and personal skills are as important as in tourism. Often it is possible to regard the role and influence of employees as a constraint on the objectives of companies. Much more satisfactory is the view that the role of employees can contribute in a positive way to the establishment and achievement of company goals.

In many countries, notably the Federal Republic of Germany, In certain circumstances employees will, by statute, be equivalent to shareholders in being represented on the management board of the company. Their objectives can thus, in theory at least, be converted' into company policy. Although this relationship is not as direct in many other countries, an input from employees should certainly be considered in the formulation of objectives, as the employee, perspective can be most valuable, derived as it is likely to be in tourism from a direct interface with customers.

Governments

In international tourism, dealing with governments in the

plural is a key fact of operation. For all but the most multinational of companies, the most important influence will be the government the home (or parent) country. Objectives will be constrained by the necessity to conform to the laws, directives, statutory requirements exhortations and ad hoc mechanisms of the country. Complicity matters of taxation, antitrust legislation, accounting practices, trade regulation, product liability and the Myriad other public policies of government is a crucial element of careful strategy formulation. However, when we deal with international operations, it is an unfortunate fact of life that the public policies of the host governments will conflict or at least not fully mesh with, those of the home government. This can involve heavy expenses, for example, in reconciling financial accounts of a conflict of objectives between different units of the firm and internal dissensions in management.

Setting objectives

It will be apparent from the review of stake-holder interests above that the process of setting objectives is essentially political in the sense of reconciling differences. The constraints on objectives are both internal and external, and the outcome will depend on the representation of those interests by the key actors, who will be in the main managers and owners. Despite these factors it is important that there should be a clear articulation of unambiguous objectives as a basis for policy choice, implementation and approval. Resistance to this process should not be ignored. It is essential to secure approval of objectives, and this can be done by consultation, attempting to achieve consensus, promotion of the objectives and linking incentives to the achievement of objectives.

The role of top management is crucial. But the process should not be confined to top management.

Corporate objectives are long term and planning too must be long term. The length of time over which objectives are defined will vary over industry segments. Many firms find it useful to have long-term objectives (10 years) within which five-year rolling plans are defined.

Strategic appraisal

It is essential that firms in international tourism should have a clear, unbiased view of their internal and external position. It is important to know where the firm is, and where it is going. Inevitably, this will involve a view of where the firm has been. Strategic appraisal has two main components: internal and external.

Internal appraisal

An analysis of where the company is an appraisal of its strengths and weaknesses is a vital and continuous process. It is necessary to cover all aspects of the firm's operations: marketing' fin personnel, research and development, production, structure, systems and procedures.

Several techniques of internal appraisal are available. The appraisal can be conducted by insiders executives, managers directly meeting and discussing the position or surveys. It may be useful to employ outsiders, whose views more objective and detached but who may not have full information. Whoever conducts the analysis, it is i be systematic, unbiased and realistic. Evidence firms within and possibly outside the industry provides against which the position of the firm can be judged. The coherence past and projected strategy can judged against the position of the firm.

It is useful to place the information necessary for a strate appraisal in a framework like the Strengths Weaknesses Opportunities Threats (SWOT) approach. Debate can then take place among the relevant managers (an& possibly other stakeholders) regarding the realism and exactitude the entries. 'Harder' information, such as profitability, share, financial ratios and personnel audits, can then be brought bear in giving coherence to the appraisal.

External appraisal

Two levels of external appraisal may be distinguished: one is the analysis of the macro environment of the firm; the other a more micro and localized approval of the firm's particular industries, market a competitive framework.

Analysis of the macro environment is important because the longterm and overall framework in which the firm operates is not static and prediction of changes that have an immediate impact often, depends' on changes at the most fundamental level. For firm in international tourism, of particular importance will be: (1) changes in demand pattern, which depends on income levels, tastes, distribution of income; (2) changes in political circumstances, both in the firm's home country and worldwide; (3) changes in technology; (4) social changes, including the ageing of the population in the most advanced countries.

Each of these key factors will influence the internal organisation of the firm and the relative costs that face it in its own markets and in others that impinge on it. Consequently, the scale and scope of the firm must adjust in order to accommodate these external changes. A change in the taste from 'sea and sun' type holidays to 'cultural tourism' will affect the occupancy rates and, therefore, the profitability of hotels in different locations, the pattern of amenity provision and travel pattern. A revolution in Ruritania will deflect holidaymakers to countries that are close substitutes. Improvements in computer technology will allow worldwide centralized booking facilities for hotels and transport companies. Each of these changes will alter the size, scope and location of firms and their investment. They will also encourage or deter entry (and exit) into the industry. The firms that are most alert to changing opportunities will gain most.

Against this general backdrop, firms must attempt to appraise their more immediate environment. This will generally mean their competitors and potential competitors, their customers and suppliers and (potential) substitutes.

Congruence between internal and external appraisal

A crucial feature of a coherent corporate plan is that there must be congruence between the internal and external approval. If the internal appraisal has shown that a major strength exists in current product offerings, then we would expect this to be reflected in current market share. Putting the two analyses together should, reveal the extent to which internal perception is external reality.

Strategy choice

In examining the various frameworks available for strategy choice, several things should be borne in mind. First, these are merely frameworks. They enable choice to take place, based on the content put into the framework. If the content is wrong, the strategy will go wrong. If the internal and external appraisals contain errors of fact, perception and interpretation, no sophisticated framework of analysis will put it right. Second, the methods of structuring strategic choice will be more or less appropriate according to the strategic position and dynamics of the firm in its context. Some of these methods are appropriate to growing firms, others to firms wishing to arrest a decline. Some pay more attention to a rapidly changing environment, others are more suitable in situations closer to equilibrium. Third, none of the frameworks is a substitute for judgement. Managerial choice, entrepreneurial flair, careful planning are all required. The function of management is to adjust to change. These methods are an aid to that, not a substitute for it.

The Boston consulting group matrix

The Boston Consulting Group Matrix, often referred to in short-hand terms as the 'Boston Box', is a device relating growth rate to relative competitive position at product level. Like many models in the strategic choice area, it presents a 2 by 2 matrix and reduction to two dimensions raises serious questions about its ability to handle complexity. It also suffers from a number of restrictive assumptions that: the market can be defined, profitability and market share are positively related, there are no barriers to entry or exit in the market concerned, the stage of industry maturity" be defined and the market is still in the growth stage. Given these restrictions, however, the model still retains some heuristic value.

The two dimensions define four product categories high-growth products where the firm has a strong relative competitive position lower-growth products with a strong market share high-growth products without a strong market share and lower-growth products with a weak market share. By mapping products according to their business growth rate and relative market share a current audit can be obtained. Strategy choice should then proceed by exiting from 'dogs' unless there is a powerful reason not to and by converting question marks into stars by increasing market share. Stars will eventually become cash cows as the market rate of growth slows and then these can be reinvigorated by using the cash flow for reinvestment. The matrix points to the need for balance between high-growth stars, which are unlikely to generate cash flow, and cash cows, which provide the wherewithal to generate new products and find investment. The assumes that a portfolio of products can be generated. It to apply the concept to a narrowly focused single-product

General electric business screen

As a contrast to the over-simplistic approach of the Boston Box, the GE Matrix can become over-complicated. It includes, again, only two variables, but as these are industry attractiveness and competitive position, they break down into as many sub-variables as can be suggested to affect a firm's profitability. In truth, the blank framework allows many interpretations. Essentially, the positioning of a firm's business units can begin only a preliminary screening of its choices.

It is essential in these approaches to pay particular attention to constraints on movement. It is costly both to enter and to exit from an industry and an industry segment. Attention to these costs is necessary to augment the analysis of strategic moves as presented by these frameworks.

Strategic growth vectors

It is often appropriate to analyse strategies around the issue of directions of growth of the company. Growth vector components presented by Ansoff enable this to occur. Take first the simple division between existing and new products, existing and new missions. Thus, by examining the product market position it possible to delineate generic growth strategies.

Product cycle models

The product cycle model makes four basic assertions: (1) Products undergo predictable changes in production and marketing. (2) There is restricted information available on products and technology; in particular proprietary knowledge, owned and controlled by firms, is crucial in attaining competitive leadership. (3) The production of goods and provision of services change over time and economies of scale are prevalent. (4) Tastes differ, so patterns of demand can vary. In particular, tastes differ according to income. This provides an opportunity for firms to standardize their offerings according to income levels. Segmentation of the market thus occurs as products travel through a life-cycle.

The process has four stages, development, growth, maturity and decline. It is a notable weakness of product cycle analysis that the cycle is programmatic, not dynamic. In other words, the programme is set, but there is insufficient explanation of the critical variables that drive this development and their relationship with elapsed time.

Stage I of the cycle is the innovation stage where a new product is created. This new product will tend to be unstandardized, high-priced and the province of one or a few innovative firms. These firms will receive quasi-monopoly returns to reward the innovation. In Stage 11, the product becomes more standardized on both the demand side and on the supply side. New competitors enter the market and drive the price down. The possibility of economies of scale (block booking, purchase of aircraft and hotels with assured full occupation) also drive down costs. Investment by established firms in this stage may well occur to forestall entry. In State 11 the product becomes mature and sells almost entirely on the basis of price. Attempts are made to secure niches within the market, but the primary imperative is to reduce costs. The product becomes susceptible to mass-marketing techniques. There is a tendency for the market to become dominated by a few large oligopolists. In the decline phase, substitute 'new products' begin to erode market share. The necessary capacity begins to decline and the product becomes much more like a commodity. This is not to say that the correct strategy is to leave mature product segments, because they are often capable of generating large cash flows. Strategies of product regeneration and segmentation can still earn a good return in such an industry. There is an imperative, however, to maintain strict cost control and this discipline may be beyond the capability of many operators.

Needless to say, there are many criticisms of the product cycle model as the basis for international corporate planning. It is over-deterministic and clearly does not apply to all products. It is also difficult to pin down exactly what constitutes a product. In many ways the model is an industry cycle rather than a product cycle. There is also a great deal of evidence that product cycles are shortening, in many cases to the point where products are innovated, standardized and differentiated almost instantaneously rather than sequentially. The use of the product cycle model in international tourism may still have validity. However, it should be borne in mind that it splits three strategic decisions which are interdependent: investment in product development and innovation, the method of approaching foreign markets and the optimum way of competing with new entrants. The major criticism that the model is outdated must be judged in the context of product development in particular industry segments.

Structured analysis and generic strategies

The analysis of industry structure, competitive behaviour and relative competitive advantages can be key factors in strategic choice. Porter's work has suggested three key generic strategies: differentiation, overall cost leadership and focus. The choice, determined by strategic target and strategic advantage, is driven by the degree of uniqueness as perceived by the customer and the cost position of the company.

Overall cost leadership rests on the ability of the firm to control costs. This means achieving economies of scale, gaining cost reduction through learning effects, tight control of overheads and reducing spending on sales costs. This strategy will tend to be linked to the achievement of high market share and maintaining a ruthless view of the product portfolio, eliminating products that do not conform to the strategy. Standardization of product and service is often the key to success in this strategy with mass marketing and advertising to maintain throughout. Examples in the tourist industry are basic package holidays and budget hotels.

A strategy based on differentiation requires that the firm's product be perceived as unique in the industry. This is usually but not necessarily a high-quality "aim at the top of the market' type of strategy. The firm thus attains a defensible position by creating an area of quasi-monopoly, giving it some price leverage. A strategy of building consumer loyalty and quality superiority are adjuncts to the strategy. Some airlines, such as Cathay Pacific and Singapore Airlines, are in the enviable position of successfully following such a strategy. There is, however, often the necessity of sacrificing overall market share in order to differentiate successfully.

Finally, the strategy of focus is built on, aiming at a particular segment, geographical area or product line. The firm must be able to service this particular niche market more successfully than its broader-based-corapetitors. It may, therefore, be lower cost or be perceived as superior by the key buyers in' the niche. As there is an element of choice in this strategy, it can be used to secure niche positions that are least vulnerable to substitutes or where competitors are weak. Examples are companies specializing in safari holidays or specialists in particular destinations or hotels catering for minority needs.

Global planning —strategic alternatives

The issues of strategy choice do not differ when international aspects are considered, but the range of options and variables increase. International modes of operation and entry strategy in detail, and this should be reviewed at this point. The mode of foreign market servicing is a critical aspect of international strategic planning and should be included in the choice of strategy. As points; out, patterns of international competition vary widely across industries and a more flexible approach needs to be taken when planning on a global scale. This will require organizational innovations to deal with increased complexity and may involve coalitions with other firms. The firm will also have more, and often conflicting, government regulations with which to deal, and will have opportunities arising from its inter national scope to generate and exploit competitive advantages. Again, a two-dimensional table can be used to illustrate the key strategy choices in international competition. These are coordination of activities and configuration issues, which centre on the location of activities. This combination of internalization and location decisions across activities permits a great complexity of strategic choice. In practice, however, in the international tourism industry, many decisions will be constrained: for example, the location of the destination, integration of key activities. Exporting also is impossible with location-dependent services. Combining the international competitive framework with the generic strategies. Porter is able to define a small number of strate alternatives where competition is global, as it is increasing becoming in large segments of the international tourism industry.. It will rarely be the that a firm follows one strategy exclusively from which the most appropriate strategy can be select as internal circumstances and environmental constraints dictate.

Strategy implementation

A much neglected aspect of corporate planning is that of implementing the strategy. Implementation will be much easier if those whose role is crucial to achieving the strategy, which is likely to be every employee of the company, have been involved as much as is practically feasible in having an input into the strategy process. Widepsread consultation and consensus seeking may seem costly and time-consuming, but it may well pay dividends at the implementation stage. The Japanese have shown that competitive advantages can be gained by having the whole workforce moving in a single strategic direction. It has been shown that decisions take longer to reach in the Japanese firm, but, once reached, implementation is more efficient and effective. It should also be noted that conflict i an essential part of strategy implementation, because the strate results from choice and choice involves taking decisions that will evaluated differently from different standpoints. Strategy involves making real resource decisions, thus depriving some members of the unit of resources in favour of others. It involves value judgements and predictions in an uncertain world. Conflict cannot be avoided, but it must be managed. The role of management in this context involves leadership, planning and control.

Leadership involves decision-taking, motivating others, monitoring outcomes and directing resources (giving orders). Leaders and managers are judged largely on the quality of their decision-taking, which is measured by the success of their outcomes. Decision-making often devolves on those with a track record of success. Successful entrepreneurs are those who are willing to back their judgement of the world against conventional wisdom. Decision-taking within a company is also linked to motivating others, largely subordinates, to carry through the decision with the greatest possible effectiveness. Thus, employee motivation becomes important. Systems can be designed to encourage motivation, including payment by results. The creation of a positive company ethic is a major support in motivating employees. Effective leadership requires the constant monitoring of outcomes. Leaders will regularly adjust their Decision-taking in order to improve outcome. Dogmatism should not be equated with leadership.

Planning, as Luffman *et al.* point out, is often relegated to budgeting. 'Systematic comprehensive corporate planning used to determine the future of a company is not widely in evidence in industrial organisations'. This is even more true in service organizations and in the international tourism industry. Commitment to implementation of the plan, particularly by top management and the chief executive officer, is crucial. Plans do not implement themselves and, as this chapter advocates, planning must be seen as a process to which sufficient time has to be allocated.

Control mechanisms must be used within planning and its implementation. Usually these will be defined as financial controls, but controls on the use of labour and management time are also clearly necessary. Naturally, there needs to be a careful balance between control and allowing innovation to take place. Controls that are too tight or require too much reporting are likely to be effective only in stifling enthusiasm. Organization design, which maximizes flexibility while ensuring effective reporting, will frequently emphasize decentralization into strategic business units (SBUs) with considerable autonomy.

As Luffman *et al.* says It should be emphasised that a highly formalised system of planning is no guarantee of success; but equally leaving things to chance constitutes the best possible guarantee of failure. It is crucial that firms in international tourism satisfy themselves that existing products and markets in which the firm operates are sufficient to satisfy future objectives.

This chapter has provided the traditional role of strategy analyses in pulling together strands from the various functional areas of the business. It needs to feed off the analyses of marketing, finance and organization covered above. In the international context, the means of doing business abroad must be integrated with the corporate planning mechanism.

Many countries look to international tourism as a source of valuable foreign exchange to alleviate balance of payments problems. The importance of domestic tourism should, however, not be understated; in many cases international and domestic tourism represent real alternatives, and therefore domestic tourism can have a marked impact on the balance of payments through its import substitute role. Tourism is playing an increasingly important role in the world economy. For example, international tourism receipts already comprise 7 per cent of the value of world exports and this figure is expected to grow. Currently international tourism is second only to oil in world trade, and it has been forecast that by the turn of the century it will be the most important sector. The scale of world domestic tourism far exceeds that of international tourism, both in volume and value terms. Total world receipts from tourism international and domestic exceed the gross national product (GNP) of any country in the world except Japan (where GNP is approximately equal to world tourism receipts) and the USA (where GNP is approximately twice the value of world tourism receipts). In recent years there has been increasing emphasis on the employment-generating potential of tourism. The general decline in traditional manufacturing activities in countries such as the UK and the USA has led to a search for alternative employment opportunities. Advantages of tourism include the facts that it is a relatively labour-intensive industry and that many of the job opportunities he in low-skill occupations where unemployment tends to be concentrated. Although interest has tended largely to centre on the economic importance and benefits of tourism, more recently increasing concern has been expressed regarding, the undesirable physical and sociocultural impacts of tourism. In particular, the effects, of pollution, overuse of facilities, social disorder, and so on, caused by massive influxes of tourists can give rise to a 'tourism backlash' in host communities, even to the extent of resulting in open resentment of tourists. These detrimental impacts of tourism need to be taken into account in tourism planning at destinations.

In order to proceed with our discussion of tourism we first need to define precisely what is meant by such terms as 'tourism', 'tourist' and so on. Wanhill defines 'tourism' as the 'temporary movement of people to destinations outside their normal places of work and residence and the activities undertaken during the time spent at those destinations'. Conventionally, 'temporary' means up to one year when referring to international tourism, and a period of up to a few weeks or months (according to the country concerned) for domestic tourism. The generally accepted definition of a visitor is a person travelling for up to this specified period 'to a place other than of his usual environment and whose main purpose of visit is other than to exercise an activity remunerated by an entity within the place visited'. When referring to domestic tourism, a minimum distance travelled requirement is sometimes included in the definitions of 'tourism' and 'visitor', and, in addition, hospital patients are usually excluded. Visitors can be divided into two categories: 'tourists' who stay at least one night in the place visited; and excursionists or day visitors' who do not stay overnight in the place visited. Although excursionists do not use accommodation facilities in the destination, they represent an important segment of the tourism market and are included within our definition of tourism.

'International' visitors are people who cross international frontiers to travel to countries other than their usual country of residence. 'Domestic' visitors are generally taken to be people travelling within their own country, although the World Tourism Organization (WTO) proposes that inbound foreign visitors should additionally be included in the definition. In the former case the terms 'domestic visitor' and 'internal visitor' are synonymous, whereas in the latter case 'domestic' visitors comprise 'internal' and 'inbound foreign' visitors. We shall adopt the more common definition in which domestic is taken to mean internal. The definition of tourism encompasses a wide variety of visit purpose: holidays, visits to friends and relatives, business visits, attendance at conferences, visits for religious or health reasons, and so on. Although the emphasis in this book is on international tourism management many of the concepts and techniques discussed are equally applicable to domestic tourism.

The measurement of tourist flows takes place in various ways. International inward tourist flows are usually recorded by frontier counts, sample surveys or registration at accommodation establishments. A problem with frontier counts is that in certain cases a substantial transit traffic element may be present, which distorts the statistics. Accommodation establishment records exclude excursionists, tourists staying with friends or relatives and those in other forms of unregistered accommodation. When different receiving countries use different measurement methods it becomes very difficult to compare arrivals data across destinations. International outward tourism flows are often measured by origin countries using sample surveys which they apply to returning residents. Other methods used to collect these data are household surveys or micro-censuses. International tourism receipts are defined as the receipts of a country resulting from payments for goods and services made by international visitors during their stay in the country visited. In general, they exclude all forms of remuneration resulting from employment, as well as international fare receipts. International tourism expenditures are defined as payments for goods and services made by residents of a country visiting abroad, and again in general exclude all forms of remuneration resulting from employment, as well as international fare payments.

Tourist expenditures/receipts data are collected in various ways. The most common method is for central banks to assemble the data using the 'bank reporting method'. Other techniques are the 'estimation method' and the 'mixed method'. In essence, the bank reporting method is based on the registration by authorized banks and agencies of the buying and selling of foreign currencies by travellers. There are many problems associated with this method of data collection, such as the identification of a transaction as a tourism transaction, the non-reporting of relevant transactions, the possible netting of some inward and outward foreign currency transactions data and the inability to capture black market transactions (which are a prevalent feature of many countries with rigid exchange control regulations). The major reservation associated with the bank reporting method is that the data are unreliable for identifying tourist receipts from a particular origin country. Any geographical breakdown provided relates to the denomination of the currency and not to the generating country; thus, for example, residents of countries with currencies that are not readily acceptable may well use US dollars on their foreign visits. The estimation method is based on sample surveys. These are usually applied to returning residents and departing nonresidents. This method provides the most reliable data on tourist expenditures/receipts. The mixed method aims to improve the statistics produced by the bank reporting method. Supplementary data obtained from other sources (for example, visitor surveys) are used to weight the transactions statistics, thereby improving consistency and reliability.

'"The tourism 'industry' may be thought of as comprising all those sectors; of the economy that contribute to meeting the needs of the tourist. Middleton breaks these sectors down into accommodation (for example, hotels, guest houses, holiday parks), transport (airlines, railways, shipping companies), travel organizers (retail travel agents, tour operators), attractions (theme parks, heritage sites, shopping facilities) and the destination organization sector (national tourist offices, regional tourist offices, local tourist offices). It is clear that tourism is a highly complex industry, and this is reflected, for example, in the problems associated with assessing the employment generated by tourism. The main complication is that the tourism industry is not defined in terms of the goods or service supplied, but rather in terms of the type of customer demanding goods and services. Thus a waiter may spend part of his time serving local customers and part of his time serving tourists, and so not all the jobs in tourism-related industries such as hotels and catering are supported by tourist spending.

The main sources of data relating to international tourism are the WTO, which regularly produces several publications containing tourism-related statistics, and the Organisation for Economic Cooperation and Development (OECD), which publishes Tourism Policy and International Tourism annually. The OECD is concerned with tourism in OECD member countries, whereas the WTO is concerned with world tourism. In particular, the WTO's Yearbook of Tourism Statistics is the most comprehensive collection of official government tourism statistics available, covering 150 countries and territories. More detailed information on individual countries is usually available directly from the country concerned; organizations such as central banks, national tourist offices and national statistical offices are often able to supply tourism-related data.

Economic environment

WTO figures show that international tourist arrivals totalled 405 million in 1989 with corresponding receipts of almost 211 billion US dollars. These receipts accounted for 7 per cent of world international trade and 18 per cent of world trade in services. When domestic tourism is also included tourism receipts rise to more than 2,000 billion US dollars. The (international plus domestic) tourism industry accounts for 12 per cent of world GNP.

Balance of payments

The balance of payments implications of international tourism are very important for certain countries and regions. The balance of receipts from inbound tourists and expenditures by tourists travelling abroad gives rise to the tourism balance, and this varies considerably from country to country and region to region. As discussed earlier, caution must be exercised when dealing with tourism expenditure/receipts data; the methods of compiling the statistics vary across countries, so the data are often not strictly comparable, and, in particular, there are serious inadequacies associated with the bank reporting method of data collection. Nevertheless, tourism expenditures/receipts data provide useful information regarding the sign and approximate size of the tourism balance.

In the tourism balance for the major regions of the world, Europe has the most favourable balance, but there are sharp differences within this total. In fact, only Southern Europe has a large positive tourism balance (reflecting the importance of sun/sea/sand tourism). The combined deficit on the tourism account for Northern and Western Europe is more than two-and-a-half times as high as the deficit for North America, the continent with the worst tourism balance. By contrast, Central America, and, in particular, the Caribbean show healthy surpluses on their tourism accounts. For Africa as a whole tourism receipts exceed expenditures, but within the continent there are great variations. In Northern Africa there is a large positive tourism balance because some countries that border the Mediterranean attract considerable numbers of European tourists, and in Eastern Africa there is also a good positive tourism balance. In East Asia and the Pacific and South Asia tourism receipts are higher than tourism expenditure.

International tourism receipts and international tourism expenditures are far greater for Europe than any other region. The most favourable tourism balance is achieved by Spain (US $12.8 billion), followed by Italy (US $7.6 billion), France (US $3.4 billion), Austria (US $3.1 billion), Portugal (US $1.7 billion) and Greece (US $1.7 billion). The least favourable tourism balance is achieved by West Germany (US $15.8 billion); although tourism receipts for West Germany exceed those of both Austria and Switzerland (which have positive tourism balances), the massive tourism expenditure of US $23.6 billion gives West Germany by 'far the worst tourism balance in Europe. The second least favourable tourism balance is achieved by the Netherlands (US $3.7 billion), followed by Norway (US $1.8 billion) and Sweden ".US $1.7 billion).

The major destination in Eastern Africa for international tourists is Kenya, and here receipts from international tourism exceed expenditure by US $323 million. This is, however, considerably smaller than the positive tourism balance achieved by Morocco (US $900 million). In North America, both Canada and the USA achieve negative tourism balances. International tourism expenditures by the USA are US $3 billion below the level for West Germany and international tourism receipts are US $8 billion higher. Thus the US tourism balance of US $5.4 billion is much more favourable than that for West Germany (US $15.8 billion) (Table 1.2). In Central and South America only Mexico has a large positive tourism balance (US $1.1 billion), similar to that of the Bahamas, and the other Caribbean countries also show healthy positive balances. In East Asia and the Pacific, Japan has a massive negative tourism balance (US $8.6 billion), second only to West Germany. In the Middle East, Egypt is a substantial earner of foreign exchange from tourism (US $1.5 billion); by contrast, Kuwait had a large negative tourism balance (US $2.4 billion). In South Asia the country with the highest level of international tourism receipts and most favourable tourism balance (US $ 1.2 billion) is India.

The contribution of international tourism receipts to the balance of payments can also be assessed in terms of the percentage of exports that these receipts represent. It can be seen that there is enormous variation among the destination countries. In certain developing countries in Africa and the Caribbean tourism plays a vital role in exports: for example, tourism receipts represent more than 40 per cent of exports in Barbados, more than 30 per cent in Morocco, and approximately 20 per cent in Kenya and Mexico. Tourism receipts also play an important role in the balance of payments for certain European countries, representing more than 20 per cent of exports for Greece and Spain, and 18 per cent for Austria, although the latter figure includes international fare payments. For Japan and West Germany, however, tourism receipts constitute only a small proportion of total ports. It should be borne in mind that international tourism generates balance of payments effects that are far more complex than those of the initial tourism receipts/expenditure (the primary effect). In particular, the extent to which tourism expenditures in a destination country generate import demand in that country will have a major impact on the foreign exchange generating ability of tourism. The secondary effects on the balance of payments include imports of supplies by the providers of tourism services (hotel operators, restaurant operators, and so on), expenditures on marketing abroad, and payments to overseas investors in the form of interest and dividends.

Employment in tourism

The tourism industry is one of the foremost generators of employment but precise figures for jobs in tourism are difficult to obtain. As discussed earlier, the major complication is that the industry is defined in terms of the customer demanding goods and services. There are many sectors serving tourists as well as other customers; for example, a taxi driver may spend 20 per cent of his/her time tourists and 80 per cent of his/her time transporting commuters. Thus, in order to obtain reasonably accurate figures for Job numbers in the tourism industry, it is not only necessary to identify all those sectors that provide goods or services for tourists, but also to estimate the proportion of the working time that a person in, one of these sectors spends on providing tourism-related goods and services.

Official figures on employment in tourism are generally not available on this basis. In many cases the figures just refer to staff employed in hotels and restaurants, but clearly many of these staff may spend some of their working time serving local customers. Staff employed in travel agencies and national tourism administrations are obviously classified correctly where they appear in the table, but the 'staff employed in other sectors of the tourist industry' component is not always an accurate classification. In the case of the UK, for example, this component includes public houses, night clubs and libraries, and for many of these sectors the tourist trade is likely to be a small proportion of total trade. Many major sectors of the tourism industry, such as transport, are not represented at all.

In order to be able to make cross-country comparisons, attention merely focuses on the 'staff employed in hotels and restaurants' category. West Germany has by far the highest figure for numbers employed in this category (992,000), followed by the UK (509,400), France (301,200), Switzerland (181,100) and Austria (116,700). The first stage in assessing tourism-generated employment is to identify which categories of employment in the official statistics are tourism related. Tourism affects many sectors of the economy, but the main tourism-related sectors are hotels and catering, transport (air, sea, rail and other inland transport), transport supporting services, retail distribution (food, clothing, filling stations, and so on), and tourism and recreational services. Estimates then have to be made of the proportions of employment in each of these sectors directly attributable to tourism. The official statistics often do not include the self-employed, but this group represents an important element of the workforce in tourism, and needs to be included. Estimates, therefore, are necessary for this group also.

An alternative approach to assessing tourism-related employment is through the use of economic impact studies. The essence of this method is to use visitor spending figures to derive estimates of job generation. If, say, $10,000 of visitor spending creates one job in tourism, the total number of jobs created as a result of visitor spending in an area can be estimated. The method can be refined to allow for visitor spending patterns in order that job generation in the various tourism sectors can be identified. The first stage in this, approach is to estimate total visitor spending split according to sector: hotels, restaurants, retailers, and so on. The second stage involves estimating the rate at which visitor spending is converted into direct employment in these various sectors.

Income from tourism

The importance of tourism to an economy can be measured by examining the ratio of income generated by tourism to gross domestic product (GDP). It is clear that Caribbean countries such as Barbados are vitally dependent upon tourism as an income earner: for this country international tourism receipts constitute one-quarter of GDP. Tourism receipts are clearly also important (albeit on a much smaller scale) to Austria, Morocco and Spain, amounting to more than 5 per cent of GDP in each case. For Australia, Japan, West Germany and the United States international tourism receipts represent less than one per cent of GDP.

Tourism multipliers

The multiplier measures the impact on an economy of

extra expenditure introduced into the economy. Tourism multipliers refer to changes in the levels of income, output, employment and the balance of payments caused by a change in the level of tourism expenditure. Tourist spending on accommodation, catering, transportation and so on in an area, tourism-related investment in the area and exports of goods stimulated by tourism generate income. Part of this income will leak out of the economy in the form of imports, savings and taxes, but the remainder will become a second round of spending in the economy, thus generating more income. The process continues, with each round smaller than the previous one owing to leakages, until the amount of expenditure becomes negligible. The concept of the multiplier is embodied in the relationship between the amount of the initial injection of tourism expenditure and the final ensuing effect on the economy.

The impact of the extra tourist expenditure on the economy can be split into the direct, indirect and induced effects. The direct effect is the amount of income (output, etc.) generated directly in the tourism sectors by the increase in tourism expenditure. The indirect effect relates to the successive rounds of inter-business transactions that are caused by the direct expenditure. It is the amount of income (output, etc.) generated by the tourism sector in purchasing extra goods and services from suppliers in the domestic economy, and by these suppliers in turn purchasing extra goods and services from domestic suppliers, and so on. The induced effect is the amount of income (output, etc.) generated by the higher level of consumer spending on domestically produced goods and services, which results from the additional personal income generated by the direct and indirect effects of the increase in tourist spending. The sum of the indirect and induced effects is termed the secondary effect.

The multiplier is generally expressed as the ratio of the sum of the direct, indirect and induced changes in the economy to the initial increase in tourism expenditure which caused the indirect and induced effects (the 'unorthodox' tourism multiplier).

Fletcher and Snee identify six tourism multipliers:

1 *The output multiplier*: this measures the extra output (direct and secondary) generated by an extra unit of tourism expenditure.

2 *The sales or transactions multiplier*: this measures the extra "business turnover (direct and secondary) generated by an extra unit of tourism expenditure. It is similar to the output multiplier, but excludes additions to inventories caused by the initial change in tourism expenditure.

3 *The income multiplier*: this measures the extra domestic income (direct and secondary) generated by an extra unit of tourism expenditure.

4 *The employment multiplier*: this measures the increased number of full-time equivalent jobs (direct and secondary) created as a result of an extra unit of tourism expenditure; alternatively, on account of the problem of differing units of measurement, it is often calculated as the ratio of the increased number of direct and secondary full-time equivalent jobs created to the direct jobs only, which result from the increase in tourism expenditure (the 'orthodox' tourism multiplier).

5 *The government revenue multiplier:* this measures the extra net government revenue generated by an extra unit of tourism expenditure, and usually includes all forms of government revenue (direct and secondary) less government expenditure on subsidies and grants to those sectors of the economy involved in the direct

and indirect provision of tourism-related goods and services.

6 *The import multiplier*: this measures the value of imported goods and services (direct and secondary) generated by an extra unit of tourism expenditure. Tourist spending in a host country comprises expenditure on both domestically produced and imported goods and services. Furthermore, suppliers to the tourism industry purchase some factors of production within the economy and import the others. In addition, some induced expenditure goes on domestically produced goods and services and the rest on imported goods and services.

Multipliers can be calculated for a country as a whole, a region or a local community. In general, the size of the economy is likely to affect the size of the multiplier; for example, the tourism income multiplier is likely to be much smaller for a small local community than for a (large) country, because of the higher proportion of goods and services that will need to be 'imported' into the area (leakages) in the former case as a result of the initial increase in tourism expenditure. A small range of economic activities within an area is likely to result in a small amount of trading taking place among these activities, and hence a small value for the multiplier.

Physical environment

The impact of tourism on the physical environment needs to be taken into consideration when planning tourism developments. A mass influx of tourists to a destination without regard to the consequences for the physical environment may well destroy the very resource that attracts tourists; the physical environment is often a powerful attraction to tourists and thus an important ingredient in the tourist product. Tourism can result in the pollution of lakes, rivers and coastlines by human waste, petrol discharged from boats, and so on. The transport tourists pollutes the atmosphere through exhaust fumes.

High noise levels can occur in previously peaceful surroundings, and litter may become a problem. Tourism on a large scale can also create congestion at, for example, airports and destinations; there is often a physical limit on the ability to absorb tourists, but before this stage is reached, the appeal of the tourist facility may well be reduced by overcrowding. Tourism can also destroy the balance of nature in an area; it can result in soil erosion, damage vegetation and wildlife, disrupt agriculture and destroy natural and manmade features. Building developments can have a marked detrimental impact on the physical environment. For example, mass tourism to coastal resorts leads to large-scale construction of hotels, restaurants, shops and so on, which often totally transform the physical environment.

In the case of natural resources, the ability of the resource to absorb tourists is an important physical constraint. Three types of carrying capacity limitation have been identified: physical capacity, environmental capacity and ecological capacity. Physical capacity is the absolute limit on tourist numbers that a resource can cope with. Environmental capacity is the maximum number of tourists that an area can accommodate without initiating a decline in the general perceived attraction of the area. Ecological capacity is the maximum number of tourists that an area can absorb before ecological decline takes place. It may, however, be possible to increase carrying capacity through the use of appropriate management techniques.

Measurement of the impact of tourism on the physical environment is a difficult task. Various techniques have been developed to try to assess this impact, but, for example, soil erosion may be a result of other land uses in addition to tourism, and it could be difficult to separate the effects of tourism from those of the other activities.

Attempts should be made to minimize the costs of tourism developments to the physical environment. In order to protect and preserve the physical environment it is necessary to instigate conservation measures, and new tourism developments, such as buildings and signposting, should be 'environmentally sensitive'. Planning controls are necessary to balance the conflicting demands of tourism (and other land uses) and conservation 'to protect and preserve the natural environment from unsystematic and unplanned human manipulation'. Also point out that:

> conservation and the preservation of natural areas, archaeological sites and historic monuments have emerged as important spill-over benefits of tourism. In turn, the protection of these prime tourist resources enhances and perpetuates tourism by maintaining its very foundation. The tourist industry has as much interest in maintaining a quality environment as organizations specifically dedicated to that cause.

In fact, tourism also may well provide the economic means whereby conservation and preservation can be effected. Finally, it should be borne in mind that other (alternative) industries also cause damage to the physical environment in the form of pollution, and so on.

Sociocultural environment

Tourism can have marked sociocultural impacts on both tourists and destination-country hosts. Many of the impacts on the host population are negative. For example, tourist-host encounters in poor countries can lead to envy and resentment on the part of hosts as they see the comparative wealth and lifestyle of the foreign visitors (the 'demonstration effect'). This may lead to dissatisfaction on the part of locals with their own standard of living, way of life and value systems, and can pose a threat to family relationships and the traditions and stability of local communities. In addition, a sizeable influx of tourists to certain Third World countries may be regarded as a form of neo-colonialism by residents of the destination country, emphasized by the 'subservient' role played by local workers in the tourism industry, such as waiters, bar staff, hotel porters and taxi drivers. More generally, large numbers of tourists may cause irritation and even antagonism in the destination as they compete with the locals for the use of overcrowded roads, beaches, and so on. Increased crime levels may also accompany high influxes of tourists. These social consequences present serious problems in certain destinations.

The negative cultural effects of tourism include the dilution and trivializing of traditional arts and crafts. Given the temporal constraints faced by tourists, they want instant culture'. The demand by foreign tourists for authentic experiences of a different culture often results in staged displays of, for example, folk dances and ceremonies. The customs and traditions of the host population are manipulated to make the experience more enjoyable for tourists; tourist attractions are often developed which conform to tourist expectations rather than accurately reflecting the genuine culture. Works of art sold to tourists may not be authentic; as mass tourism and visitors with less per capita spending power than those independently arrive, the destination may react by selling produced poorly made artefacts.

Although the detrimental sociocultural impacts of tourism have been emphasized, there are also beneficial impacts. International tourism can promote better understanding between people of different cultures and nationalities, particularly as far as those tourists are concerned who tend to travel independently and actively try to fall in with, meet and talk to the local population. Cohen suggests a typology of four tourist roles: organized mass tourist, individual mass tourist, explorer and drifter. For the mass tourist categories most arrangements are preplanned and prebooked in the tourist's home country through a travel agent, and these tourists have little direct contact with the host community. They tend to stay largely within the micro-environment of their home country, where familiarity is at a maximum and novelty at a minimum. The explorer', by contrast, arranges his trip alone and tries to get off the beaten track, but nevertheless still requires reasonable accommodation and transport. He attempts to associate with the host community and to speak their language here novelty plays a much greater role than for the mass tourist. The 'drifter' ventures furthest away from the sphere of familiarity; he attempts to live the way the people he visits live, sharing their accommodation, food and customs, and is almost completely immersed in the host culture. Clearly, the contacts between the explorer/ drifter tourists and the host community can result in considerable beneficial social impacts in terms of promoting better understanding between different nations. Tourism also has positive cultural effects; in many cases local customs and culture have been revived in host communities because of the interest shown by foreign visitors. Measurement of the impact of tourism on the sociocultural environment presents the problem of isolating the behaviour associated with tourism from that associated with other influences, which is a difficult task.

Political environment

The extent of government involvement in the tourism

industry will depend upon the political philosophy of the ruling party, the country's history, socioeconomic conditions and level of development, and the extent to which tourism supply is already in existence. Government actions can aim to support or control the tourism market, and can be directed towards the supply of or demand for tourism services.

Tourism supply

The government can play a role in facilitating tourism development by improving the tourism infrastructure of a country: for example, by building new roads and airports and raising the level of public services provided (water systems, sewers, and so on). The provision of adequate education and training facilities to meet the requirements of the tourism industry is a further means by which governments can support the tourism industry. A major method by which the authorities can encourage tourism development lies in the provision of investment incentives. These have three main purposes:

Acceleration of realization of development. By providing incentives the government can enjoy the resultant (usually economic) benefits sooner. Although a project may eventually be realized anyway (even in the absence of incentives), the provision of incentives may hasten the development.

Satisfaction of profit motive. Investment incentives may assist in the generation of profits at a level sufficient to meet corporate objectives, and thus enable an otherwise unprofitable project to go ahead.

Project discrimination. Investment incentives can be used to increase the profitability of tourist developments in certain areas (such as depressed inner cities in need of regeneration), or of certain types. Such incentives, while encouraging developments in these areas ' also make investment in locations which are not favoured (for example, holiday destinations suffering from the effects of overcrowding) relatively less attractive.

Investment incentives fall into two categories

Reduction of capital costs. This may be executed through he provision of capital grants, loans at subsidized rates, interest rate subsidies, tariff exemption on construction materials, provision of land at below market value, and so on.

Reduction of operating costs. This may be brought about by the provision of accelerated depreciation allowances, tax holidays (5 to 10 years), tariff exemption on materials and supplies, training subsidies, and so on.

'Typically tourist projects, such as the construction of hotels, have a relatively high level of fixed costs arising from the initial capital and relatively low operating costs, that is, a high Operating leverage. In order to reduce the business risk and encourage investment, the preferred type of financial help, therefore, is that which reduces capital costs (Wanhill, 1989). Investment incentives may be provided automatically for tourism industry projects, or be discretionary and biased to encourage developments in specific locations or of specific types.

In order to encourage foreign investment in the tourism industry, it may be necessary for the government to guarantee repatriation of capital and profits.

Legislation can be used to protect those resources which represent tourism attractions, for example, historical sites, national parks and monuments. Governments can also either use public funds to acquire such resources, or provide financial support for their restoration, maintenance and improvement. Governments play an important role in controlling the various sectors of the tourism industry, for example, through the imposition of fire regulations on hotels and health regulations on restaurants. In many countries there is a compulsory or voluntary system of registration and classification of hotels and other accommodation establishments. Public transport companies, tour operators, travel agencies and tour guides are often controlled through a system of licensing. The major objective of the government in this sphere is the protection of the consumer. Obstacles in relation to the foreign supply of tourism services are often imposed by governments in the form of foreign exchange restrictions, rules governing the right to establish a business, and so on. These mainly stem from concerns regarding competition. Thus, even within the European Community, national airlines have various advantages over foreign competitors. For example, foreign airlines are usually not allowed to compete in domestic air transport markets.

Tourism demand

Governments are usually involved in the stimulation of tourism demand, both domestic and inbound international, through tourism promotion. A country's national tourist office (NTO) is the organization that generally is officially responsible for carrying out this marketing function. Some of the activities of the NTO are aimed at the tourism industry and others at the consumer; with the growth in inclusive tours the marketing emphasis has had to shift from appealing merely to the independent traveller to also catering for tour operators and other sectors of the trade.

Some governments provide positive incentives in the form of subsidies to encourage their residents to take domestic holidays, for example, holiday vouchers are given to the low paid in France and subsidised holiday centres have been run by some governments in Eastern Europe. Obstacles in relation to the demand for international tourism can be imposed by governments in generating and receiving countries. Exchange controls on outbound tourists in the form of restrictions limiting the amount of currency that may be purchased for travel abroad are in effect in many countries, and departure taxes discourage foreign tourism. Time consuming administrative formalities also act as a disincentive to foreign travel. Entry visa requirements of the host country are an impediment to international tourism because of the costs in money and time. Destinations may also impose special taxes or minimum exchange requirements on tourists.

The nature and extent of government involvement with domestic international inbound and international outbound tourism varies considerably from country to country; governments can pursue active or passive roles, and seek to support or control the industry and the tourists.

In economic data terms, tourism is not defined as an industry —it is not designated a Standard Industrial Classification (SIC) code. Those industries serving tourists directly may be designated tourism-related industries. A major complicating factor is that for many of these industries tourist spending will only generate part of the total output of the industry, and, therefore, it is necessary to ascertain how much of each tourism-related industry's activities are generated by tourism gives the following percentages for tourism-generated activity in certain UK tourism-related industries in 1985: hotels and catering 42 per cent; recreational and cultural services 25 per cent; transport and travel services 23 per cent; and retail distribution 3 per cent.) The tourism 'industry' may then be viewed as follows:

> to the extent to which particular activities supply tourist rather than other markets, the sum total of the parts represents an entity, which may be described as an industry that part of the economy which has a common function of meeting tourist needs.

The tourism industry can be categorized into the following sectors: accommodation and catering, transport, travel organizers, attractions and destination organization.

Accommodation and catering sector

Many elements are included in the accommodation and catering sector. Serviced tourist accommodation includes hotels, motels, guesthouses, bed and breakfast establishments, farmhouses and cruise ships. Here, staff are at hand to supply other services in addition to the provision of rooms, which may include, for example, restaurants, bars, room service and porterage. Selfcatering tourist accommodation includes rented villas, chalets and apartments, camping sites, caravan sites, time-share properties, second homes and motorhomes. Some types of tourist accommodation can be either serviced or self-catering, for example, holiday camps/centres/ villages, and educational institutions such as universities and colleges. Tourist accommodation can also be split into the commercial and non-commercial sectors. Whereas serviced accommodation generally falls within the commercial sector, there are many types of self-catering accommodation that do not, for example, second homes, private yachts and staying with friends and relatives.

The purpose of visit of a tourist will often determine the accommodation used. Most visits for business purposes will entail the use of serviced accommodation such as hotels and these are often located in city/town centres. By contrast, holiday camps/centres/villages tend to be just used by holidaymakers, as are caravan and camping sites.

As well as being categorized into hotels, guesthouses, caravan sites, and so on, tourist accommodation can also be classified and graded. Classification denotes the splitting up of accommodation by such physical features as the number of bedrooms with and without private facilities. Grading generally relates to the number of restaurants and other facilities provided, the availability of night porters and car-parking space, and so on, although it can include subjectively assessed features such as 'atmosphere' and quality'.

Location is critical for accommodation units and, once established cannot be changed. This can be a particular problem in periods of changing tastes, on account of the fairly long time-lag between the initial plans for, say, a large hotel and its actual coming into operation. Location is important with regard to both the destination and the unit's position within the destination itself. If the destination is 4 resort, the accommodation should appeal mainly to holiday-makers, whereas accommodation in city centres is used mainly by business tourists. These distinctions are obviously not clear cut, in that many resort areas also attract convention business and many city centre hotels, which cater largely for businessmen during the week, frequently offer highly discounted rates at weekends in order to attract holidaymakers.

The hotel sector accounts for the major part of commercial serviced accommodation. There are several very large international companies in the hotel sector, and many of the major chains are enjoying considerable growth. Concentration is increasing in the hotel industry —the potential economies of scale to be enjoyed in the areas of marketing, finance, training and purchasing provide the appropriate inducements and the various systems whereby growth can come about. It should be home in mind, however, that the grouping of hotels into chains is not necessarily an indication of ownership. A recent development has been the emergence of consortia of independent hotels in order also to benefit from marketing economies of scale. In fact, most hotels graded as three-star or higher belong to hotel chains or consortia.

At the other end of the spectrum there is an enormous number of single-unit independently owned and operated accommodation establishments numerically the small business dominates the accommodation sector. Most hotels are still run by owner-operators.

A recent phenomenon has been the increasing emphasis on market segmentation in the hotel sector. Thus we have leisure hotels, country house hotels, all-suite hotels, budget hotels, and so on.

Almost one half of the total number of rooms and bed-spaces (49 percent) are located in Europe, and another 28 per cent of rooms and bed-spaces are located in North America. Europe and North America thus account together for 77 percent of rooms and bed-spaces in hotels and similar establishments throughout the world. Furthermore, it can be seen that there is an almost exact correspondence between the percentage of rooms in the world total and the percentage of bed-spaces for the various regions. Food and drink account for a substantial proportion of tourist expenditure. Catering services are provided for the tourist by a wide variety of restaurants, coffee shops, bars, etc. In addition, food and drink is provided for tourists when travelling by air, rail and sea, and sometimes on coaches. Rapid growth has taken place in the fast-food segment of the catering sector over recent years, primarily through franchising. Fast-food chains such as McDonald's, Burger King and Pizza Hut provide standardized meals in locations throughout the world, thus providing the tourist with relatively low-cost, risk (surprise)-free dining experiences.

Transport sector

The commercial transport sector of the tourism industry includes airlines, shipping lines, coach and bus operators, railways, car-rental firms and taxi operators. The non-commercial section of the transport sector, is dominated by the private car, although a few tourists travel to their destinations by privately owned aircraft or yachts.

Air transport

Air transport is by far the major form of travel to medium-haul and long-haul destinations. On the other hand, the private car is the most popular transport mode to nearby destinations, in particular for day-trips, domestic tourism and international tourism involving a land boundary.

Air transport can be divided into scheduled and charter services. Scheduled services operate on specific routes in accordance with published schedules. Charter services, on the other hand, can be cancelled if demand is insufficient; they are used mainly for holiday purposes, and seats are often sold as part of an inclusive tour, Charter flights operate on short, medium and long-haul routes, but their major concentration is in the short-haul and medium-haul high-volume markets. For example, most short-haul air travel for holiday purposes within Europe takes place on charter aircraft. By contrast, the scheduled flights which operate on short and medium-haul routes carry mainly business tourists. On long-haul routes the large majority of transport services are provided by scheduled aircraft, which cater for all tourism purposes.

Sea transport

Shipping lines comprise cruise lines and ferry operators. Medium and long-haul sea transport has largely been replaced by air transport, but on short-haul routes ferries can provide vital access between areas. Ferry services usually link road networks and are widely used by cars, buses/coaches and goods vehicles; they provide transport for all purposes. For example, a substantial proportion of UK outbound international tourism comprises tourists travelling by private car, and this involves a sea crossing.

Cruise lines have enjoyed a revival in recent years in certain areas. The large ships usually function as self-contained resorts and are targeted at holidaymakers. They tend to operate most successfully in warm/hot climates, such as the Caribbean and Mediterranean, and the recent substantial growth in the cruise market has mainly occurred in North America, with the majority of ships sailing from Florida to the Caribbean region. Fly/cruise packages enable tourists to get quickly to the chosen destination area, and, therefore, to have a worthwhile short cruise.

Coach/bus transport

Coach and bus operators play a significant role in the provision of tourist transport for non-business purposes they are the cheapest form of commercial transport. They can operate as either the main or sole form of transport, or in a subsidiary role to complement the main transport mode. An example of the former is a coach tour. An example where coach transport plays a subsidiary role is when inclusive tour travellers are transferred from the destination airport on arrival to their accommodation. Coaches are also used in destinations for excursions, In addition, scheduled express bus/coach services, mainly on intercity routes or city-resort routes, are important in the overall provision of tourist transport. In order to compete more effectively with other transport modes over longer distances, considerable efforts have been made to upgrade coach travel. The provision of improved on-board facilities such as toilet facilities, drinks and snacks, on coaches travelling on the longer routes is now quite common, and on some there are also video facilities.

Rail transport

Railways were at one time the major mode of travel in many countries, but with the private car coming to dominate short-haul transport and air travel competing over longer distances, railways have generally gone into severe decline. The main use of rail travel for tourism purposes is on the intercity services, where trains can compete effectively in terms of speed, comfort and cost with other transport modes. Time savings often occur because trains usually have the advantage that their routing goes to and from city-centre locations. The successful development and operation of highspeed trains in certain countries, such as France and Japan, has resulted in journey times over medium distances that are considerably less than those of either car or air transport (in the latter case because of the travelling time to and from airports, which are usually situated some distance from city-centres, and also the checking-in time at airports)

Car transport

The rapid rise in car ownership during the last forty years has meant that the majority of households in North America and Western Europe now possess a car, and this is the dominant transport mode for domestic tourism, as well as for much international tourism. Car travel provides accessibility and convenience that cannot be matched by other modes, but, as distances between origin and destination get longer, there is increasing competition from air transport in terms of the saving in travel time. Car-rental firms are playing an increasingly important role in the provision of tourist transport. Clearly, rented cars may simply be a substitute for private cars, but where substantial growth has recently taken place has been in the fly/drive travel market. Here, the advantage of speed in reaching the destination by air is combined with the convenience of having a car available for use in the destination. Fly/drive travel is used by both business and leisure tourists.

Taxi companies generally provide a complementary service to other transport companies, but one that is vital in the overall provision of transport for tourists. A major role lies in the provision of local transport between, say, an airport, shipping port or railway station and accommodation units. Taxi companies also service within-destination travel by tourists.

Travel organizers sector

The two main groups of travel organizers are retail travel agents and tour operators, although other groups, such as conference organizers, also go to make up this sector.

Retail travel agents

Most travel principals sell their products to tourists via retail travel agents, who receive a sale commission, but travel agents do not accept liability for the services offered by the principal. This sale outlet is extremely important in the cases of airline tickets and inclusive tours abroad. As with the retailing of services generally, the role of the retail travel agent differs from that of the retailer of manufactured goods. In the latter case, the shopkeeper makes purchases from the goods manufacturer, with which he stocks his shop. By so doing the shopkeeper takes some of the risk of production off the manufacturer. In turn, if the manufactured goods retailer finds that he is being left with unsold stocks of a particular product he will try very hard to promote sales in order to avoid losses. By contrast, the retail travel agent does not purchase travel to resell to his/her customers no stock of aircraft seats, hotel beds, and so on, is carried, and so the principal bears all the risk of production. It is only when a customer has taken the decision to purchase, say, an airline ticket or an inclusive tour that the retail travel agent approaches the principal on behalf of the potential tourist. As the retail travel agent is not in the position of having to dispose of products that he/she has previously purchased, he/she tends to display less brand loyalty towards specific companies (principals) or products than is likely to be the case with other retailers, which presents a marketing problem for the principals.

As far as consumers are concerned, the lack of brand loyalty should be an advantage in terms of obtaining more impartial advice from travel agents. In addition to the provision of information and advice, and a booking service for air, sea, rail and coach transport, inclusive tours, hotel accommodation and car hire, retail travel agents often supply various ancillary services such as travel insurance, travellers' cheques and foreign exchange, and arrange travel documentation. In order to receive a commission payment from the principal for selling the principal's services, the retail travel agent often needs to be a member of a particular association or some similar arrangement, which demonstrates that certain minimum standards of competence, financial responsibility, and so on, have been achieved. In the UK, for example, for inclusive tours arranged by tour operators who are members of the Association of British Travel Agents (ABTA), the travel agent must also be an ABTA member. Furthermore, travel agents must be licensed by the International Air Transport Association (IATA) in order to receive commission from ticket sales of IATA member airlines, which is crucial for sales of seats on international airlines. Formal approval is also necessary from British Rail, shipping companies, and so on. In the USA, travel agents need to possess a 'conference appointment' to be eligible for commission payments from the Airlines Reporting Corporation for sales of seats on domestic airlines, from the Passenger Network Services Corporation for sales of seats on international airlines, from the Cruise Lines International Association for selling cruises, and from the National Railroad Passenger Corporation (Amtrak) for sales of rail tickets.

Tour operators/tour wholesalers

Most inclusive tours involve air travel, and, particularly for short-haul and medium-haul destinations, charter flights are the dominant form of transport used in air inclusive tours. The basic inclusive tour comprises a combination of accommodation (usually hotel beds), transport (usually aircraft seats) and ancillary ground transport to effect the transfers between the destination airport and hotel. However, the use of self-catering accommodation, such as villas and apartments, in inclusive tours is proving increasingly popular, as are self-drive packages in the case of UK outbound tourism here the transport element of the inclusive tour is a ferry crossing. The basic inclusive tour can be extended to incorporate excursions and various other forms of entertainment.

Holiday packages are prepared by tour operators on a speculative basis, and it is, therefore, important for tour operators to be able to forecast likely trends in the demand for inclusive tours.

The tour operator business is characterized by horizontal integration often a few very large mass-market tour operators dominate this sector. The large mass-market tour operator business is, in turn, characterized by vertical integration, with many operators in combination with airlines and/or hotel chains.

Attractions sector

Tour operators combine accommodation and transport (and possibly other services) to give an inclusive tour, which is then sold as a holiday package at an all-inclusive price (the individual costs of the components cannot be separately identified). The majority of tour operators are tour wholesalers in that the holiday package is sold through retail travel agents, but some tour operators are tour wholesalers and retailers.

The all-inclusive price for which inclusive tours (or package holidays) are sold is usually considerably lower than would be possible if an individual tourist booked the accommodation and transport separately. The bulk buying power of tour operators enables significant savings to be made, part of which is generally passed on to the consumer. Further advantages of inclusive tours from the consumer's point of view are the convenience factor in so far as the tourist merely purchases a single travel product, and reduction in terms of product assurance when buying tour operator. In addition, in the UK, holidaymakers who book inclusive tours with ABTA member tour operators receive a financial guarantee to cover holiday payments if the tour operator should become bankrupt. The tourist attractions sector of the tourism industry is very diverse and is made up of natural and built resources; it comprises gardens, national parks, country parks, wildlife parks, stately homes, cathedrals, castles, ancient monuments, museums, industrial heritage sites, art galleries, theatres, theme parks, amusement parks, sports facilities, scenic railways, casinos, shopping malls, shops selling tourist products, and so on. In addition to these 'permanent' attractions there are many temporary attractions such as events and festivals. Attractions possess the characteristic of being able to draw people to them, and the bundle of attractions available in a destination may well have a considerable impact on its popularity.

In order to attract tourists to a destination for, say, one or two weeks, it is necessary to have a sufficient breadth of attractions. Attractions thus often tend to be clustered. Examples of successful developments in the tourist attractions sector are the growth in skiing holidays and the huge popularity of leisure/theme parks. A leisure park can be defined generally as:

> a site, uniting in a single enclosure, a series of attractions and activities and completed with a number of important side services, such as cafeterias, restaurants, shops and lodgings.

The very large growth rates experienced in ski holiday demand during recent years have led to the construction of more ski lifts and ski lodges, and greatly increased production of ski equipment and ski clothing.

Theme parks have been among the most successful tourist attractions ever developed, in particular, Disney World in Florida (which attracts about 20 million visitors per year) and Disneyland in California (which attracts about 10 million visitors per year). Disney World is much more than just a theme park based on the characters and scenes from the Disney cartoons it also has a considerable number of additional displays and features, such as the EPCOT Center (Experimental Prototype Community of Tomorrow), which is themed on the future.

The types of events and festivals that can attract tourists include sporting events such as the summer and winter Olympic Games and tennis and golf tournaments, commercial expositions, and music and garden festivals. The attractions sector of the tourism industry differs from the accommodation and catering sector and the transport sector in that it is concerned almost wholly with leisure-related tourism (although the education market can be significant for individual attractions).

Destination organization sector

The destination organization sector of the tourism industry comprises the various tourist offices and tourist associations. At the country level we have national tourist offices (NTOs); these are government-funded organizations and most of their operations are performed on a non-commercial basis. NTOs are supplemented at a lower level by regional (or state) tourist offices and local (usually town/city/resort) tourist offices. These are often reliant on local authority and/or private sector support in addition to (possibly) central government support.

NTOs are responsible for tourism matters at the national level, and their functions vary considerably from country to country. 'U, Wally the main function of an NTO is to engage in marketing of the country in order to attract more tourists. NTOs are sometimes also involved in planning for and regulation of the tourism industry, and many perform a coordinating function. Some NTOs also have certain financial responsibilities.

The marketing function of an NTO includes advertising the country internationally (and often also nationally) as a tourist destination it aims to emphasize the various general attractions that the country offers to tourists. An NTO should also undertake appropriate public relations activities. NTOs usually also have a market research department, which enables studies to be made in order to identify appropriate policies to be pursued: for example, the markets that should be targeted for promotional activities. Further marketing activities undertaken by NTOs include the provision of appropriate literature and information centres.

The planning role of NTOs may include assessing personnel and training requirements for the tourism industry in the country, and ensuring that adequate provision is made. In addition, NTOs can be involved in the presentation and improvement of the tourist products in the destination. NTOs may also be required to assess the infrastructure requirements of a country, which would be necessary in order to cope with expected future patterns of tourism demand, and then make appropriate recommendations. The development of infrastructure is generally a public sector responsibility, and includes provision of water supply, sewage disposal, power supply (electricity, gas, etc.), communication networks (telephone, fax, etc.), roads, airport runways, railway lines, and harbours. These facilities are used by local residents and tourists alike, but must be designed to accommodate usage at times of peak demand (often at the peak of the tourist season). If the infrastructure at a destination is inadequate, then the full potential of the tourism superstructure hotels, restaurants, entertainment facilities, etc. will fail to be realized. The regulatory and coordinating function of NTOs may include licensing of certain sectors of the tourism industry, regulation of accommodation standards and prices, coordination of national promotional activities with those of individual participants in the industry (airlines, hotels, and so on), and acting as the coordinating link between the various regional and local tourist offices and tourist associations in order to ensure maximum effectiveness.

A major financial duty of some NTOs is to contribute funds from government sources for approved projects. These NTOs are usually responsible for directing the aid towards certain types of tourism projects in order to achieve particular objectives for example, if one objective is to extend the tourist season, this may be achieved by encouraging the construction of all-weather leisure facilities.

Regional or state tourist offices have a similar working pattern to that of an NTO. A major part of their activities is concerned with marketing the regions to potential tourists, and includes advertising campaigns, exhibitions and provision of regional literature on accommodation and attractions. They also provide development advice to private sector tourism operators within the region, and undertake market research in order to be able to disseminate more detailed local information. Local tourist offices are mainly concerned with promoting the town/city/resort.

International tourism: the future

One thing can safely be said of tourism in the future: it will increase. Nothing but a global war can prevent that. Current forecasts suggest a 5 per cent yearly growth in international tourist flows through the 1990s, and that means a lot of tourists; expenditure is likely to grow even faster in real terms. But where will the increase occur? And where will there be a decline? These are more difficult questions. They will be answered partly by innovatory practices and new products, and the next question is what will they look like? This chapter examines a number of issues that are likely to be landmarks of the future including:

> directions of growth and decline; products; the role of government: intervention and market forces; economic and social consequences of tourism; working conditions; ownership; tourism backlash; blockages and clearances including: currency exchange and frontier formalities; the transport infrastructure; nationalism and violence; pricing; health; the affairs of Eastern Europe.

Directions of growth and decline

Factors that influence the decision to journey abroad have already been identified. Overwhelmingly, tourism is related to personal expenditure, although international tourism is also influenced by exchange rates. A recent publication suggested that a 1 per cent growth in private consumption leads to a 0 per cent growth in tourism; but a 2.5 per cent increase leads to 4 per cent more tourism, while a 5 per cent figure adds up to a 10 per cent growth.

This accelerating relationship between economic and tourism growth rates leads to some interesting speculations for Europe, where the 2.5 per cent rate coincides exactly with forecasts for growth during the 1990s, which suggests that crossborder tourism both within and from Europe will increase rapidly; the increase will be assisted, no doubt, by the physical and psychological influences of the single market. The increase will be all the greater if the growth rates in the poorer countries of the Community, such as Spain, are higher.

Similar growth figures are anticipated for the other major industrial countries United States, Canada, Japan and Australia suggesting that for them also there will be considerable increases in tourist flows. The extra tourists generated will no doubt mainly follow conventional routes, although the numbers will certainly lead to an increasing popularity for destinations that are currently less popular. The 5 per cent figure leads to some even more intriguing speculations about countries outside Europe, because it is *below* the anticipated growth forecasts for the newly industrializing countries of South East Asia. This suggests a new source of tourism flows. It is possible, indeed, that even smaller growth rates than four or five per cent will increase the flow of tourists from developing countries. This arises from the unequal distribution of wealth in the poorer countries; where this applies, in a country like India, a relatively small growth in wealth could produce a larger increase in the demand for tourism. A growing middle class will be interested in foreign travel.

Growing wealth in Asia, and the move to use part of

the growth in longer holidays, will help to change the directions of tourist travel, with an increase in holiday resorts in the Pacific. Japan will contribute to this when more of its wealth is translated into shorter working years by longer holidays. In that country, too, there is now government encouragement to travel abroad in order to reduce the balance of payments surplus.

But the increase in tourism from the newly industrializing countries and certain other developing countries is likely to be matched by an increase in tourism to those countries. This will happen because domestic tourism will also increase and with it the necessary facilities and infrastructure will emerge. Ile industry will then have stronger incentives to promote tourism from abroad. Aggressive marketing and a reduction in air fares in real terms will combine with a general growth in business to produce new directions of travel.

Traditional sunshine and seashore holiday resorts—such as the Mediterranean coast are near capacity already and some decline may be expected with the rising popularity of inland holidays. On the other hand, ageing populations in the industrial countries will lead to the promotion of more offpeak holidays.

A sideeffect of the increase is that nations and wouldbe suppliers will read the statistics and be encouraged to enter the holiday market. As a result, it is likely that supply will move ahead of demand. This can be expected to increase competition and produce a general rise in standards.

Against all the pressure towards expansion stands the possibility of a world slump. A decline in the disposable income of the richer countries is unlikely to affect international tourism in the short term. The old (with enhanced pensions, including lump sum payments) and the young (with two incomes to a household) will retain some protection against setbacks and a propensity to use spare income on travel. But, in the longer term, the gearing effect that has rapidly increased tourist spending can work the other way equally rapidly.

Demographic factors are often quoted, like the fact that the over 50s will outnumber the 25 to 50 year olds in Europe by the end of the century and that there will be less young people around but those less will be much more prosperous. Also significant will be the general increase in the population, which continues against all the fluctuations in the birth rate.

Products

A major new product looms in the next century in the form of space travel.' This may be a long way off, although pressure to make possible a limited number of highcost flights will build up as soon as techniques are devised to make capsules more inhabitable. Meanwhile, more mundane changes must be expected nothing even as revolutionary as the package tour once was. Product innovation is more likely to be about unpackaging rather than packaging, providing more individual attention within a number of price bands. This means at the top level, more high luxury, individual, escorted tours with every possible need met. At a lower levei, it will mean that tour operators exercise considerable ingenuity to combine individual arrangements in much the same way that freight is bulked now. The result will be an arrangement that appears personal to the tourist, but is less expensive than it would otherwise be because a block booking of facilities has been made. Even so, package holidays are not going to disappear. Indeed, they may increase in number as third world countries come into the market; they will make international tourism available to a wider population, one whose expectations have been raised. It is the relative importance of package tours that will decline.

Package tours and individual holidays

Some sectors of the inclusive tour market will continue to grow, but the core business of hotelbased summer tours is in decline. Air trafficcontrol delays are one factor in this decline, as are health scares in the major Mediterranean resorts, but there does seem to be an underlying dissatisfaction with traditional packages. Clients have become tired of the increasingly developed and overcommercialized sun and sand resorts. Moreover, the pricebased market share battle between the major operators has in reality or in perception lowered the quality of the holidays on offer. The traditional package holiday has become unfashionable, and the concern is that this is permanent rather than temporary.

Several factors have combined to depress the market in Britain. Shortterm high interest rates have reduced discretionary spending and the price wars waged by competitors have reduced the quality of the product and profitability. Add to these the costs of congestion and bad publicity about overcrowding at destinations and there may be a longterm reaction against the package tour. This has not been the reaction in the rest of Europe, howeveror at least not yet. Other package tour markets, such as West Germany, appear to have avoided the low price and low quality trap; as a consequence, they seem quite healthy. In Britain, despite the dramatic fall, there wii still be 89 million package holidays sold in 1990, which, if not the hoped for 13 million, is still a large number. The accessibility of package holidays is still an attractive option for many. For the market to survive it has to maintain its quality. This means a higher price, because good accommodation and attendant support services do not come cheap. However, the general signs are that the traditional package holiday has become less popular in the industrial countries. All tour operators are having to adjust to a market that demands independence but wants the advantages of bulk purchase as well as independence of action. In addition, the market for holidays specially tailored to specific segments (such as birdwatching and hiking) is large and growing rapidly. It will be in this market that the smaller operators will have good prospects.

Individual holidays are already increasing through the letting of individual accommodation (like the gftes in France), the growth of timeshare and the purchase of holiday homes. There is scope for expansion in all three, especially for timeshare, in spite of recent setbacks in Britain. Reservation systems especially those used by airlines will increasingly be able to cope with customized arrangements.

The role of government

Governments generally favour tourism unlike some of their subjects. The visitor brings foreign currency and assists the balance of payments; for countries with special problems, there is the bonus that a high proportion of the tourists bring hard currency. This situation is not going to change, but the forms of government intervention will. One likely change is from direct assistance to indirect.

Within limits imposed by government policies, investment incentives and grants for the development of tourism have become universal. The more interventionist-minded governments have given loans up to 100 per cent of the capital costs of new hotels on easy terms, sometimes interest free for an initial period. In countries with less interventionist governments, measures for encouraging new investment, at least, have been applied to tourism. In addition, the transport infrastructure is statesupported in most countries. Further local government assistance may well be available, even in countries where national governments do not provide support.

In the future, however, direct aid by government or local government is likely to decline as tourism increases. A cycle, already evident, will become more pronounced. If we assume that the cycle starts with areas that are seen as having potential for tourism, such areas will attract direct aid, especially if there is also high unemployment. As direct aid becomes less necessary, other measures become more important such as attempts to relieve overcrowded areas or to help spread the season by publicity or offseason entertainments and special events. Other forms of official assistance include aid to special groups, such as farmers, to enhance farm incomes by offering accommodation and farm tours. Help to the voluntary sector is yet another form of assistance. Not only has voluntary effort been the basis of tourism developments in many countries, but hardpressed groups in the performing arts can find justification for official support by claiming that they encourage foreign visitors.

But the role of government is not likely to be confined to direct or indirect support for tourist facilities. Two controversial issues are safeguarding standards and training. On these issues, also, there seems to be a cycle of official support that waxes and wanes.

Countries such as Switzerland have a highly developed system for both standards and training, while the degree of acknowledged professionalism in the industry is higher in some countries than in others. It is doubtful whether any other country has equalled Swiss standards; it is certain that many aspire. The controversy is between state-sponsored or voluntary standards for facilities and for training. The climate of opinion in much of the world today is in favour of selfregulation and privatization. In a fragmented industry such as this, it may well turn out that some official control is necessary in view of the competition. As supply creeps ahead of demand, countries considered to have lax controls over, for instance, standards of accommodation may well find themselves losing out.

A controversy that has influenced official policies over the last twenty years is that between economic growth and the limits to growth. Once considered a minor issue that, in any case, was only of interest to the richest countries, the argument is rapidly becoming universal stimulated by events like floods in Bangladesh, partly caused by agricultural changes in India. The argument is mainly concerned with the use of natural resources, in agriculture or in forestry, but it also affects road and rail building, and the use of fuel. A new road that may be economically desirable may not be wanted on social or environmental grounds. It may even open up sensitive areas to overvisiting.

Government initiatives aimed at improving the transport infrastructure will be more carefully scrutinized in the future; this can be expected to stimulate research into new technologies, which will themselves need assistance to become viable. Infrastructure problems are discussed below.

Economic and social consequences of tourism

International tourism has been credited with benefits such as improving the balance of payments, providing employment and helping citizens of different countries to understand one another. This last consideration has influenced the European Commission to arrange visits and educational programmes between member states and to launch a European Year of Tourism with, among its objectives, 'bringing Europeans still closer to one another.'

Inevitably, each of these advantages has its characteristic drawback. The balance of payments is only benefited by inward tourism, the type of employment is sometimes considered undesirable often as a last resort by local nationals and hostility can arise as well as understanding. European countries, such as Spain and Portugal, owe part of their success with foreign tourism to their prices. These are likely to increase rapidly, partly as a sideeffect of a favourable balance of payments, which will also raise the value of the currency, and partly as a consequence of continuing industrialization causing wages to rise. As a result, the two countries are likely to experience strong competition from tourist facilities on the North African shores of the Mediterranean.

The professionalism of tourism staff, it has already been indicated, varies from country to country; it has also been suggested that competition will lead to upgrading in many countries. Continuing efforts will be made to dispel the image of lowpaid workers in poor conditions. There will remain, however, a strong lure for providing employment for immigrants, legal and illegal, and for temporary workers who are themselves tourists. The increasing availability of international tourism will do nothing to lessen the ambitions of those who cannot afford it.

Rival pressures from demand for more professionalism and higher pay on the one hand (a pair of factors that do not necessarily support one another) and a continuing supply of cheap labour on the other are likely to increase the current trend towards a twotier labour force. Ultimately, mechanization of the more menial tasks may reduce the lower tier. Currently, tourist facilities, like the service sector in general, are noted for being labourintensive, but this is likely to change. One reason why hotels, for instance, have become more labourintensive is because of the general move upmarket, which became apparent in the 1970s. In the 1990s, it is not improbable that selfservice will move upmarket.

The facilities sector, as opposed to transport, has always demonstrated in an exaggerated form an ownership structure common to other industries concentration at one end and fragmentation at the other. The fact that catering and tourism facilities are an attractive way into a business of one's own is not going to change, nor are the opportunities for building empires in hotels or theme parks. In this sector the extremes support one another: major companies operate franchising arrangements for small firms as well as supporting tourism activities which it is not economic for them to own. The larger owners are likely to put much effort into anticipating or finding new tourist centres. This will extend large company ownership to regions that have not known it before.

Running through this chapter have been themes that are likely to intensify the backlash against tourism, first noted as a growing threat since the early 1970s. The industry is an easy target for criticism, and will become easier as it grows ever more universal, raising and dashing expectations in the process and bringing more foreign ownership to overpower more local businesses. Perceptions about the character of tourism employment have already been mentioned: a major grievance is that the periodical influx of foreigners disturbs the calm and injures the culture of a locality. Whatever the economic benefits to the country or to the town, many local inhabitants do not benefit. They form a core of opposition, which may centre around local issues such as culture or care of the countryside. It is likely that environmentalism will be increasingly seen whether justly or not as opposed to tourism.

The tourism backlash will probably spread, but will

generally focus around local issues. Neither national nor international organizations are likely to treat it seriously as a world phenomenon; at the most, it will be looked upon as a curable problem of little relevance to policymakers. The following factors, which are related to general world issues, are likely to feature more prominently on the agenda of world organizations in the years to come.

Currency exchange and frontier formalities

One of these factors is currency exchange. There can be little doubt that irresistible pressures towards a European currency are building UP and thatgive or take a hiccough or twothiswill become a reality in the next few years. The next question is how long before the adoption of a world currency comes on the agenda? A European currency, if successful, will surely stimulate a demand elsewhere. Back in 1988, *The Economist* forecast that a world currency (provisionally entitled 'The Phoenix') would come into existence in about thirty years' time. 2 Although a world currency would not take over all countries in the world at once, any more than a European currency would be acceptable to all Europeans at the same time, it would be a boon to tourists and tour operators.

The psychological boost, resulting from becoming accustomed to money that can be used almost anywhere, may well prove even more significant than overcoming the relatively minor inconvenience of exchanges and travellers'cheques. The change will obviously not be so welcome to banks and other organizations that provide exchange facilities, although they may benefit in other ways money transfer will become less expensive.

Another probable change that will not be welcome to a number of interests, including the tourists themselves, is the abolition of 'duty free' goods. The demise in Europe of this survival from the days of sailing boats has been forecast for many years and has yet to happen. If vested interests and public opinion are strong enough to retain in Europe a practice that is clearly incompatible with the principles of a common market, it must be a long time before duty free is brought to an end globally. Nevertheless, it is surely true that this special privilege to the traveller will be ended eventually.

A consequence of this abolition, at least in the short term, will be a tightening of frontier controls there will be a temptation for travellers to become petty smugglers. In the longer term, there is the prospect of international agreements on excise duties and sales taxes that make smuggling less worth while. But this prospect has still not produced an agreement within the European Community, where excise duties vary widely. The difficulties of producing standard rates of value added tax and excise in the Community provide an idea of the problems likely to be encountered worldwide. Nevertheless, the growth of travel is going to persuade governments to look hard at the possibilities of reducing frontier formalities.

The transport infrastructure

Congestion is a word currently associated with all forms of transport. Airports and air routes are crowded, roads are at a standstill and trains are filled beyondcapacity. Forairtransport, thenextten years appearto be a holding period. An anticipated growth rate of 46 per cent per year can just be supported by better management and improvements of the existing infrastructure and increases in aircraft size. Passengers will have to accept some penalties in less convenient scheduling and a greater use of differential pricing to encourage offpeak travel. Some relief will be provided by improvements in other forms of transport, but the growth of longerdistance travel for both business and leisure will wipe out the effects of many of the shortterm measures. In the next century, at least three important technical developments are likely to lead to a steep expansion in air travel. One is the emergence of a new generation of shorttakeoff aircraft and another is the finding of a solution to the noise problem. The latter development is needed to make the former acceptable. These developments could transform air transport early in the next century. Quieter aircraft could mean airports closer to city centres and to the relaxing of restrictions on night flights. Already, the existence of allegedly quieter planes has led operators to demand that airports remain open for longer hours. A third technical change will take longer: thirty years has been suggested as a likely period before space technology is applied to intercontinental travel. The possibility of travelling from Tokyo to Paris in an hour must surely stimulate research and investment.

Congestion in the air has stimulated investment in surface transport; rail against all the expectations of a decade ago is making the running with technical advances meaning that speed increases will make rail competitive for lengthening journeys. A further stimulus is being provided by the growth of fixed links, such as the Channel Tunnel between Britain and France, the series of bridges and tunnels that will link Scandinavia to the rest of Europe by the end of the decade and the routes joining the islands in Japan. These links have also stimulated road building. Evidently the car is going to be the principal means of transport for the foreseeable future, but a greater use of multiple modes of transport is a possibility. The current low technology version loading cars on to trains currently accounts for a very minor part of the industry. Indeed, cheaper and more efficient car hire blocked growth in carbyrail systems many years ago. The revival of the multimode transport for freight, especially in North America, may well stimulate new inventions that will affect road and rail transport but never to a great extent. A bigger change will come with the development of a form of transport that combines the advantages of both. Indeed, when railways were first invented, they experimented with attaching private carriages to trains. Intermodal transport is a major topic of discussion nowadays.

Nationalism and violence

Uprisings and riots are much publicized, but have little effect on tourism in the longer term. A few years ago violence in Greece caused a decrease in tourism to that country, but the decrease only lasted a short time and is now forgotten. Similarly, a bomb on a plane causes cancellation during the following twelve months, but bookings revive after that. In some circumstances, violence can be an attraction. Tourism to Fiji increased after the revolution there, because pictures of the violence also showed the beauty of the islands.

Pricing

A considerable stimulus to international tourism has been the price. For a richer country a combination of weak currencies and lowwages has made holidays in even distant poor countries attractive. This combination changes, sometimes quickly. Relative exchange rates change and wages increase. For the foreseeable future, there will always be poorer countries to take the place of those that raise their prices unduly and this will further the trend towards longdistance travel.

Longestablished threats to health, such as contaminated water or infectious diseases, have been much reduced; malaria, once a strong disincentive to travel in both Africa and Asia, has been largely overcome by readily available tablets that are also easy to take although the emergence of fresh strains immune to existing drugs may still cause scares. One infectious disease AIDS has caused a setback in some areas, or at least a rethink of certain tourist attractions. A possible influence on future attitudes is the danger of skin cancer from overexposure to the sun. This is hardly likely to be more than a passing scare for a fortnight's holiday; but health consciousness is still likely to affect tourism patterns.

4

Tourism in Developing Countries

In many developing countries there is a scarcity of resources, a lack of expertise, and limited involvement in tourism by the private sector. For these reasons, government has often had to play a central role. Also, in the initial stages of tourism development, the government might be the only body which has resources to invest in the sector. It may also be the main guarantor for overseas investment. Government, in addition to providing the necessary infrastructure for tourism, has, in a number of countries, actually engaged as an entrepreneur in the tourism sector. This may have been done for political reasons or, usually, has reflected the absence of private investors with the capital, experience and willingness to invest in tourism. However, over the last ten years, there has been growing concern that tourism has not delivered its expected benefits. To a large extent this might be a condition of the fact that tourism has given rise to expectations which were beyond its capacity to meet. There are many reasons for this, not least being the economic imperative which has long been associated with tourism. For these reasons, it is now appropriate to reappraise the role of tourism in the development process and to ask whether a new approach is necessary? This reappraisal is something which is exercising the interests of politicians, planners and, not least, academics because of the growing importance of tourism in the global, regional and national economics. A further factor is that, as tourism has become more important in global economic activity, then not only governments, but also a very wide range of international agencies and interest groups are concerned with its future.

This chapter considers these issues and examines what are the options for change and, in particular, examines whether a greater degree of private sector involvement in tourism policy formulation, planning, and implementation would be a major improvement on the current situation.

It is this wide-ranging and complex nature of tourism that requires careful analysis. Individual, ad hoe responses to tourism opportunities and problems do not constitute a policy for tourism. Such responses may merely provide short-term solutions to essentially long-term problems. There is no simple consensus of what is meant by the term policy.

There is a strong linkage between policies, planning and implementation strategies. In many countries, particularly in the developing world, the formulation of policies and plans for the tourism sector have usually been undertaken by foreign consultants; implementation has been almost neglected with the host government being expected in most cases to undertake this for itself. Perhaps this is one of the fundamental weaknesses of tourism development where much emphasis has been placed on the technical coherence of the plans but where a lesser amount of attention is given to implementation. This weakness is probably one of the major reasons that tourism, in many countries, has been unable to match the high economic expectations which the sector has been accorded. The traditional approach to tourism planning There are a number of general characteristics which can be ascribed to the planning process for tourism in developing countries.

1. There has been a dominant role played by government. As noted in the introductory section, there are many good reasons why government has been given this role.
2. From its introduction as part of development strategy, there has always been a major emphasis on the economic benefits which tourism could generate. This is not surprising given the need in many developing countries to create jobs and incomes, and to generate the necessary foreign exchange to help with the development effort. It was regarded very much as a 'growth point' activity.
3. The major expertise for undertaking planning and assisting with policy formulation for the tourism sector was usually, and still is provided and financed by international agencies. For this reason, tourism was developed very much as a by-product of the experience of the developed countries. As a consequence, development was usually guided and managed by foreign advisers, financed by foreign investors, and created what was, and is still regarded in some countries, as 'a foreigners' industry run by foreigners for foreigners.'
4. In addition to its traditional role of providing general infrastructure and also for the tourism sector, government sometimes had to undertake the role of entrepreneur to 'kick-start' the sector. There are many examples of tourism development investments wholly owned by governments which undertake what are operational and entrepreneurial roles. For example, the Indian Tourism Development Corporation invested extensively in hotels and airlines, and also provided travel agency and transport services. State ownership of airlines is common throughout the world.

As this scenario unfolded, and when the expected benefits from tourism were not achieved or only partly achieved, a more critical attitude towards the sector evolved. Governments and development agencies began to ask why tourism was not producing the volume of benefits which most of its adherents had promised. There was also a noticeable lack of investment in the tourism sector by the World Bank, the African Development Bank and the Asian Development Bank, all agencies which were strongly represented in regions of the world where tourism was a growing and major activity. In the case of the Asian Development Bank and the African Development Bank, direct investment in tourism, other than in general infrastructure, really did not occur until the late 1980s. The main institutional support for tourism was made by the United Nations Development Programme, particularly in providing technical assistance, usually through the World Tourism Organisation. The European Community has become arguably the principal support for tourism in the developing world, particularly facilitated by the LOME IV Convention. It currently has major tourism support initiatives in the South Pacific, the Caribbean and Asia.

Although there was widespread recognition of the potential of tourism to stimulate economic growth, there were apparent a number of problems which required analysis.

There are a number of general problems which can be associated with the history of tourism development. As mentioned above, there has been general disappointment with the economic returns from the tourism sector. Perhaps this is not surprising. In the early 1970s the major emphasis on tourism as a development option was based on a very high expectation of its ability to generate economic advantages, usually related to foreign exchange earnings, to the creation of jobs, to the generation of both personal and government incomes, and to its acting as a stimulant to regional development. Strategic importance was placed on increasing the number of visitor arrivals, increasing the per visit spend, and increasing the length of stay. Priority was given to the gross volume of tourist expenditure. What was not considered in sufficient detail was the input necessary to retain a high proportion of that expenditure. It is well known that within developing countries leakages from the tourism sector are high, particularly in island economies.

The major criticism must be that tourism planners simply concentrated on creating more tourist expenditure without addressing the attendant issues of how to retain a higher proportion of that expenditure within the country. The net retention factor should have been the major economic target, but surprisingly this was not greatly addressed by planners. The growing volume of leakages out of the tourism sector often reflected the state of underdevelopment of a particular country's economy and its inability to take advantage of intersectoral linkages to provide the inputs necessary to the tourism sector. To a large extent these problems are structural and can only be addressed over a long period of time. However, their accumulated effect was to create disappointment with the economic returns received from tourism.

This disappointment was exacerbated by insufficient knowledge of the market mix of international tourism. It is recognised that for most developing countries tourists are generated from the relatively wealthy advanced developed countries. The flow patterns have not greatly changed over the last fifty years or so and we find that the scale and type of development in third world countries is determined not by themselves, but by the market demands which are interpreted by the foreign tour operators. Cohen's term ecological bubble' has stood the test of time in the sense that it describes the expectations of tourists from developed countries travelling to developing countries. Without any doubt, these expectations are still maintained and therefore determine what should be provided in the developing countries for the foreign tourists. It causes a situation where within third world countries you often have first world facilities which are provided on an enclave basis for foreign visitors. This, of course, then gives rise to social and political discontent. Egypt, unfortunately, is a current example of this situation.

Although there is social and political discontent with Tourism we have to accept the reality that tourism is essentially an international industry and one which is market-driven. This means that what has to be supplied has to meet international standards and international demands it is not sufficient to provide what a country wishes to offer without reference to expected standards. To a large extent, the problem has been that government has created facilities, aided by advisers, without realising that it is the market which determines acceptability and not government or planners.

This comment does not imply that the market for tourist destinations and level of services expected is homogeneous; it is not. Supplies of tourist amenities and services should identify those market segments which best match what the destination country has to offer and what it wants to offer. Demand is still driven by consumer preference, but that preference is linked to what a country perceives to be its desired form of development. Low-volume, market-specific tourism (eco-tourism) might be suitable for some destinations, e.g. the Maldives, but high-volume, general beach tourism could be more suited for others, e.g. Spain.

The inability of governments to react to market changes is not surprising. Government mainly provides infrastructure or limited revenue-generating facilities such as hotels, transport services, and travel agencies in some cases, which provide services to tourists. However, government with its bureaucratic structure is unable to react quickly to market changes and often lacks the flexibility in managerial approach and vision that allows a high quality service to be developed. Government, for these reasons, is not a very useful or effective source of tourism management and this is one of the critical areas where much of the disappointment with tourism has to be focused.

Criticisms of the noneconomic aspects of tourism have also increased. In the early 1970s, probably until the mid-decade, the major arguments for tourism were related to the economic benefits it could bring to the developing countries. Very little attention was given to the social, cultural and environmental impacts of tourism. These concerns certainly became more apparent in the late 1970s and 1980s, but to a very large extent the major thrust in development policy was on creating facilities which would attract foreign visitors and maximise economic impacts. A further consideration was that little attention was given to the host communities. Planning was essentially for foreign tourists and to meet the demands of the foreign markets.

There was also a growing political awareness that because of the nature of tourism and its reliance on the international market it was a sector over which the host country and governments could exercise only limited control. This gave rise to a feeling that it was an industry which had a great risk attached to its investments, because markets, that is tourists, could virtually disappear without any cause other than political or social instability. We see the effect that economic depression in the 1990s in the developed countries had on tourist flows to the developing world. Major political factors, e.g. the Gulf War, have had worldwide effects on tourism flow patterns. It is these unforeseen fluctuations, induced by events often outside the control and influence of the tourist receiving countries, which have made many investors wary of the tourism sector.

The very low levels of development in certain tourist -receiving countries meant that indigenous people simply did not have the income to participate in tourism. The provision of facilities for tourists, very much in accordance with the 'ecological bubble' concept, meant that there was a tendency to create advanced enclaves within third world countries. Tourism, not surprisingly, was seen as a foreigners' industry creating facilities for a privileged elite which many indigenous people would never likely be able to afford. It is this type of image which has often caused problems for tourism, where many people argue that it is a demonstration of affluence in the midst of squalor. It is difficult to repudiate this argument except in economic terms. Investment in tourism should be justified on the basis of having a comparative advantage *vis-a-vis* other investment possibilities. The surplus generated from tourism investment then can, in part, be used for other development purposes. Too often, governments and national tourism organisations have failed to relay this message to local national populations; ignorance of tourism often breeds suspicion and misunderstanding.

Given the circumstances described above, there appeared to be three scenarios for change which can be considered.

1. *Status quo*: In this situation it is envisaged that the planning for tourism in developing countries will proceed as it has traditionally proceeded, that is, in

giving a central focus to government and in trying to develop the sector based on maximum visitor flows. However, there is a modification to this scenario in that planners now are much more sensitive to the needs of the host community and are also recognising that not all types of tourism are necessarily beneficial. This means that a greater emphasis is being placed on the appropriate type and scale of tourism development in various countries.

2. *Technical tinkering* Technical tinkering reflects a situation where there is no intention to change the status quo described above except to try and improve the benefits from tourism by taking into account the economic structure of the country and ensuring that better linkages are achieved. This, if successful, would obviously have the effect of increasing the net retention of tourism earnings, but it would still envisage a planning scenario driven by a central role for government.

3. *Radical change* In this case the central role of government is diminished and a much greater emphasis is placed on the involvement, both at policy and planning levels and through implementation, of the private sector. It is this scenario which seems to be gaining support, particularly from the international agencies.

In order to obtain enhanced benefits from investment in tourism, a new approach has become apparent in the last three or four years. This approach does not necessarily change the planning dimensions applied to tourism but rather reorders the priorities and places greater emphasis on the indigenisation of ownership and operation within the tourism sector.

Some developing countries, e.g. India, the Bahamas and Kenya, have generated considerable expertise in tourism, but most countries still rely on the international agencies to fund initial development and to assist with the technical expertise required to develop the sector. The United Nations Development Programme is increasingly expecting countries either to become the executing agency for tourism projects or to carry out this task in conjunction with specialist agencies such as the World Tourism Organisation. A major change, therefore, is the increased determination to ensure that there is a transfer of knowledge and expertise from the consultants to their indigenous counterparts.

Second, there is a growing realisation that not all types of tourism are appropriate in certain countries or within regions of the countries. To a large extent this change in emphasis has been a product not only of developing expertise in tourism planning, but also of the growing number of interest groups who are now concerned about the scale, type and nature of tourism projects. The emergence of terms such as 'ecotourism', 'green tourism', 'responsible tourism' reflects the fact that there is more interest now in the noneconomic impacts (and benefits) arising from tourism than there were before. There is also a realisation that if tourism is to be sustainable in the long term, its sustainability is not based on economic criteria alone; it also has to be sustainable by becoming acceptable to the host communities. In countries where the tourist host community is essentially rural, then this usually means that rural people are the poorest people in the country and those with the lowest incomes. A growing concern, therefore, is that tourism should stimulate regional development and raise rural incomes and should do this in such a way that there is a growing indigenisation of ownership of tourism facilities and operations of those facilities by local people. The idea that tourism can simply be imposed on a country or a region has now been largely rejected in favour of a much more balanced approach to the needs of visitors and hosts.

The issue of indigenisation is important. One of the general grievances against tourism in developing countries is that much of the investment is owned by foreigners and managed by foreigners, and that the profits leak from the country. There are good reasons why this situation has prevailed but there are no good reasons why it should prevail indefinitely. Governments, by training and educational policies, must try to develop a management cadre and, eventually, an indigenous top managerial class. However, there is also a need to encourage indigenous investment in the tourism sector to ensure that benefits from tourism accrue to local people. As Richter has noted 'those who shape tourism policy must recognise its complexity and be more responsive to those who challenge sanguine assumptions about tourism benefits'.

In addition to this change of emphasis there has also been a change in attitudes towards how the benefits of tourism are best secured. As we see in the former Soviet Union, the political changes there have led to the emergence of the private sector and the market as the major determinants of economic growth. More tourism planners are accepting that flexibility is essential to take advantage of market opportunities and to react quickly to market changes. It is felt that this flexibility can only be obtained through an increased private sector involvement in tourism.

Privatisation usually refers to an economic situation where the major developments in the economy are stimulated by private sector investors. This classically is the situation in most of the developed countries of the world. The argument is that market sensitivity is essential for sustainable development. Market sensitivity can only be acquired by those most involved in the marketplace. This involvement is mainly the concern of the private sector firms which provide the services for tourists. As profit-driven organisations, they need to be providers of good service standards at acceptable prices in order to survive. It is very interesting to note that in most developing countries it is the government-owned services which usually are loss-making, most obviously in hotel and airline activities.

Market-sensitivity and the need for a greater involvement of the private sector diminishes the role of government in an operational but not in a control sense. Government still is responsible for the overall acceptability of the type of tourism that is developed. It also has a social responsibility to ensure that the benefits of tourism are not gained to the major detriment of social, cultural and environmental standards.

A movement from a centralised planning and operational system to one of complete privatisation has dangers, The current chaos in the states of the former Soviet Union indicates the perils of a rapid structural transformation. In this sense many of the developing countries are in no position to move towards a fully privatised tourism sector, but rather there is a movement towards more decentralisation and a greater attempt to operate government services at a more commercial standard. In China, for example, the new economic policies espoused by the government have designated certain zones where private enterprise is the dominant economic force. In tourism the Chinese authorities have also invested heavily, but the operation of most facilities has been left to the private sector.

Privatisation should not be regarded as a point of political dogma but rather as a pragmatic shift in policy which may have to be implemented in stages.

Governments are under increasing pressure from the international lending agencies to move towards more market sensitive economies. If this movement is too rapid, as some structural adjustment programmes have been in African countries, then economic and political disturbances are likely. The tourism sector is perhaps only different in that it is, for most developing countries, an export sector where competitive standards and prices are determined by the international market. Most suppliers of tourism services in the developing countries are price takers rather than price-makers. If tourism prices are subsidised, then this is not usually a deliberate policy of government but rather a consequence of the bargaining power of foreign tour operators.

Given these international pressures and the varying levels of economic development in third world countries, privatisation measures have to advance cautiously and selectively.

Limits to privatisation in tourism For most developing countries the government will still have a major role to play in development strategy. This reflects the situation that in most of these countries the private sector is still embryonic, and in certain parts of the economy, may not be represented at all. This is not an argument for continuing centralisation of policy and operation of facilities. It may, at a point in time, simply reflect the situation as it is seen.

Given this particular background then the first stage of privatisation is to move towards a more commercial aspect of development. This may be done through the setting up of parastatal companies which, although owned by government, will have the flexibility to operate in the private sector and to offer services at a commercial rate. This so-called commercialisation will make the operation of tourist facilities much more sensitive to market trends and forces than if these facilities were managed from a ministry. Over a period of time, a movement towards more privatised services can be made, either through the setting up of joint venture companies or by the privatisation of certain designated services, e.g. travel agency services, hotels, transport, etc.

The problem facing the development of tourism in the third world countries is that tourism often is most influenced by externalities. These externalities, such as the Gulf War or a serious downturn in the economies of major tourism generating countries, can have dramatic and rapid effects in the tourist-receiving countries. It is for these reasons that governments often find it difficult to react to market changes. Private sector companies whose very existence relies on tourism will make such changes because of the need to ensure that business continues. It is the competitive nature of the market which suggests that the private sector is likely to best influence tourism development and can be proactive rather than simply reactive to market forces.

As a general concept it is difficult to know how far privatisation can extend. The considerations must be based on the levels of economic development, on tourism experience and on the political expectations of specific countries. An over-rapid movement towards privatisation will obviously cause as many problems as it produces benefits.

There is a growing body of opinion which suggests that the involvement of the private sector should not be limited to the provision of tourism services, but that the private sector should also be involved in tourism planning and policy formulation. This not only meets the general understanding that private sector companies are best able to read the market, but it also reflects the fact that governments have very limited budgets and therefore cannot invest in tourism or in any other sector of the economy without limitation. It is usually the case that government will be involved in creating and approving the international image that is projected for the country in the tourism marketplace. International publicity and the servicing of the travel trade is very expensive. Most developing countries, even those with the most advanced tourism sectors, still find that international promotion and marketing is a heavy outlay in terms of foreign exchange. Increasingly governments are attempting to involve the private sector companies in these activities. However, often the private sector companies feel that government does not have the market-based understanding or the flexibility to react to market demands.

There is a long experience of governments developing tourism facilities through tourism development corporations. These initiatives often were the means for governments' involvement in entrepreneurial activities, for example, not only building but also operating hotels and other facilities. They are vehicles on the road towards privatisation; through joint-participation with private companies, governments do become involved in commercial operations and have been so for many years. As the tourism sector develops and strategic objectives are met, the governments may choose to sell off their assets and reinvest in other tourism developments or in other sectors of the economy. Governments' intervention should be selective and specific.

Tourism development in China has not been excluded from the tensions created by the pace of economic and social change in that country in recent years. Increasingly, the impact of tourism on host communities requires greater understanding if negative impacts are to be minimized and positive impacts maximized. Where conservative rural communities are confronted with tourism development, the processes of acculturation, westernization, modernization and sometimes urbanization may be accelerated. Conflicts often arise, some of which may be functional and some dysfunctional. In this context the sociocultural impacts of tourism are among the least understood phenomena of the tourism industry.

250 kilometres southwest from the capital, Guangzhou (Canton), is a 100-square-kilometre area of karst (isolated limestone) hills where some of China's largest and most spectacular caves are found. The surrounding area of calcareous soils is agriculturally poor and sugar cane is the main crop grown by the village communities. Paddy (rice) fields are confined to narrow river valley bottoms where the soil is a little more fertile and not quite so porous, Farming incomes at 700 yuan per annum are among the lowest in Guangdong.

Ling Xiao consists of a huge cave 90 metres high with thousands of geological formations and a river running through the mountain which is accessible from both the north and south sides of the karst. Yu Xi consists of the Jade River which takes the tourist through three different karst caverns over a two kilometre stretch. The boundary of Yang Chun and Wan Fau Counties runs along the bank of the Jade River and over the top of Ling Xiao cave mountain.

Tourism to Ling Xiao began in 1974 in a very small way with one or two thousand visitors a year. After 1978, as tourism began to expand, Yu Leung Hang village in Yang Chun County and Lam Po village in Wan Fan County (both communities are situated on opposite sides at the base of the Ling Xiao caves mountain) began to organize tours in competition with each other, with both sides claiming territorial rights to do so. Conflict ensued. The Guangdong Province government mediated in the dispute and in 1984 Yang Chun County was given responsibility for developing Ling Xiao and Yu Xi sites under an agreement termed 'The Four Centralizations' (centralized control, planning, development and management). The decision was based on the fact that the county boundaries placed the Yu Xi caves and the southern entrance to Ling Xiao in Yang Chun, and on the fact that Wan Fau was relatively rich because of extensive marble deposits (the county is called 'the Italy of the East') while Yan Chun had only an impoverished agricultural economic base.

Yang Chun County established the 'Ling Xiao Caves Scenic Region Management Company' (LXMC) in the vicinity of Yu Leung Hang village, and in 1984 invested more than 6.5 million yuan (US$1.6 million) in infrastructure (restaurant, powerhouse for internal lighting, recreation area, stairs and paths inside the cave, boats for river trips through the caves, facilities for tour coaches, management office, bridges over the river, a landing, public toilets, etc.) and visitation grew dramatically. In 1992 and 1993 more than two million tourists visited the sites, making them the third most popular destination in Guangdong Province, Total revenue of more than 4 million yuan (US$0.5 million) each year was generated for the company. An estimated 1.5 million additional yuan (US$150 000) per year was earned by the local Yang Chun peasants with sideline industries—souvenir stalls, pony rides, refreshment booths, and calligraphy (interview with the company manager).

The people of Ling Xiao and Yang Chun County officials used the 1984 decision to block entry from the Wan Fan side by sealing the three northern cave entrances with reinforced concrete. However, the Lam Po people still gained entry via the river. But the river being narrow, the boats were 'always crashing into each other and causing arguments'. Competition for the economic benefits of tourism continued when Wan Fan County built a road from Lam Po village to the northern bank of the Jade River in 1991/1992 and began to organize rival boat trips through the three caves.

After a series of incidents between both sides in which guides were beaten, tourists harassed and boats destroyed, the Provincial Government issued an edict in October 1992 which reiterated that management of the sites rested with Yang Chun and that both counties were to:

> counsel the locals (clans) not to cause trouble, nor to destroy any scenic resources or tourist facilities in order to protect the stability of the scenic region and the normal operations of tourist activities.

The LXMC immediately moved to shut Wan Fau County and Lam Po village out of the operation altogether by blocking the Wan Fau river entrance and entry to the Jade River caves with boulders. Tension between the two communities rose and, after several confrontations, violence erupted on 26 January 1993, the fourth day of the Chinese Lunar New Year, when several hundred Lam Po villagers invaded the Ling Xiao cave and fired shots at an estimated 1000 tourists, Over the next three days the villagers systematically blew up the facilities with more than 700 gunpowder bombs, before a contingent of Yang Chun police reasserted control. The villagers also seized a boatload of 50 tourists and their Yang Chun guide on the Jade River and held them hostage for several hours.

The provincial government subsequently established an Investigation Working Party with representatives of both communities and counties' officials in an attempt to determine the cause of the attack, apprehend those guilty of breaking the law, settle the conflict once and for all and consider the question of claims for compensation. Evidence indicated that the situation had its origins in a clan boundary dispute reaching back several decades, but that until the advent of tourism and the relatively huge amounts of wealth it was generating, the resources of the caves were not directly coveted.

The problem of defining the issues involved in the Ling Xiao situation confronts the Western observer with Chinese and socialist perspectives and values. 'Facts' as defined by Chinese socialist bureaucrats may not be 'facts' as defined by Western scholars. Indeed, Western scholars have frequently been accused of 'intellectual imperialism' in their use of Western values and standards to analyse issues that are both Chinese and communist. As Ogden wrote:

> Which values are used is a subjective determination ... and profoundly affects the conclusions reached. The real question is, do students of China really understand the Chinese situation better when Western . . . values, concepts and models with which they are familiar form the analytical framework? Or does their use simply distort understanding, since different values, concepts, ideals and objectives motivate the Chinese communists?

Pye considers that in practice the application of contemporary Western social science theories (to tourism developments) in China can be 'a tricky business'. This is not because of the 'grossly overexaggerated dangers of ethnocentrism and intellectual imperialism', but because the concepts and theories of the Western disciplines were developed out of assumptions about systems which operate quite differently from their Chinese counterparts. According to Pye, the very notion of 'system', that is, of a set of interacting variables with a close fit between cause and effect, has to be modified in the case of China where:

> social and economic changes may have only

> marginal consequences for politics and even such dramatic developments in parts of the economy as those in southern China may be limited and the effects on the national government hard to predict.

Scholars sympathetic to the goals of the Chinese communist revolution, in rejecting Western evaluative standards have by inclination been ready to accept the Chinese leadership's definition of the situation. According to this viewpoint, 'what really matters are Chinese and communist values, ideals, models and objectives and whether or not they have been realized'. Harding has attributed much of the United States's uncritical academic writings of the 1970s about China to a too-willing embrace of Chinese values and the suspension of Western models, standards and perspectives, with consequent loss of objective appraisal. This he argued was because, in the past, American academics had been influenced by the prejudices of the Cold War and had largely ignored China's achievements while exaggerating its shortcomings. Their writings had more to do with American politics than with Chinese reality and Chinese politics. As Rose noted: 'What we do not command at this point is a mode of discourse that is culture or value-free. When we write about other cultures that is itself a political act'. Uberoi commented that: 'By way of permanent solution, I think that there is nothing for it but to lift our false limitation and admit all theories, native and Western, new and old, classical and vernacular, to fresh scrutiny and independent judgement, for or against, in the light of the relevant facts'. This has begun to happen in contemporary Western ethnography/ethnology/anthropology/sociology, where Western ideas are used to elicit but not to dominate the ideas and practices of the peoples Westerners study.

A cross-cultural and multi-disciplinary approach is necessary for building up a comprehensive understanding of the dynamics of tourism development in China because the complexities of Chinese society and culture do not always lend themselves easily to Western concepts. The social sciences, as practised in both China and the West, are reviewed to assess their applicability to the conflict at Ling Xiao since: 'The impacts of tourism are the most fundamental and of particular concern to anthropologists and other social scientists because established (anthropological) scholarship stresses the validity of maintaining group cohesion as a bulwark against disruption with its accompanying internal conflict and stress'. The paper draws upon a range of social science disciplines as it attempts to take account of Chinese approaches and definitions to the issues as well as utilizing paradigms from Western research.

The CCP regimes in China from 1949 until 1978/79 were ambivalent about tourism as an appropriate form of economic activity. Both domestic and international tourism were almost nonexistent. Entry was strictly controlled, as indicated by the euphemism: 'the Bamboo Curtain'. Tourism activity was held tightly in the hands of the state machinery and reflected the pattern common to other communist states. That is, what little foreign tourism that existed was sanctioned on the grounds that the successes of communism could be paraded before a selected international audience. From 1954 to 1978 the China International Travel Service (set up to arrange visits by 'foreign friends') played host to only 125 000 overseas visitors. Access was restricted to 'showcase' attractions and destinations and contact between tourists and locals was strictly regulated. Guides accompanied foreign tourists at all times and were able to 'quickly and proficiently report the great strides society and the economy had made under socialism'. However, Hong Kong Chinese, although required to register with the authorities prior to 1978, were able when visiting friends and relatives to interact freely with the local people. Segregation in hotels into the categories of foreign tourists, overseas Chinese, Hong Kong and Macau Chinese, and locals, was rigidly enforced.

Mao died in 1976 and in 1978 the Bamboo Curtain was pulled aside as Deng Xiaoping introduced his 'open door' policies, also referred to as 'socialism with a Chinese face', Deng overturned three decades of repression of intellectuals, acknowledging that the creative energies of educated specialists were essential for implementing the 'Four Modernizations'. This is a four pronged effort to marshal national resources to modernize agriculture, industry, the defence forces, and science and technology. To the extent that some market forces of supply and demand had to be accepted to accomplish modernization, socialist values were compromised in a limited way (the supply and price of some 800 basic commodities remained under government control, for example).

Intellectuals who had been banished to the countryside for manual labour were rehabilitated, and universities were encouraged to reopen disciplines, faculties and research institutes. The social sciences, which had been banned since the 1950s after Mao's 'Let one hundred flowers bloom' campaign and his 'Anti-Rightist Campaign' reemerged. The 'twenty bad years' (as they are called in China) of these two campaigns, the 'Great Leap Forward' and the 'Cultural Revolution' whose repression of intellectuals had continued until 1976, were quietly put aside. As part of Deng's modernization programme the Chinese door opened to world tourism. The first national conference on tourism was held in 1978 to formulate guidelines and organizational structures for its development. Politically, tourism as an acceptable industry was justified in socialist ideology on the grounds that it would advance economic reforms and the policy of opening to the outside world, it would further friendship and mutual understanding between the Chinese proletariat and other peoples of the world, and it would contribute to world peace. In three different speeches in 1979 Deng Xiaoping stated the need for swift growth and development of tourism

The decision to embrace the industry was not reached lightly because international tourism was recognized by the Chinese government as a major vehicle for modernization which inevitably promoted the penetration of Western values and Western culture. According to Ogden:

> The Chinese leadership developed a far greater tolerance for market forces of supply and demand which challenge socialism, than for Western values that might pollute Chinese culture: the government was more willing to sacrifice socialist values than Chinese cultural values in the pursuit of economic development.

In this context, tourism, a valuable new industry and a potentially large generator of foreign exchange earnings, was to be developed around Chinese culture and tradition. Funds were provided for the restoration of cultural sites such as the Ming Tombs, the Xi'an 'terra cotta army' of warriors and horses, and repairs to the Great Wall. Access to a wide range of Chinese cultural heritage sites was approved. In the early 1970s fewer than 12 cities were open to foreign tourists; by 1979, 60 destinations were open; by 1984 there were 200; and by 1987, 469 cities and destinations were approved for foreign visitation

Nunez's observation about the development of tourism in third world countries in general is pertinent in the case of China:

> the situation indicates an interesting irony: in order to survive and perpetuate their cultural identity and integrity, emerging new nations . . caught up in a competitive world economy encourage and invite the most successful agents of change (short of political or military agents) active in the contemporary world.

Recognizing the danger, and in order to mitigate such impacts, the Chinese leadership determined to keep planning and development firmly under its control. Tourism authorities were established at the national, provincial and county levels, with responsibility for the development of attractions and associated infrastructure. The national government initially assumed responsibility for international promotion and marketing and the provision of travel agency services, although in the last few years provinces and counties have been permitted to engage in their own marketing and set up their own travel agencies.

The growth of China's tourism industry following the ,open door' policy was nothing short of spectacular. In 1978, a total of 1.8092 million tourists visited China. In 1979 that figure expanded to 4.2039 million, an increase of 232%. By 1985 the figure had grown to 17.833 million, an increase of 986%. By 1988, prior to the June 1989 Tiananmen Square incident, the total had swelled to 31.695 million. Tourism receipts grew from US$263 million in 1978 to more than US$2.25 billion by 1988.

In 1989, however, there was a drastic decline in response to the bloody suppression of the Tiananmen Square democracy demonstrations. Only 24.5 million foreign visitors were recorded and international tourism receipts fell to US$1.86 billion as general travel, package tours and cruise-line schedules were cancelled worldwide. In 1990 the figure was 27.462 million. By 1991, however, the figure had risen to 33.345 million and tourism receipts to US$2.845 billion. In 1992, tourist arrivals reached 38.115 million and international tourism receipts totalled US$3.947 billion, almost 40% more than the previous year.

The fluctuations in tourism visitation mirrored the political changes in China. In the early 1990s in the aftermath of the Tianamnen Square demonstrations, and in the wake of the collapse of communist regimes throughout Eastern Europe and the USSR, China's more conservative leaders gained control of the helm. The legitimacy of communist regimes worldwide had been undermined. Ideology in China gained ascendancy over pragmatism and 'he 'open door' policy, because it provided a crutch to support the principle of party 'infallibility' based on socialist 'purity' and that could be used to justify the right of the CCP to govern.

However, in response to the PRC's violent suppression of student protesters, foreign economic sanctions were imposed. The drying up of foreign investment, the halting of all World Bank loans except those for humanitarian purposes), and the 25% reduction in tourism receipts exacerbated economic problems. The period of rigidity, austerity and recentralization tried by the conservatives contributed to bringing, China's economic growth to a virtual halt.

By the end of 1991 their policies were discredited and Deng was able to reestablish his leadership in 1992 on the catch-cry of the need to develop China and speed up the pace of economic reform. It should be stressed that Deng's apparent embrace of capitalist market forces was not acceptance of capitalism per se but in fact a close and logical 'fit' with Lenin's philosophy of political evolution. This stated that capitalism had to precede socialism because only the wealth created by capitalist market forces could build the base needed for socialism. Deng postulated that China had moved too quickly in the

1950s to dismantle an embryonic capitalism which was only just beginning to challenge feudalism—that in effect China had tried to leapfrog over the capitalist stage of evolutionary development. The result had been to delay the eventual succession to socialism. However, feudalism was still rampant and responsible for China's 'backwardness'. It had to be countered by capitalist techniques and structures as an intermediary step necessary to achieve the ultimate goal of socialism at some undefined time in the future.

Socialism as redefined by 'Deng's Thought' permitted China to develop by whatever means would be successful: 'It does not matter if the cat is black or white. If it can catch rats it is a good cat'. Market values were reasserted, the importance of tourism was reiterated and tourism numbers expanded.

The development of a major tourist attraction at Ling Mao only became possible after 1978 in the context of the emergence of the policies of 'socialism with Chinese characteristics' which gradually moved China away from a centrally administered economy to a more decentralized, market-oriented system. Over the next 15 years some 20 million village-run and town-run enterprises were created which led to the 'rural urbanization' of much of China. Hundreds of tourism sites were developed by local interests. The Ling Mao Nyam Scenic Region Management Company is one of them.

There were two specific policies which permitted this. The first was 'the responsibility system of contracted production' authorized by the Third Plenum of the Eleventh Central Committee in 1978. The second was the decision by the government in 1984 to allow peasants to settle in cities and towns and to engage in business and service industries on condition that they provided for their own grain provisions.

The first policy in effect replaced the village brigades and production teams by devolving responsibility for production down to individual households. This was accomplished by 'de-collectivization'—returning traditionally owned lands to the peasants who were ,assigned' the land for up to thirty years. In this way Chinese socialism was maintained by the continued legal ownership of the land remaining with the state; thus, it was argued, a new landed upper class was not being created. But households were awarded freedom of usury rights and the right to pass on land to descendants, as if ownership resided with the peasants. Wealth that might accumulate under this system was acceptable, provided the rich did not trample on the socialist principle of non exploitation of labour.

Since then households in the countryside have found that from the limited farmland they have been contracted to work 'a massive workforce can be released for other lucrative propositions'. In a study of four municipalities covering twenty counties, Fei found that one-third of the workforce in the countryside would belong to the category of surplus labour if calculated on the basis of one farmhand taking care of four mu (about one hectare) of land. Chen Ximen, Director of the Department of Rural Development (State Council Development Research Centre), said at a conference on rural reform in December 1993 that of China's total rural workforce of 440 million, 110 million worked in factories and service industries. The remaining 330 million worked on the country's 100 million hectares of farmland but had work for only one-third of the year.

This surplus rural labour, who used to be submerged by the practice of 'everyone dipping into the common pot', becomes a new workforce in the countryside once they are given the opportunity to work in enterprises they set up on their own. In consequence, village and town-run enterprises have blossomed everywhere in the countryside. It can be said that village and town industry is the off spring of the combination of surplus labour and new means of production and objects of labour.

The second policy was fundamental to the 'rural urbanization' of China, which freed more resources for non-agricultural pursuits. For example, in the four countries in Guangdong surveyed by Xu and Zhang 1988-89) there were only nine towns in the four counties n 1978. By the end of 1984, however, there were 64. In 1978, town populations totalled 275 303 (10.27% of the total population of the four counties); by 1984, town populations had risen to 434508—15.78% of the total population of the counties.

In 1992, the State Bureau of Statistics recorded that township enterprises registered a gross output of 1.76 trillion yuan, accounting for 31.6% of the country's total non-agricultural output. In 1993, the gross output of township enterprises was estimated to total 2.7 trillion yuan. 'Having the peasants leave the land without leaving the village' to participate in village-run and town-run enterprises has been acknowledged as a guiding principle of national strategic importance.

If we have accounted for the development of a thriving tourist enterprise such as Ling Xiao in the depths of rural China, how do we account for the violence that erupted there in January 1993? The answers to this question are complex and require further investigation.

Wu developed an analytical framework to examine social problems in rural China. He identified 'nine trends, seven evils, six scourges and five diseases' based on 'six sources of all ills'. His model may be likened to 'cheung nga kau', or the Chinese ivory artefact in which a series of concentric ivory balls are carved one inside the other (the trends encircling the evils which in turn encircle the scourges which themselves encircle the diseases), resting on a carved wooden base (the sources).

In the context of Ling Xiao, the Lam Po clan carried out systematic harassment of Ling Xiao guides and villagers. They created problems inside the caves on the rivers, staircases and paths. They constantly created a management headache for Yang Chun because they could not be controlled.

Distinctions in the Western world between the social sciences as applied to tourism analysis have begun to blur. Anthropology, for example, has traditionally been seen as a 'four fields' discipline encompassing cultural anthropology, archaeology, physical anthropology and linguistics, and many Western scholars move in and out of these four fields freely. Increasingly, more radical thought in Western academic circles challenges the 'owner ship' of bodies of knowledge claimed by different disciplines and expounds the need to adopt a multi-disciplinary and 'polyphonic' or 'multi-genre' construction if there is to be a future for the social sciences. Writers such as Rose, claim that the past decade has witnessed:

> the dissolution of boundaries between literature, sociology, anthropology, critical theory, philosophy, cinematography, computer science, and so on: and an ultimate transparency and probable liquidation of that series of sacred centers ... that now constitute, somewhat precariously, each of the academic disciplines in the human sciences.

This is in marked contrast to the social sciences in China where the Soviet model of the 1950s resulted in very narrow definitions of disciplinary boundaries and very clear distinctions being drawn between the different disciplines, For example, anthropology was (and still is) defined as 'physical anthropology', involved in the study of biological types; and ethnology was (and still is) restricted to the study of China's ethnic minorities with the pragmatic task of 'uplifting them'. In examining the dynamics of events at Ling Xiao, Western social sciences offer a richness of analytical models. These might include attribution theory, social exchange theory, conflict theory, the concept of 'new-want formation', dependency theory, compensation theory, the concept of empowerment, deviance and social control, modernization theory, development theory and others, which would all appear able to make a contribution to understanding the events. Constraints of space prevent a synthesis of those being utilized in this paper. Instead, the Weberian concept of patrimonial authority will form a central but not the only analytical tool for taking a Western academic-oriented view of Ling Xiao. In this context it is postulated that the violence at Ling Xiao can be related in part to the reemergence of clan structures in rural China since 1978.

When the Communist Party came to power in 1949 it set about establishing a monolithic centralized power structure. It reached out into a majority of villages throughout the country with its grass roots councils of party members wielding authority and with responsibility to implement policies and ensure conformity with central dictates. In part this system was designed to eradicate the last vestiges of the feudal, patriarchal clan structures which had traditionally dominated the Chinese countryside for several thousand years. In many villages, clan elders were removed from power and the communist system of local government set up.

Despite three decades of communism accompanied by massive rural upheaval, including the imposition of the death penalty for thousands of 'capitalist' clan leaders and their families purged during the revolution, the clan system never disappeared completely. Utilizing the Weberian concept of patrimonial rulership, McCormick has advanced a telling three-point argument for the enduring nature of clan structure in China:

1. it fits longstanding Chinese cultural traditions; many thousands of villages are 'single name' clan-based viri-local communities;
2. it is, with its accompanying forms of corruption (i.e. institutionalized payments to officialdom), 'a rational response' to China's 'rigid and inefficient bureaucracy'; and
3. patrimonial relationships are an integral part of elite relations in China's Leninist system,` where 'connections' are vital for getting anything done.

Judd has described this 'patrilineal, effectively androcentric social organization' as 'a living element in contemporary rural China'. Cohen describes the role of patriliny in rural China as 'a fixed genealogical orientation which provides one set of referents for the assertion and negotiation' of community wants and needs. It constitutes what Pye has called 'Confucian Leninism' and what Walder has termed 'organized dependency'.

With Deng's rural reform programme of 1978, old ideas began to make a comeback. The contract responsibility system returned the land to individual households and villages, with the inevitable result that the control structure established by the party and government began to weaken, 'Decollectivization' during the 1980s meant the demise of the former brigades and teams whose leaders were the linchpins in state control and authority as they imposed community quotas and implemented state policies.

Ownership' of the land empowered the clans as it had empowered their ancestors (and subsequently the

Communist Party). The traditional system of clan structure, which had been based on land ownership, gradually began to reemerge and descendants of clan elders began to reassert clan values and authority. Judd rioted that to the extent to which informal, lineage based organizations were efficacious in the rural political economy in competition with official structures, they were a major concern for the government. This was highlighted in a government report which identified 'spontaneous organizations' based on ties of kinship, neighbourboods and 'networking connections' as common in the countryside following de-collectivization and as 'problematic' for the bureaucracy.

According to a survey carried out in Hunan Province in 1989 by the official communist newspaper Legal Daily, by the late 1980s the reappearance of clan structures had become 'endemic'. Nearly one-third of all the villages in the north of the province had set up clan organizations, with that figure rising to nearly 80% in some counties, 'There appears to be a striking phenomenon of replacing administrative power with clan power and replacing laws and regulations with clan rules', the newspaper reported.

With the reemergence of clan power came the subsequent revival of age-old clan disputes. The Legal Daily noted that there had been more than 600 clan battles between 1988 and 1989, accounting for 60% of all rural disputes in Yueyang. More than 500 people had been killed or injured. The disputes between rival clans and between clans and government officials often turned into 'pitched battles with peasants using explosives and home made weapons to settle old scores'. The SCMP quoting Chinese official sources reported that: 'Although the official media has tended to play down the clan problem, there is considerable evidence that clan organizations and clan disputes are still very much a part of rural China'. It reported a pitched battle in September 1993 between 5000 peasants from two rival clans in southern Hunan which left five dead and 12 seriously wounded before it was finally broken up by a battalion of 200 paramilitary police.

In Ling Xiao, much of the available evidence points to a clan dispute over territorial claims which go back many years. 'Wan Fan' means 'floating cloud' and historically, Lam Po village and the County have claimed and occupied land 'wherever the cloud rises to' despite boundary demarcations to the contrary, according to Ling Xiao residents who dispute those claims. Guangong Province officials assert that the dispute was settled by the CCP in 1949 with a survey of the boundary. However, conflicts over rights to exploit the trees on the hill-slopes produced a Province-negotiated settlement in 1964 which gave the southern slopes of the Ling Xiao caves hill to Lam Po village 'in order to meet their need for wood for cooking and daily life'. The boundary was sited along the top of the hill. For the next two decades there appears to have been only very minor disagreements between the clans on either side of the boundary.

Only in 1984 when tourism began to increase and generated a level of income far in excess of normal levels for Yang Chun did conflict again break out into the open. Competition for the tourist dollar resulted in continuing violence between the two communities.

Part of the problem lay in the application by the provincial government of the philosophy of 'Everyone dipping into the common pot' to justify its decision to grant development rights of Ling Mao to Yang Chun rather than Wan Fau. Under this Maoist edict, the wealth derived for Wan Fau County from its marble deposits was expected to provide for the needs of all. But it disregarded the reality that, with the reemergence of clans, redistribution of wealth was not occurring that Lam Po had no marble deposits, and that Lam Po village was as poor a farming community as its counterpart village on the other side of the Ling Xiao caves hill. The clan members, supported by Wan Fan County officials, therefore established their own tourist enterprise to access the benefits from tourism in defiance of the provincial government and in opposition to Ling Xiao.

The situation was one of an imbalance of power between the actors. In our variation of Emerson's power dependence relation framework, it can be stated that Ling Xiao had become dependent upon the income derived from tourism, was in control of the resources and therefore perceived the host-guest relationship in a positive light. It had the political support of the provincial government, a legal agreement verifying its rights to manage the tourism resources of Ling Xiao and Yu Xi, and a territorial presence manifested by the infrastructure the Yuang Chun County had developed at both sites, and the residence of villagers there. Lam Po, on the other hand, desired access to the tourist-generated income, derived some benefits from the limited access it had achieved informally, but lacking control over the resources, found itself in an inferior position with little capacity to change the situation. When its access to even a limited amount of income was denied by the actions of Yang Chun, as the disadvantaged actor Lam Po developed negative perceptions and attempted to redress the situation through violence in a vain attempt to gain control of the resources.

Tourism in Greater Mexico

A study of minorities, their 'culture' and the impact and relationship with Westernstyle tourism immediately raises issues of definition, domination and 'dead-culture'.

What is a minority and what is culture (and can it be 'owned')?—these are often emotive and politicised, and, in the context of developing countries, laden with the cry of cultural imperialism. Indeed, tourism and the tourists' pursuit of authenticity in ancient minority situations could be seen as the ultimate David v. Goliath culture clash, with the outcome inevitably not of the Hollywood-biblical happy-ending variety.

The extent to which academic research and analysis can deal with these issues does therefore require not only a multi-disciplinary approach (anthropology, geography, economics, politics, culture, art/history etc.), avoiding 'misplaced concreteness', but also an acknowledgment of the limitations of Western thinking and assumptions in applying value-judgements and explaining observed behaviour in 'other' sociocultures.

An obvious example, relevant to the study of cultural heritage, is the fact that native languages of indigenous Indians (Indigenas) do not contain a word that can be regarded as synonymous with the Western concept of art or heritage, which is usually seen as something separable from the rest of everyday life. The role of culture is therefore inextricably bound up in everyday living and beliefs in non-eastern cultures, from Africa, Asia, Australasia, to the Americas. The oral tradition also separates these societies from our reliance on the written word. The Mexican-Indian traditions and the continuity between life and the afterlife (epitomised in the 'Day of the Dead' celebrations) also offer a different view of living culture and 'heritage'. This European disregard for oral history and expression is reflected in the Western academic and curator's line drawn between prehistory and history, the latter signifying the first stage of civilisation (sic), the written (European) word: 'My culture, the Lakota culture, has an oral tradition, so I ordinarily reject writing. It is one of the white world's ways of destroying the culture of non-European peoples'. In Mexico, prehistory 'ended' with the Spanish conquests in the 16th-century. The modalities of white v.'other' value systems can be epitomised in tourism interaction and impacts on host communities:

> the white cultural framework attempts to universalize *exchange-value* to the exclusion of all other.. formulas for the translation of speech into writing, of time into money, labor into a commodity, language into language, land into property—into money, versus 'non White' cultural emphasis on *use value*: stewardship of the land... on the home as a place to live (rather than visit), not to sell... work that is satisfying in itself.

Basis of study

This comparative research in Greater Mexico (Meso america) based upon separate study tours, in 1990, of New Mexico, Southwest USA, including accessible Pueblo villages and cultural festivals, and in 1992, of Mexico—the Independencia region and Tlaquepaque/ Guadalajara in Central Mexico, and the Oaxaca region in the south, including Oaxaca City (a recent Unesco-designated World Heritage Site), Puerto Angel, Puerto Escondido and Bahias de Huatalco. These three resorts on a coastal stretch of 103 km, respectively represent differing stages of commercial tourism development, from the *limited* to the *expanding* (local/national owned, sensitive-scale, but foreign investment proposed) and the *overbuilt*.

The study offers a comparison of heritage tourism management and impact on Native Indian sociocultures between New and 'Old' Mexico and thus at national/ state policy levels, between the USA and Mexico. Both are epitomised as 'tricultural', meaning Indian, Spanish ('Hispanic') and Anglo; and, until the separation in 1846,

New Mexico formed part of greater Mexico—both, therefore, were under Spanish rule for 200-250 years. Tourism, 'fourth world' arts and culture are viewed in the broader context of the political and economic development affecting Indian communities, and the sociocultural continuity and change they experience through the gap between 'primitive and modern', for which tourism, arguably, provides a special bridge.

The context and political economy relevant to the timing of this research, are the 500th anniversary celebrations of Columbus's 'discovery' of the Americas, and disputed state elections in Mexico during 1992, and the progression towards the North American Free Trade Agreement (NAFTA), between the USA, Mexico and Canada, which came into force on I January 1994. 1993 was the United Nations International Year of Indigenous People and, shortly before the end of the year, the UN launched the 'International *Decade* of the World's Indigenous People'.

Minorities of all kinds—cultural, religious, linguistic, ethnic and racial—are ubiquitous today; few nation-states do not have one or more minority group within their national territories and minorities are frequently divided by state borders. Tribal people typically have stable, low energy, sustained-yield economic systems, based more dependently on their specific environment. Whilst leadership and internal democratic systems exist, Indigenas generally lack national representation, and few, if any, political rights. The treatment and relationship between dominant and minority groups presents both a moral and political problem, with national and international implications, not least for tourism and other forms of economic development. These have been recognised by external agencies in project evaluation criteria.

This is no more so, than in the case of Native

Indians of the Americas, whose place in history is rooted in European myth and imperialism. In Mexico, native Indigenas are numerically and geographically in the minority, with less protection and land-reserves than Southwestern (USA) contemporaries, whilst in neighbouring Guatemala, Indians as a whole occupy the majority (c. 55%), but are made up of over 20 tribal groups, receiving even more effective domination and discrimination than in Mexico. Numerical size is therefore only one measure of socioeconomic minority status and institutional racism is often concentrated in post colonialist style power (e.g. Afrikaners)

From a peak of 57 million Native Americans in 1492, there are estimated to be only 33 million today. In Mexico the Indian population has fallen over 60% from 21+ million in 1492 to 8 million in 1992 (8% of the population), Indian communities are concentrated in poorer, less developed regions of Mexico, including tourist trail, heritage sites and potential tourist resort areas.

The Columbus quincentenary anniversary focused attention on past and present conflicts: '(which) exemplified *par excellence*, heritage and tourism in the global village today—with the raw flesh showing'. These 'celebrations' were partially muted by demonstrations in Central and South America, as well as the USA, and used by indigenous populations to protest against miserable living conditions, discrimination and land expropriation, as well as the reenactment and rewriting of the history of 'Old and New Worlds': 'a sterile argument between triumphalism and political correctness'.

Against this backdrop, tourism development and operations sit uncomfortably between continuing repression and exploitation, and this dreadful inheritance. In Mexico, this is masked by a continuity of a benign form of democracy ('perfect-dictatorship', Mario Vargas Llosa) since independence, the relative success of its tourism industry in economic and product terms and paradoxically, the adoption of Indian cultural heritage as the image and expression of what is Mexico:

> since the 19 10 Revolution in Mexico, archaeology has been officially encouraged in order to promote national unity (sic) by celebrating a pre-Hispanic past (and thus including the large indigenous population) and to claim Mexico's uniqueness... sites that double as museums and tourist sites.

The preservation of the past now serves political and economic ends: nationalism and tourism.

One could be forgiven, when the social, environmental and economic impacts on Indigenas are examined (including tourism development), for feeling that such a 'celebration' represents at best, tokenism, and at worst, continued 'internal colonisation', and cultural imperialism by the Mexican State. Images of ancient sites and ruins, museum collections and ethnic art, provide not only the unique selling point for domestic and international tourism, but the cultural emblems and identifications in Mexican society itself, including government communications and media; 'it has become a standard photo-opportunity for PRI (Institutional Revolutionary Party-PRI, more Institutional than Revolutionary) candidates, to appear in the brightly coloured Indian poncho'. The image of the Indian, artefact and heritage site is equivalent to the British Beefeater, or American Cowboy; the difference here is that this 'heritage' is still 'living', but has little control over its own culture, or its exploitation. Tourism development in Mexico

International tourism development in Mexico originated in the 1950s. In 1961 a National Tourism Council was established, made up of five members appointed by the President. The national Fund for the Promotion of

Tourism, FONATAUR, provides state funding and credit finance for government-approved tourism projects, and the Secretariat for Tourism also funds agencies responsible for control and regulation of hotels and travel organisations. Mexico has a highly centralised tourism development system, emphasising its national economic importance.

Unlike other less developed countries (Turkey, Spain) embarking on rapid development subsequently, Mexico was seen as a relatively successful example in economic development terms. This was due to the mix of its destination offer and experience, from ancient heritage sites, colonial towns and cities, to beach resorts in both Pacific, and Caribbean (Cancun, Cozumel) coasts. These complementary attractions and seasonal periods combine with Mexico's proximity to the USA and Canada, which provide over 85% of overseas tourists, predominantly on short breaks. The high level of nationalisation, from oil to airlines, and a proportionately high unskilled labour requirement, also reduced the degree of leakage; by the 1970s net foreign exchange earnings were over 80% of gross.

By the late 1970s and early 1980s, Mexico's expansion, consequent public debt, trade deficit (increased by 366%) and over reliance on oil sales in the volatile international oil market, led to rapidly increasing inflation and public debt. At a time of low US dollar rates, growing competition from other destinations, Mexico became more expensive to its prime market and tourism numbers and spend suffered. Its market position and concentrated economy were also its Achilles' heel.

'The government's main response was to devalue the peso successively, in 1976 by 37.5%, in 1977 by 14%, against dollar. The effect of devaluation on international tourism was short-term; in fact net foreign exchange earnings front tourism and its proportion of GDP did not improve between 1975 and 1982, when the peso was floated and exchange controls imposed.

The overriding determinant was world and North American recession, exacerbated by high domestic inflation/noncompetitive prices and airfares. The tourism I account began its recovery after 1982 and tourism has increased its positive balance $1136 million, or 210% of exports by 1986. Tourism is the second highest foreign currency earner, with receipts of $5324 million. Mexico's regained competitive position combined with the North American upturn resulted in spectacular visitor increases. As destination, however, Mexico was 'mature' in terms of its prime source-markets and tourists now had lower per capita expenditures; mass charter-based packages increased. Domestic inflation also fuelled imports, border transactions and the benefits from tourism growth were diminished.

The Mexican government has continued to pursue a policy of growth in international tourism and border transactions—hence the keen interest in the adoption of the North American Free Trade Agreement. The latter will require an even more open economy, open to foreign investment (inward and outward); import licences have been removed and trade tariffs reduced. One manifestation, of this is a privatisation regime prior to the NAFTA, including State Airlines, banks and the most politically sensitive, the national oil corporation (Pemex), as well as diminishing manufacturing sector. Mexico is moving towards a service and satellite economy, of which tourism is a prime sector. Ironically, this may accelerate as a result of both NAFTA and the recent GATT agreement.

Despite increased border manufacturing activity, leakage will be high (value-added goods and services will be retained by the USA) and agricultural products will be increasingly uncompetitive against mass grain imports from the USA. This will directly impact on indigenous production and land use. Full Free Trade (NAFTA and GATT) is forecast to reduce Mexico's income in real terms over the next ten years, despite short term annual growth. The urgency to capitalise on the momentum from these trade agreements and footloose investment, ahead of Presidential elections in 1994, promises a headlong development regime, which is likely to have scant consideration for social, cultural, or environmental impacts.

Foreign involvement in tourism development, with state incentives, promises a second wave of mass tourism development in undeveloped areas, many on existing and expropriated Indian lands. The 1993 government target of 50000 extra hotel rooms and a 20% increase in tourist arrivals therefore promise a post-Fordist scenario of state encouraged private-sector tourism development and related infrastructure expansion, dominated by US, Japanese and Mexi-American corporations, targeted at these markets, European and *nouveaux* riches Mexican tourists. This may be 'optimum' for the private sector, but not for the Mexican economy, environment and community. Power criticises such 'self-defeating' strategies of growth and offers a list of goals for local development: (1) the availability of satisfying and useful work for members of the community; (2) security of access to biological and social necessities; (3) stability; (4) access to the qualities that make life varied, stimulating and satisfying; (5) a thriving, vital community.

The political and macro-economic issues are noted here, not merely for the potential impact on host communities, but to put tourism economic development into its broadest context. The opportunity costs of alternative investment strategies, impacts from other economic activities and improved efficiency—in Mexico this includes oil, manufacturing, agriculture—all have produced the effects of acculturation (social, cultural and religious), mechanisation and loss of land. In fact, without the socioeconomic policies pursued by third world nations playing a first world 'growth' game, international tourism would not seriously feature in a country such as Mexico. (Perhaps only in smaller, island communities could tourism be said to have the leading dominating influence the prime agents of change.)

Demonstration effects cannot easily, or solely be traced to tourism; Mexican national TV mixes Anglo images and forms, from game shows to blonde bimbos, with national (ethnic) pride in Indian heritage (more emphasis on the dead-inanimate than the living): 'Faces on the murals may be copper, but those on television are white'. However, per capita tourist spending by Mexicans reached $62 in 1990 (compared with $154 in the USA) and Mexican tourists in Britain were, remarkably, the highest spenders in 1992 (£4312 for a family of four—higher than tourists from the Middle East, Japan and the USA). The imbalance of wealth in Mexico is extreme; one-third live below the official (i.e. understated) poverty line, and just 35 of the richest families (Mexico has one of the highest numbers of dollar billionaires in the world), earn more than 15 million of the poorest Mexicans, of which over 50% are Indigenas.

With only 10% of the population able to afford foreign travel, a status symbol (mostly to the USA and South America, but increasingly to Europe), domestic travel, predominantly visiting friends and relatives, is strong, based on a network of cheap and often hair-raising bus routes, and a growing internal air transport system, as a result of partial air privatisation and deregulation. The latter is under pressure, not only from debt financing and free trade requirements, but also in order to finance upgraded fleets, which will be required to meet US environmental standards.

Post-revolution Mexico continues discrimination and expropriation of Indian land and livelihoods. In the 1970s, the Institute Nacional de Indigenas (INI) followed a policy of modernisation of Indian farming, forcing the introduction of fertilisers, intensive farming and centralisation.

In contrast to Mexico, the Native Indians in the southwest of the USA, although also suffering from the cycle of exploitation-separation-integration, have achieved a greater degree of control and acceptance in reservation systems and Pueblo settlements, covering over 17 million acres. Many reservations are now self-governing, with similar powers to those of states, and in 1978 the First Amendment extended protection to native religions. The Navajo 'Nation' of over 250 000, covering an area twice the size of Israel, may be the first 'Indian state'. As unlikely as it may seem, this would be the first 'return' to indigenous control of a part of the Americas, which are unique, continuing 'colonies' in a post-colonial world.

In New Mexico, 'pre-tourism' developed in the late 1800s and was well-established by 1920. The encroaching railroad was the main factor of change and promotion of settler immigration and relocation. Natives were allowed to ride for free on trains as romantic exotica and the Sante Fe railway company used Indian symbols in their promotional literature and encouraged Indians to set up craft stalls outside stations. An enterprising 'tour operator', Fred Harvey Corporation, even devised 'Indian Detours' which offered passengers a few days off the train and excursions to Indian villages and sites. During this period, Indian groups began to see tourists as sources of income.

In fact, some tribes, such as the Mescaleros (Apache), promote tourism more than other groups. This includes the management of a luxury ski-resort ('Ski Apache', 'Inn of the Mountain of the Gods', 'Apache Haven Motel') and game-hunting tours. More recently, exploiting state legislation, reservations have opened popular gambling centres, much to chagrin of non Indian Americans, some of whom are claiming spurious Indian ancestry, in order to receive reservation status!

Amongst Pueblo settlements, some are more open than others; over two-thirds do not allow cameras or recorders a degree of choice and destiny-control is evident, therefore, unlike for their equivalents in Mexico. The effective access to political power has been one key to this degree of self-determination; Indian communities in New Mexico have exercised a block vote and the US-federal system perhaps provides a more representative form of democracy for minority groups and greater devolved power of land use and economic development, including tourism, and consequently over cultural affairs. These 'rights' were not of course given (nor could they be), but have been fought for, increasingly through the politicisation of Indian communities and the rising profile of leaders in the political and campaigning struggles, Indian consciousness and a modern 'movement' had arrived in the southwest states and elsewhere in North America, not just an assertive and self-determining force, but as a rejection of the domination and assimilation of minorities by majority-rulers and of the related social anthropological processes:

> No European can ever teach a Lakota to be a Lakota, a Hopi to be a Hopi. A master's degree in Indian studies... cannot make a person into a human being, or provide knowledge into traditional ways. It can only make you a mental European, an outsider.

These oppositional movements are gaining force through out aboriginal societies and situations worldwide and present parallels with black power movements—the natural desire for rediscovering both their roots and recognition of the present-day situation as functions of colonial and post-colonial domination: 'There is no longer any excuse for ignoring the viewpoint of the "discovered", the vanquished, the colonized. MacCannell's notion of 'constructed authenticity' can be observed in the degree of control, acceptance and rejection of tourism amongst Pueblo and other Indian communities on the one hand, and their collaboration through pan-Indian and ethnic art trade and tourism with the White society.

The extent to which Mexican Indian communities have emulated their US counterparts is harder to assess. As part of the political process their powers and numbers are limited and issues of land use, expropriation and development control are often subsumed into regional economic disputes arising from agrarian reform, privatisation and political corruption. They share common complaints with subsistence farmers and oil workers—a workingclass struggle against an urban elite, perhaps, but given the continued discrimination, their special needs and threats are not fully recognised. Unlike in the US southwest, Indianbased tourism promotion is managed by the national/international tour industry and at a local level by intermediaries (Ladinos—Spanish/ White—and Mestizos —mixed Indian/Spanish blood), who are therefore almost always non-Indians.

The overriding distinguishing factor is tourism's role and relationship to a third-world developing economy, compared to a diversified and developed economy such as the USA. It is likely, therefore, that where development opportunities present themselves, public or private-led, minority heritage and communities will continue to lose, as Mexico strives for first world status. Indeed an almost surgical approach to the first wave of resort development created Cancun on the Caribbean coast: 'Once virtually uninhabited, the area was computer-selected because of its near-perfect climate, peerless white-sand beaches, proximity to major populations and its pre-Columbian archaeological sites'.

The aggressive approach to tourism development was seen more recently in the Pacific area of Bahias de Huatalco. This area in the Oaxaca State contains the highest proportion of remaining Indian population in Mexico and was settled in pre-Hispanic times by Zapotec and Mixtec tribes. In 1984, locals heard rumours of large scale tourist development of their coastline. Without consultation it was subsequently announced that, by the year 2000, Huatalco was due to have 9000 hotel rooms, 800000 visitors a year and a permanent population of 100000 (then only 500).

This development cycle now threatens Puerto Escondido, further north along this coastline, following the construction of an international airstrip. Now an off beat surf-centre, with smaller-scale accommodation, US and Japanese developers plan major hotel developments and the expansion of existing facilities is likely to kill off the local fishing industry and small firms, and widen the 'ring-fence' area from which indigenous populations are expelled and are self-excluded.

The third of these resorts, Puerto Angel, reflects the first wave of tourist development, and a few fading hotels remain, several family-owned and occupied. One of these, the Posada 'Canon de Vata' (Green Canyon), has been developed over 20 years by a North American university educated Indian, who has reclaimed an and valley through tropical tree-planting. This has created a micro climate, and a source of self-generating pumped water and shade, in a subtropical environment. Meals are taken with the family and staff, and this early model of eco-tourism might have thought to have attracted interest from state and private organisations; however, to date no assistance or cooperation has been forthcoming from either. The attitude of private and public developers to environmental impacts and alternatives (solar, low energy, recycled), both here, in the environmentally sensitive Baja peninsula, and 'An tribal lands generally, shows little consideration, of sustainable development, environmental standards, or lessons from the past. This is at odds with the lip-service and fancy brochures on sustainable and environmental policies issued by international airlines and hotel operators who are active in Mexico. These are exclusively directed at the physical, not human, environment.

Huatalco is modelled on the Acapulco example, and represents one of the worst kinds of tourism development, with maximum benefits for international operatois and minimum opportunity or consideration for local economy or communities. This approach ignores the prime beneficiaries of local economic development—the local population: a complete lack of 'Pareto gain'—in favour of questionable national economic maximisation. Beach tourism represents nearly 90% of Mexican tourism; the remaining 10% is represented by cultural tourists. Resort development does, however, increasingly take place in remoter areas, which in Mexico are unsafe havens for indigenous populations. The impact on these sociocultures comes not only from the site development and worker-support areas themselves, but also from the transport infrastructure, which precedes them. Resorts also serve as 'hubs' for explorer-tourists going into sensitive tribal areas themselves.

The greater control by New Mexico Indians in tourism development, from accommodation, sightseeing and craft sales to staged performance in tourist areas, is a model to which Mexican Indigenas may aspire. For some communities, however, the business of tourism will remain undignified and threatening, and further encroachment and relocation will be resisted. This will require not only a more accountable tourism policy and equitable land use, but also, if sustainable tourism and environmental protection are to be effective, the recognition that minority ethnic communities require protection and consideration at least to the same degree as the built and natural heritage sites—that 'live culture' is given the same recognition as 'dead-culture': 'mass tourism can result in loving something to death'.

The various environmental and sustainable tourism initiatives, from industry-sponsored research centres to the UN's World Heritage Sites, are biased towards the latter. The protection of ruins is clearly less sensitive than that of indigenous populations, whose inheritance is of such 'concern'. Questions of ownership, access and management of heritage sites and collections, although increasingly raised by indigenous groups and their vocal leaders, seldom feature in tourism promotion and planning.

In sacred sites around Mexico, including regional museums and-the-jewel-in-the-crown—the National Museum of Anthropology in Mexico City, their access and exploitation has been institutionalised along Western lines. Entry is charged and controlled, by state bodies who are staffed largely by non-Indians. The economic benefits from their inherited culture is effectively denied, Local Indians can be found in ruins such as Mitla or Monte Alban and operate as informal guides; they are tolerated, but are outside the museum system itself.

As an area of cultural and tourism investigation, the southwestern USA and Mexican Indian communities are rich in both history and material and, given their proximity to the USA, anthropologists, art historians and 'socio-tourist' investigations are many and wide-ranging. Given the predominance of the White-American tourist, the dominance of the US academic and art trader are also evident. A study of impacts on minority ethnic groups could easily fall into the trap of investigating the 'other' and disregarding and projecting the views of the tourees themselves: 'Reifying culture is fundamental to cultural tourism and fits well with the general sense in Indian folklore that the whiteman is a slave to consumerism'.

Studies of 'flow "We" see "Them" ' provide useful insights into the rationales and reactions of tourists and can demonstrate the cultural gaps that exist:

> I never really feet that I'm welcome in any of the pueblos..... I don't know how I would feel about tourists coming and looking at me either... I get the feeling they're disgruntled but they'll do it. On the other hand when we go to Europe... nobody seems to worry about it there. Why is it all right to wander around a Dutch town and take pictures and not okay to wander around Acoma and take pictures?

Members of the majority culture are socialised to value intellectual curiosity and to ask questions, but the Pueblo people feel that when outsiders learn their religious secrets, the spiritual power of the ceremony is lost. Given the degree of knowledge and experience of these socio cultural differences that has been built up among travel firms, and through frequent American visitor-experience, it seems that the travel industry and those information sources are failing to provide even basic ground rules, and even guide books present a negative image: 'frankly an unfriendly pueblo... a visit cannot be recommended'. This even extends to criticism of the extent of tourist development itself:

Indians should capitalise on tourist curiosity by creating pueblo hotels, restaurants serving Indian food, or even a pueblo theme park... You don't see them exploiting in a sense, their own best qualities and heritage. So it doesn't seem like they take advantage of their own traditions.

The 'worldview' and adaptation of Native Indians to tourist situations, has been less studied from their standpoint: 'the attention of social scientists has been elsewhere focused on cultural relativism, ethnic identity and symbolic systems. This leaves the impression that cultural enclaves are all inward-looking populations, disinterested in the world outside'.

Academics do not escape this ethnocentricism: 'field workers are tourists and the two share characteristics that become the butt of Indian jokes and stories that ridicule them'. Deirdre Evans-Pritchard's study of host group attitudes to guests, paints a universal and sanguine Indian-view, with jokes and humour a key reaction, and one means of dealing with tourist contact and their often gullible and pathetic behaviour. This is no less so in the tourists' misconceptions of authenticity and inner-meanings, which Indian artists and guides choose to ignore, or 'they respond to tourists' needs for cultural significance by telling them just what they want to hear'.

In 'Burlesquing the "Other" in Pueblo performance', the Pueblo people 'for the most part regard tourists as fools' and categorise tourists based on origin or interest:

1. tourists from back-east (the most 'ignorant', Hollywood images...);
2. tourists from Texas (*tejanos*'—loud, pushy....')
3. hippie-tourists ('a nuisance—joined in when not appropriate...');
4. save the whale tourists (backpackers, 'right-on...')

All of these are generally derogatory; however, frequent visitors are invited to share more genuine celebrations, epitomised as 'White, or Anglo friend'. Art-trade brokers also develop, over time, a degree of trust and mutual respect, which is effectively earned.

Burlesquing as a phenomenon can be seen as another example, not of acculturation, but of cultural interaction, keeping separate those aspects of white-consumerist society by mocking them, adapting to those cultural forms and emblems (e.g. fashion), which they choose to integrate into performance. This can include contemporary and political issues and therefore follows a tradition of *realpolitik* in art, as a form of social comment, demonstration. The resistance to and then absorption of the Catholic religion into Indian beliefs and ceremonies can be seen throughout Latin America. The banning of traditional/national performance can have the effect of ensuring survival of cultural forms and practices, as well as fusion between religious cultures themselves.

5

Tourism Development and Socio-Cultural Change

Tourism development in China has not been excluded from the tensions created by the pace of economic and social change in that country in recent years. Increasingly, the impact of tourism on host communities requires greater understanding if negative impacts are to be minimized and positive impacts maximized. Where conservative rural communities are confronted with tourism development, the processes of acculturation, westernization, modernization and sometimes urbanization may be accelerated. Conflicts often arise, some of which may be functional and some dysfunctional. In this context the sociocultural impacts of tourism are among the least understood phenomena of the tourism industry. This paper examines the impact of tourism on two rural communities in Guangdong Province, southern China, where conflict has arisen over a tourism development centred on the limestone caves of Ling Xiao on the boundary of Yang Chun and Wan Fau counties.

250 kilometres southwest from the capital, Guangzhou (Canton), is a 100-square-kilometre area of karst (isolated limestone) hills where some of China's largest and most spectacular caves are found. The surrounding area of calcareous soils is agriculturally poor and sugar cane is the main crop grown by the village

communities. Paddy (rice) fields are confined to narrow river valley bottoms where the soil is a little more fertile and not quite so porous, Farming incomes at 700 yuan per annum are among the lowest in Guangdong.

Ling Xiao consists of a huge cave 90 metres high with thousands of geological formations and a river running through the mountain which is accessible from both the north and south sides of the karst. Yu Xi consists of the Jade River which takes the tourist through three different karst caverns over a two kilometre stretch. The boundary of Yang Chun and Wan Fau Counties runs along the bank of the Jade River and over the top of Ling Xiao cave mountain.

Tourism to Ling Xiao began in 1974 in a very small way with one or two thousand visitors a year. After 1978, as tourism began to expand, Yu Leung Hang village in Yang Chun County and Lam Po village in Wan Fan County (both communities are situated on opposite sides at the base of the Ling Xiao caves mountain) began to organize tours in competition with each other, with both sides claiming territorial rights to do so. Conflict ensued. The Guangdong Province government mediated in the dispute and in 1984 Yang Chun County was given responsibility for developing Ling Xiao and Yu Xi sites under an agreement termed 'The Four Centralizations' (centralized control, planning, development and management). The decision was based on the fact that the county boundaries placed the Yu Xi caves and the southern entrance to Ling Xiao in Yang Chun, and on the fact that Wan Fau was relatively rich because of extensive marble deposits (the county is called 'the Italy of the East') while Yan Chun had only an impoverished agricultural economic base.

Yang Chun County established the 'Ling Xiao Caves Scenic Region Management Company' (LXMC) in the vicinity of Yu Leung Hang village, and in 1984 invested more than 6.5 million yuan (US$1.6 million) in infrastructure (restaurant, powerhouse for internal lighting, recreation area, stairs and paths inside the cave, boats for river trips through the caves, facilities for tour coaches, management office, bridges over the river, a landing, public toilets, etc.) and visitation grew dramatically. In 1992 and 1993 more than two million tourists visited the sites, making them the third most popular destination in Guangdong Province, Total revenue of more than 4 million yuan (US$0.5 million) each year was generated for the company. An estimated 1.5 million additional yuan (US$150 000) per year was earned by the local Yang Chun peasants with sideline industries—souvenir stalls, pony rides, refreshment booths, and calligraphy (interview with the company manager).

The people of Ling Xiao and Yang Chun County officials used the 1984 decision to block entry from the Wan Fan side by sealing the three northern cave entrances with reinforced concrete. However, the Lam Po people still gained entry via the river. But the river being narrow, the boats were 'always crashing into each other and causing arguments'. Competition for the economic benefits of tourism continued when Wan Fan County built a road from Lam Po village to the northern bank of the Jade River in 1991/1992 and began to organize rival boat trips through the three caves.

After a series of incidents between both sides in which guides were beaten, tourists harassed and boats destroyed, the Provincial Government issued an edict in October 1992 which reiterated that management of the sites rested with Yang Chun and that both counties were to:

counsel the locals (clans) not to cause trouble, nor to

destroy any scenic resources or tourist facilities in order to protect the stability of the scenic region and the normal operations of tourist activities.

The LXMC immediately moved to shut Wan Fau County and Lam Po village out of the operation altogether by blocking the Wan Fau river entrance and entry to the Jade River caves with boulders. Tension between the two communities rose and, after several confrontations, violence erupted on 26 January 1993, the fourth day of the Chinese Lunar New Year, when several hundred Lam Po villagers invaded the Ling Xiao cave and fired shots at an estimated 1000 tourists, Over the next three days the villagers systematically blew up the facilities with more than 700 gunpowder bombs, before a contingent of Yang Chun police reasserted control. The villagers also seized a boatload of 50 tourists and their Yang Chun guide on the Jade River and held them hostage for several hours. Total direct damage was estimated at more than 4.4 million yuan (US$0.6 million) (*Sing Pao Daily News*, 8/2/93; *Sing Tao Daily*, 8/2/93, 9/2/93, 10/2/93; *Wah Kiu Yat Po*, 9/2/93; *Ming Pao*, 9/2/93, 11/2/93; *South China Morning Post* (*SCMP*), 9/2/93). All tourism ceased.

The provincial government subsequently established an Investigation Working Party with representatives of both communities and counties' officials in an attempt to determine the cause of the attack, apprehend those guilty of breaking the law, settle the conflict once and for all and consider the question of claims for compensation. Evidence indicated that the situation had its origins in a clan boundary dispute reaching back several decades, but that until the advent of tourism and the relatively huge amounts of wealth it was generating, the resources of the caves were not directly coveted.

Chinese versus Western interpretations of issues

The problem of defining the issues involved in the Ling Xiao situation confronts the Western observer with Chinese and socialist perspectives and values. 'Facts' as defined by Chinese socialist bureaucrats may not be 'facts' as defined by Western scholars. Indeed, Western scholars have frequently been accused of 'intellectual imperialism' in their use of Western values and standards to analyse issues that are both Chinese and communist. As Ogden wrote:

> Which values are used is a subjective determination ... and profoundly affects the conclusions reached. The real question is, do students of China really understand the Chinese situation better when Western . . . values, concepts and models with which they are familiar form the analytical framework? Or does their use simply distort understanding, since different values, concepts, ideals and objectives motivate the Chinese communists?

Pye considers that in practice the application of contemporary Western social science theories (to tourism developments) in China can be 'a tricky business'. This is not because of the 'grossly overexaggerated dangers of ethnocentrism and intellectual imperialism', but because the concepts and theories of the Western disciplines were developed out of assumptions about systems which operate quite differently from their Chinese counterparts. According to Pye, the very notion of 'system', that is, of a set of interacting variables with a close fit between cause and effect, has to be modified in the case of China where:

> social and economic changes may have only marginal consequences for politics and even such dramatic developments in parts of the economy as those in southern China may be limited and the effects on the national government hard to predict.

Scholars sympathetic to the goals of the Chinese communist revolution, in rejecting Western evaluative standards have by inclination been ready to accept the Chinese leadership's definition of the situation. According to this viewpoint, 'what really matters are Chinese and communist values, ideals, models and objectives and whether or not they have been realized'. Harding has attributed much of the United States's uncritical academic writings of the 1970s about China to a too-willing embrace of Chinese values and the suspension of Western models, standards and perspectives, with consequent loss of objective appraisal. This he argued was because, in the past, American academics had been influenced by the prejudices of the Cold War and had largely ignored China's achievements while exaggerating its shortcomings. Their writings had more to do with American politics than with Chinese reality and Chinese politics. As Rose noted: 'What we do not command at this point is a mode of discourse that is culture or value-free. When we write about other cultures that is itself a political act'. Uberoi commented that: 'By way of permanent solution, I think that there is nothing for it but to lift our false limitation and admit all theories, native and Western, new and old, classical and vernacular, to fresh scrutiny and independent judgement, for or against, in the light of the relevant facts'. This has begun to happen in contemporary Western ethnography/ ethnology/anthropology/sociology, where Western ideas are used to elicit but not to dominate the ideas and practices of the peoples Westerners study.

This paper postulates that a cross-cultural and multi-disciplinary approach is necessary for building up a comprehensive understanding of the dynamics of tourism development in China because the complexities of Chinese society and culture do not always lend themselves easily to Western concepts. The social sciences, as practised in both China and the West, are reviewed to assess their applicability to the conflict at Ling Xiao since: 'The impacts of tourism are the most fundamental and of particular concern to anthropologists and other social scientists because established (anthropological) scholarship stresses the validity of maintaining group cohesion as a bulwark against disruption with its accompanying internal conflict and stress'. The paper draws upon a range of social science disciplines as it attempts to take account of Chinese approaches and definitions to the issues as well as utilizing paradigms from Western research.

Tourism development in China

The CCP regimes in China from 1949 until 1978/79 were ambivalent about tourism as an appropriate form of economic activity. Both domestic and international tourism were almost nonexistent. Entry was strictly controlled, as indicated by the euphemism: 'the Bamboo Curtain'. Tourism activity was held tightly in the hands of the state machinery and reflected the pattern common to other communist states. That is, what little foreign tourism that existed was sanctioned on the grounds that the successes of communism could be paraded before a selected international audience. From 1954 to 1978 the China International Travel Service (set up to arrange visits by 'foreign friends') played host to only 125 000 overseas visitors. Access was restricted to 'showcase' attractions and destinations and contact between tourists and locals was strictly regulated. Guides accompanied foreign tourists at all times and were able to 'quickly and proficiently report the great strides society and the economy had made under socialism'. However, Hong Kong Chinese, although required to register with the authorities prior to 1978, were able when visiting friends and relatives to interact freely with the local people. Segregation in hotels into the categories of foreign tourists, overseas Chinese, Hong Kong and Macau Chinese, and locals, was rigidly enforced,

Mao died in 1976 and in 1978 the Bamboo Curtain was pulled aside as Deng Xiaoping introduced his 'open door' policies, also referred to as 'socialism with a Chinese face', Deng overturned three decades of repression of intellectuals, acknowledging that the creative energies of educated specialists were essential for implementing the 'Four Modernizations'. This is a four pronged effort to marshal national resources to modernize agriculture, industry, the defence forces, and science and technology. To the extent that some market forces of supply and demand had to be accepted to accomplish modernization, socialist values were compromised in a limited way (the supply and price of some 800 basic commodities remained under government control, for example).

Intellectuals who had been banished to the countryside for manual labour were rehabilitated, and universities were encouraged to reopen disciplines, faculties and research institutes. The social sciences, which had been banned since the 1950s after Mao's 'Let one hundred flowers bloom' campaign and his 'Anti-Rightist Campaign' reemerged. The 'twenty bad years' (as they are called in China) of these two campaigns, the 'Great Leap Forward' and the 'Cultural Revolution' whose repression of intellectuals had continued until 1976, were quietly put aside. As part of Deng's modernization programme the Chinese door opened to world tourism. The first national conference on tourism was held in 1978 to formulate guidelines and organizational structures for its development. Politically, tourism as an acceptable industry was justified in socialist ideology on the grounds that it would advance economic reforms and the policy of opening to the outside world, it would further friendship and mutual understanding between the Chinese proletariat and other peoples of the world, and it would contribute to world peace. In three different speeches in 1979 Deng Xiaoping stated the need for swift growth and development of tourism

The decision to embrace the industry was not reached lightly because international tourism was recognized by the Chinese government as a major vehicle for modernization which inevitably promoted the penetration of Western values and Western culture. According to Ogden:

> The Chinese leadership developed a far greater tolerance for market forces of supply and demand which challenge socialism, than for Western values that might pollute Chinese culture: the government was more willing to sacrifice socialist values than Chinese cultural values in the pursuit of economic development.

In this context, tourism, a valuable new industry and a potentially large generator of foreign exchange earnings, was to be developed around Chinese culture and tradition. Funds were provided for the restoration of cultural sites such as the Ming Tombs, the Xi'an 'terra cotta army' of warriors and horses, and repairs to the Great Wall. Access to a wide range of Chinese cultural heritage sites was approved. In the early 1970s fewer than 12 cities were open to foreign tourists; by 1979, 60 destinations were open; by 1984 there were 200; and by 1987, 469 cities and destinations were approved for foreign visitation

Nunez's observation about the development of

tourism in third world countries in general is pertinent in the case of China:

> the situation indicates an interesting irony: in order to survive and perpetuate their cultural identity and integrity, emerging new nations . . caught up in a competitive world economy encourage and invite the most successful agents of change (short of political or military agents) active in the contemporary world.

Recognizing the danger, and in order to mitigate such impacts, the Chinese leadership determined to keep planning and development firmly under its control. Tourism authorities were established at the national, provincial and county levels, with responsibility for the development of attractions and associated infrastructure. The national government initially assumed responsibility for international promotion and marketing and the provision of travel agency services, although in the last few years provinces and counties have been permitted to engage in their own marketing and set up their own travel agencies.

The growth of China's tourism industry following the ,open door' policy was nothing short of spectacular. In 1978, a total of 1.8092 million tourists visited China. In 1979 that figure expanded to 4.2039 million, an increase of 232%. By 1985 the figure had grown to 17.833 million, an increase of 986%. By 1988, prior to the June 1989 Tiananmen Square incident, the total had swelled to 31.695 million. Tourism receipts grew from US$263 million in 1978 to more than US$2.25 billion by 1988.

In 1989, however, there was a drastic decline in response to the bloody suppression of the Tiananmen Square democracy demonstrations. Only 24.5 million foreign visitors were recorded and international tourism receipts fell to US$1.86 billion as general travel, package tours and cruise-line schedules were cancelled worldwide. In 1990 the figure was 27.462 million. By 1991, however, the figure had risen to 33.345 million and tourism receipts to US$2.845 billion. In 1992, tourist arrivals reached 38.115 million and international tourism receipts totalled US$3.947 billion, almost 40% more than the previous year.

The fluctuations in tourism visitation mirrored the political changes in China. In the early 1990s in the aftermath of the Tianamnen Square demonstrations, and in the wake of the collapse of communist regimes throughout Eastern Europe and the USSR, China's more conservative leaders gained control of the helm. The legitimacy of communist regimes worldwide had been undermined. Ideology in China gained ascendancy over pragmatism and 'he 'open door' policy, because it provided a crutch to support the principle of party 'infallibility' based on socialist 'purity' and that could be used to justify the right of the CCP to govern.

However, in response to the PRC's violent suppression of student protesters, foreign economic sanctions were imposed. The drying up of foreign investment, the halting of all World Bank loans except those for humanitarian purposes), and the 25% reduction in tourism receipts exacerbated economic problems. The period of rigidity, austerity and recentralization tried by the conservatives contributed to bringing, China's economic growth to a virtual halt.

By the end of 1991 their policies were discredited and Deng was able to reestablish his leadership in 1992 on the catch-cry of the need to develop China and speed up the pace of economic reform. It should be stressed that Deng's apparent embrace of capitalist market forces was not acceptance of capitalism per se but in fact a close and logical 'fit' with Lenin's philosophy of political evolution. This stated that capitalism had to precede socialism because only the wealth created by capitalist market forces could build the base needed for socialism. Deng postulated that China had moved too quickly in the 1950s to dismantle an embryonic capitalism which was only just beginning to challenge feudalism—that in effect China had tried to leapfrog over the capitalist stage of evolutionary development. The result had been to delay the eventual succession to socialism. However, feudalism was still rampant and responsible for China's 'backwardness'. It had to be countered by capitalist techniques and structures as an intermediary step necessary to achieve the ultimate goal of socialism at some undefined time in the future.

Socialism as redefined by 'Deng's Thought' permitted China to develop by whatever means would be successful: 'It does not matter if the cat is black or white. If it can catch rats it is a good cat'. Market values were reasserted, the importance of tourism was reiterated and tourism numbers expanded.

Tourism development in rural China

The development of a major tourist attraction at Ling Mao only became possible after 1978 in the context of the emergence of the policies of 'socialism with Chinese characteristics' which gradually moved China away from a centrally administered economy to a more decentralized, market-oriented system. Over the next 15 years some 20 million village-run and town-run enterprises were created which led to the 'rural urbanization' of much of China. Hundreds of tourism sites were developed by local interests. The Ling Mao Nyam Scenic Region Management Company is one of them.

There were two specific policies which permitted this. The first was 'the responsibility system of contracted production' authorized by the Third Plenum of the Eleventh Central Committee in 1978. The second was the decision by the government in 1984 to allow peasants to settle in cities and towns and to engage in business and service industries on condition that they provided for their own grain provisions.

The first policy in effect replaced the village brigades and production teams by devolving responsibility for production down to individual households. This was accomplished by 'de-collectivization'—returning traditionally owned lands to the peasants who were ,assigned' the land for up to thirty years. In this way Chinese socialism was maintained by the continued legal ownership of the land remaining with the state; thus, it was argued, a new landed upper class was not being created. But households were awarded freedom of usury rights and the right to pass on land to descendants, as if ownership resided with the peasants. Wealth that might accumulate under this system was acceptable, provided the rich did not trample on the socialist principle of non exploitation of labour.

Since then households in the countryside have found that from the limited farmland they have been contracted to work 'a massive workforce can be released for other lucrative propositions'. In a study of four municipalities covering twenty counties, Fei found that one-third of the workforce in the countryside would belong to the category of surplus labour if calculated on the basis of one farmhand taking care of four mu (about one hectare) of land. Chen Ximen, Director of the Department of Rural Development (State Council Development Research Centre), said at a conference on rural reform in December 1993 that of China's total rural workforce of 440 million, 110 million worked in factories and service industries. The remaining 330 million worked on the country's 100 million hectares of farmland but had work for only one-third of the year.

This surplus rural labour, who used to be submerged by the practice of 'everyone dipping into the common pot', becomes a new workforce in the countryside once they are given the opportunity to work in enterprises they set up on their own. In consequence, village and town-run enterprises have blossomed everywhere in the countryside. It can be said that village and town industry is the off spring of the combination of surplus labour and new means of production and objects of labour.

The second policy was fundamental to the 'rural urbanization' of China, which freed more resources for non-agricultural pursuits. For example, in the four countries in Guangdong surveyed by Xu and Zhang 1988-89) there were only nine towns in the four counties n 1978. By the end of 1984, however, there were 64. In 1978, town populations totalled 275 303 (10.27% of the total population of the four counties); by 1984, town populations had risen to 434508—15.78% of the total population of the counties.

In 1992, the State Bureau of Statistics recorded that township enterprises registered a gross output of 1.76 trillion yuan, accounting for 31.6% of the country's total non-agricultural output. In 1993, the gross output of township enterprises was estimated to total 2.7 trillion yuan. 'Having the peasants leave the land without leaving the village' to participate in village-run and town-run enterprises has been acknowledged as a guiding principle of national strategic importance.

6

Information Technology in Tourism

Developments in information and telecommunication technologies (ITT) and computer reservation systems (CRS) undoubtedly change rapidly both business practices and strategies. Unexceptionally, the tourism industry has received several influences from these developments. This chapter concentrates on the implication of ITT for the tourism and hospitality industries (THI) and more specifically for the small and medium tourism enterprises (SMTE) section of the market. Further, the chapter concentrates on the contribution of SMTE to the prosperity of destinations. Examining SMTE's advantages and disadvantages, the chapter explores the major threats for the SMTE which jeopardise their future welfare, namely changes in consumer preferences, ITT and CRS domination, emergence of multinational corporations, and rising conflicts within the distribution channels of tourism products. ITT is proposed as a potential strategic tool for strengthening SMTE's competitive position in the international tourism arena. Computer reservation systems (CRS) in particular have a leading role in contemporary issues, effecting the best practices in the industry. An overview and a classification of the existing CRS is offered.

Hitherto, most ITT applications have concentrated on improving efficiency within the organisation context, though SMTE can achieve great benefits by building electronic networks for destination coordination. Thus, the idea of the regional integrated computer information reservation management systems (RICIRMS) is analysed. The chapter is based on ongoing research aiming to provide strategic solutions and strengthen SMTE. It benefits from a pilot field research survey which incorporated 'in-depth semi-structured' personal interviews with 18 hospitality SMTE and eight incoming travel agencies (ITA) in two Aegean islands (Kos and Hios). In addition, four British tour operators (TO) (both small and large) and four outgoing travel agencies (OTA) (both chains and independents) have been interviewed in early 1993.

The first results of a proper survey in more than 300 Aegean SMTE are also incorporated. Furthermore, lengthy discussions with academics, consultants, entrepreneurs, information technology experts and computer reservation system representatives of the last three years contribute also. Useful inferences from the pilot application of a RICIRMS on the Greek Aegean islands (AEGEO) are also drawn. The emphasis is to explore the information and reservation needs by the entire distribution channel and to identify specific requirements for every member. In addition, practices and conflicts in the existing channels are investigated. The chapter does not aim to provide a quantitative analysis or statistically accurate results, owing to the small sample, but provides insights into the perspectives and needs of the various actors. Quantitative analysis based on a larger sample is due at a later stage in this research.

Since the early 1970s ITT has played a radical role in the competitiveness of enterprises worldwide and it became one of the most important strategic weapons of organisations. Empirical data have demonstrated that ITT is used as a strategic resource in the following areas: cost competitiveness (66.67%), customer service (64.29%), product/service differentiation (45.24%), market segmentation (41.67%), new product planning (32.14%), supplier relations (28.57%), other (26.19%).

Thomas defines technology as 'consisting of society's pool of knowledge concerning the industrial, mechanical and practical areas'. In addition, 'telecommunications networks provide the information highways over which new products and services can be offered, thereby redefining concepts of customer service, opening up new arenas of innovation, and altering the economies of distribution'. Porter recognises that ITT is reshaping the nature of industrial competitiveness by changing the nature or conduct of business. Consequently, 'the primary use of strategic information systems is to support or shape the competitive strategy of the organisation and its plans for gaining (or maintaining) competitive advantage', especially if ITT can deliver cost advantage or differentiation against competitors.

However, ITT is not a panacea for organisational problems. Strassmann proves that there is little correlation between spending on information systems and profitability. Moreover, there is criticism that ITT often fails to add value to the organisation's operations, while the associated cost (capital, training staff) exceeds the benefit. High technology by no means guarantees profitability and it may even worsen a firm's competitive position in industry attractiveness. A variety of organisational redesigns and alterations on management control systems may be required in order to benefit from ITT. Moreover, managers' attitude and degree of capitalisation on ITT's potential play a critical role in the successful contribution to the organisation.

The ITT revolution had severe implications to the tourism and hospitality industries (THI) as it changed the 'best operation practices' and provided opportunities for business expansion in the geographical marketing and operational sense. THI has become more flexible, quicker in response to consumer requests, more efficient. ITT has also reduced the costs of operations while it has delivered tools for flexible and competitive pricing. The rapid increase of the reliability, capabilities and capacity of telematics, combined with the decrease of their cost, has encouraged THI to adapt and use these new strategic tools heavily. 'A whole system of ITT is being rapidly diffused throughout the tourism industry and no player will escape its impacts'.

Further, adoption of ITT is forced by the enormous growth of the THI. Millions of schedules and prices are applied in the deregulated transportation industries daily, while numerous tourist destinations and unlimited tourist products have been developed lately. All these international business activities could never be handled without using ITT. Moreover, the proliferation of computers in society and the fierce competition force enterprises to increase efficiencies and consequently drive ITT in the THI. Poon probably describes it best: 'Tourism is a very information intensive activity. In few other areas of activity are the generation, gathering, processing, application and communication of information as important for day-to-day operations as they are for the travel and tourism industry'. Unlike durable and industrial goods, the intangible tourism service cannot be physically displayed or inspected at the point of sale before purchasing. Tourism services are normally bought well before the time of their use and away from the place of consumption. In the marketplace, tourism products are almost completely dependent upon representations and descriptions (information) imprinted and audiovisual forms. Thus, communications and information transmission tools are indispensable to the tourism trade.

On the tourism demand side, a new/experienced/sophisticated/demanding traveller is seeking more destinations and experiences. Consequently, tourists request a wide variety of specific information on the areas, accessibility, facilities, attractions, and activities at destinations. Timely and accurate information relevant to the consumer's needs is often the key to successful satisfaction of tourism demand. Therefore, it can be concluded that radical development of ITT usage in the THI is driven by both the development of the size and complication of the tourism demand as well as by the rapid expansion and sophistication of tourism and hospitality supply.

The rapid growth of multimedia technology which combines time-based media such as voice animation and video—along with space-based media such as text, graphics and image—provides the opportunity for interaction between the system and the user and thus will have radical effects on the tourism industry. Integrated services digital networks (ISDN) will formulate high-speed networks which will be able to handle large data volumes offering a revolutionary medium for distribution of tourism products.

Although until recently consumers were reluctant to utilise home holiday purchasing the increasing computer literacy of the younger generations, the wider availability of information technology in more households and the rapid growth of ITT's capabilities are expected to increase the direct involvement of consumers with ITT, in order to get a wider range of information on destinations and their attractions/facilities before making their ideal choice. Holiday shopping at home is gradually becoming a serious alternative or complement to traditional travel agent visits. It is estimated that 2.9 million viewers in the UK use the travel section of the teletext. In addition, the wide spread of videotex technology, such as Minitel in

France, has also provided a convenient communication media for home holiday shopping. Minitel claims 42% of travel reservations in France, with agents just one point ahead with 43% of bookings. The development of shopping channels through satellite and cable TV is another potential method of home shopping.

Ultimately direct booking by the customer via home computer and interactive systems will become a reality. Holiday home shopping through ITT incorporates several advantages which can support its growth. Firstly, it enables the consumers to access a wider range of information, enabling them to acquire specific replies to their personal needs. The provision of some tangible elements, such as video sights and music from destinations, hotels, attractions and local environment, instead of relying on small, inadequate and often ill-informed or misleading brochures produced by tour operators, can reduce some of the 'intangibility' of the tourism product, especially for destination-naive tourists. Moreover, ITT offers a greater flexibility, as travelling partners do not need to visit a travel agency together, at what are often inconvenient shopping hours or location, to discuss and book their holidays. Consumers have often suffered from travel agencies' inadequacies in providing quality service for various reasons, such as: inexperienced staff; holiday sold out of the brochure without any effort to customise the product; bias towards operators who provide higher commissions or special incentives; and lack of backup information resources. Holiday home shopping will never replace traditional high street travel agencies though, but it complements them and forces them into travel consulting. Thus, ITT is more likely to offer an additional distribution channel, targeted at ITT-literate consumers, those who have used the travel services before and therefore feel somewhat secure with the destination environment and those with specific requirements which cannot be accommodated by mass products. Destination-naive travellers, elderly people and ITT-illiterate customers would probably keep to the traditional paper brochure and travel agency combination.

Leisure destinations often consist of SMTE networks producing a blend of independently provided services, which are combined in order to create an integrated product—the tourism experience. THI are regarded as highly value added chains where the performance of one activity affects the cost and effectiveness of the other. ITT plays a dominant role in interconnecting SMTE and provides the communication network which enables the THI to perform their services delivery. In this sense, ITT is the lifeblood or the cement that holds together the producers and the distribution channels. Thus it enables the creation of a multi-integrated business and technology network in which integrated ITT provides the platform for efficient communication in an integrated tourism industry, which in its turn is integrated with the local business and economic community.

Porter suggests that 'the world of the next decade is going to be a world where people struggle with how to connect systems, how to make them compatible, how to deal with the complexity of systems that span many activities within the firm and cross functional boundaries'. This could not be more applicable than in the THI. ITT is effectively playing an executive role in managing and unravelling the complexity generated by the interrelationships within the tourism industry. The systemic adoption of ITT by all segments of the industry provides the necessary ground for a total system of wealth creation for the supply side and a total system of consumer satisfaction for the demand side.

Small and medium enterprises (SME) dominate the

global economy. It is estimated that 70% of turnover generated within the European Union (EU) is produced by the small business sector, 22% by micro enterprises (< 10 employees), 48% by small and medium enterprises (< 500 employees) and only 30% by large companies (> 500 employees); while 70% of Europe's workforce is employed by small business (29% by micro enterprises, 41% by SMEs and 30% by large companies). Almost 92% of all EU enterprises are micro enterprises (13.6 million), 6 million of which had no salaried employees; 7.9% of all enterprises are SMEs (911000 small and 70 000 medium firms), while large enterprises account for only 1 in 1000 companies (13 000 in total). The average size of an EU enterprise is seven persons.

Classifying enterprises into small, medium and large is not an easy task. Two major approaches can be employed: a quantitative/objective and a qualitative/subjective approach. In the first case, three criteria are normally used: number of employees, annual turnover and number of beds, especially for hotels. The European Union characterises as SMTE all enterprises which have less than 500 employees, less than 75 million ECUs net fixed asset, less than 38 million ECUs net turnover and less than one-third of the company being held by a larger firm. When the employment criteria are applied then companies with 09 employees are characterised as micro, or very small, and the ones with 1099 employees small, while 100499 employees signifies a medium company and more than 500 employees a large enterprise. When hotels are classified, the number of beds criterion can be applied.

Most authors seem to agree that accommodation establishments with less than 50 beds are small. Further Moutinho characterises as small all hotels and travel agencies employing fewer than 10 people. When qualitative methods are employed, a wide range of criteria can be used, such as the organisational structure, participation in hotel consortia or chains, turnover, responsibility distribution in decision making, financial strength, operational procedures, recruitment and training practices, decision-making process, entrepreneurial involvement and control, integration level, family domination in running the property, internationalisation of operation; marketing functions and managerial experience.

Traditionally, SMTE have played a dominant role in the THI. They are particularly important in destination development, not only by providing tourists with direct contact with the character of the destination, but also by facilitating rapid infusion of tourist spending into the local economy. It is estimated that more than 90% of hotels are SMTE and family-managed. Most of the hotel establishments throughout Europe are small, independent, flexible and seasonal. More than 90% of Swiss hotels have 50 rooms or fewer and only 2016 have more than 100 rooms. In France, 80076 of the tourism firms employ fewer than 10 people. The average hotel in the UK has 25 rooms while 70% in the Scottish Western Isles have fewer than five letting bedrooms. The average hotel and restaurant establishment in Greece employs 2.5 persons while on the Greek Aegean islands the average number of beds per hotel is 63. Finally, almost 90% of US hotels have fewer than 149 rooms.

SMTE have, in most cases, informal organisational structures with great involvement by the proprietor's family. Often it is found that household traditional roles are adopted in the everyday running of the business. Research in small Greek hotels demonstrated that in many cases women have cooking, serving, cleaning and room setting responsibilities, while men look after the reception, the bar, construction, technology, negotiating prices and signing up contracts, purchasing, marketing and financial functions. As a result, businesses are run on family principles rather than proper business practices while people in the SMTE rarely have formal education or training. This often causes both managerial and emotional problems.

A wide range of strengths and weaknesses of the SME are due to their size. More specifically, in the THI a range of strengths are often attributed, such as flexibility, direct control of service delivery, personalised and tailor-made service, entrepreneurial activity, strong local character, catering for special interest groups, employment of family members, flexible timetable and multi-skilled personnel.

However, SMTE have significant weaknesses as well. Management often suffers because of inadequate education or vocational training, ignorance of modern management and marketing techniques and lack of strategic planning. Family domination in SMTE can be a weakness because rational decisions have to be avoided in order to preserve family cohesion. The small size of operation provides little opportunity for the division of tasks, professional employees and proper training. Since no quality standards are introduced, service delivery varies according to the occupancy, service provider and timing. Moreover, SMTE face financial weaknesses, lack of economies of scale in purchasing raw material, low bargaining power, and lack of advanced facilities. As the THI becomes more professional, embraces quality management and responds to an increasingly discerning customer, the SMTE's typical lack of business expertise and minimal standardisation may become a liability.

Marketing, and specifically the distribution channels, is the greatest weakness and threat for the SMTE. Unable to understand the consumer behaviour process, they rely on a canonical and seasonal demand, until of course it dries up. Consequently, they offer a 'product-oriented' service rather than one which is market-oriented. Moreover, SMTE cannot afford to launch their own marketing campaign and they lack the know-how. Inability to follow current trends and developments in the distribution channel field is evident. In a recent research study of more than 250 hospitality establishments only a handful had ever heard of computer reservation systems and one of them had such a misunderstanding that it had installed a travel agencies' version of a major CRS. Recent field research by this author on the SMTE of the Aegean islands provides plenty of evidence that this marketing weakness is capitalised on by members of the distribution channel in tourism, namely tour operators (TO) and major travel agencies. Being aware of SMTE's handicap, TO promote themselves and in fact are regarded by SMTE, as the only way to fill empty rooms.

However, TO rarely pay deposits to guarantee 1 their bookings and no formal obligation is normally given to fulfil their allotment. In addition, there is a 'release period' of only one to two weeks, which is insufficient for hoteliers to sell their rooms elsewhere in the event of their not being used. In most cases no compensation or cancellation fees are offered if rooms are not used. These practices we followed almost globally, regardless of the destination. As a consequence, TO minimise SMTEs' profit marlins by negotiating discounts of up to 70% on the official rates of hospitality enterprises. Special offers, contributions to advertising and brochure production, representatives' expenses at destination and complimentary hospitality for 'educational trips' are also requested.

In several Aegean hotels, TO offered a 0% increase for the 1994 rates. As there had been an inflation rate of almost 15%, an increase in labour cost of 22% and a capital cost of up to 35%, there was little room for optimism. In addition a constant devaluation of the drachma increases the profit margins for TO and allows them to offer reduced prices to their customers in order to compete in their market. In other tourist enterprises, such as restaurants, bars, night clubs, jewellery, souvenir and fur-leather shops, heavy commissions and/or a fee per tourist are requested by locally based representatives in order for the particular enterprise to be included in the 'suggested list' or to be made one of the stopovers in the city bar crawl organised at die destination.

This 'blackmailing' situation is evident, specifically in destinations where supply exceeds demand and the area is reaching its maturity stage. Several TO practices, utilised in order to preserve their power in the distribution channel, were reported consistently by Aegean SMTE. The most common ones are: quoting that a particular hotel is full in order to promote committed hotels; downgrading customers' ratings for a hotel and consequently reducing its appeal; offering a disadvantageous space in brochures; offering a very short release period and thus minimising the opportunities for a hotel to sell its unused rooms; timing contract signing in low periods in order to achieve minimum rates; and leading tourists to different resorts every year, in a periodical way, in order to suppress demand and prices in all regions. Reducing the profit margins of the SMTE affects other enterprises in the area through multiplier effects. Consequently the entire local economy is endangered should SMTE fail to achieve a successful performance owing to inabilities to distribute their products adequately.

Moreover, the rapid development of the THI and global competition has increased the professionalism required in the market. Transportation technology has removed the geographical barriers in travel behaviour, while media have reduced the distances and increased the understanding between different countries and cultures. Consequently, tourists have a much wider spectrum of destinations to choose from, most at very competitive prices. Furthermore, globalisation of the industry suggests that SMTE compete in a multinational environment where only organisations which can provide exceptional value or cost advantage, would be able to survive. The rapid development of ITT is often regarded as a facilitator for the globalisation of the THI.

The opportunity of gaining economies of scale in all non-operational functions of the hospitality industry, such as distribution channels, reservations, marketing, advertising, administration, personnel management, technology adaptation, new product development, training and bulk purchasing of raw material and equipment, has forced the creation of major hotel chains, international consortia, management contracts and multinational franchising companies, and placed the independent operator at a disadvantage. The overall trend in the hotel industry is towards a gradual but steady switch from independently owned and operated hotels to hotel chain affiliation. Unfortunately for the SMTE, globalisation goes hand in hand with increased concentration in the THI as large corporations consistently gain market share and market influence. SMTE seem to be the weakest and most vulnerable members of the industry, and therefore need to seek competitive advantages to be able to compete in the international arena and maintain their market share.

The development of the 'new' tourist who is becoming knowledgeable and is seeking exceptional value for money and time, and participation in special interest activities is another major challenge for SMTE. Thus, the relative importance of package tours which are based on low-quality, low-prices, is expected to decline in favour of independently organised tourism. Poon has led the debate on tourism metamorphosis by suggesting that the 'old tourism' is gradually replaced by the 'new tourism'. The old tourism is characterised by 'mass, standardised and rigidly packed' tourism with little attention to tourists' personal needs, capitalising on the Ford model of mass production. It has been appealing to the mass markets based on economies of scale and has primarily served the sunlust and inexperienced consumer. Using charter flights and undifferentiated, inexpensive accommodation, TO gather all elements of a trip in a 'package' which they sell as a commodity in its own capacity. However, since the 1990s the *new tourism* has emerged, offering new best practices. It is characterised as 'flexible, segmented, customised and diagonally integrated'. Utilising new technology, the tourism industry is able to offer a much more tailor-made product to a new/experienced/ sophisticated/ demanding tourist who is looking for authentic experiences and has a wanderlust as well as an independent attitude. A relatively new movement towards environmental preservation and appreciation for the local society is also evident. Tourists tend to participate in the experience by being active and spend their time on their special interests. Flexibility in both consumer choice and the service delivery process is a key element. Brackenbury President of the IFTO, recently admitted that

> the traditional annual family holiday, mostly in a Mediterranean beach resort, will not play a dominant role in the future. We have to accept that multi-interest travel is replacing part of our present bread and butter products. At least it has to be a combination of beach holidays plus pleasure of some kind or culture.

Every tourist is different, bringing a unique blend of experiences, motivations and desires. Jones suggests that 'leisure life-styles are inconsistent, contradictory and individual'. In the 1990s tourism is following the trend towards customisation. Cooper and Buhalis suggest that 'to an extent the new sophisticated traveller has emerged as a result of experience. Tourists from the major generating regions of the world have become frequent travellers, are linguistically and technologically skilled and can function in multicultural and demanding environments overseas'.

In a similar sense Buhalis proposed that the traditional '4Ss' of the tourism industry (Sun-Sea-Sand-Sex) are transformed into Sophistication-Specialisation-Segmentation-Satisfaction. Hitherto, holidaymakers from northern countries escape to the sunny south to 'recharge their batteries' for a heavy winter back home. However, *Sea* pollution, health dangers resulting from *Sun* exposure, *Sand* degradation and modern *Sexually* transmitted diseases gradually limit the appeal of these elements. An increasing demand for more individualised, authentic and enriched tourist experiences signify the transformation of the traditional '4Ss' to four modern ones which framework the trends of the emerging tourism demand. Educated, experienced and demanding tourists require *Sophisticated* tourism products which can satisfy their cultural, intellectual and sporting interests.

As a result a demand for tailor-made, authentic and enriched experiences is leading the tourism industry to a sophisticated market place. Since every prospective tourist has almost unique needs and wants a certain amount of Specialisation, it is expected to dominate the future tourist product. Thus, the focus is turned to individuals and mini-mass markets which can share common activities and desire to experience similar activities. The identification of these mini-markets can only be achieved through detailed market Segmentation, based on life-style rather than on demographics. This process could demonstrate the similarities of the consumers and result in the formulation of feasible specialised activities. The ultimate aim for every tourism enterprise and destination should be the total customer Satisfaction throughout the tourist consumption chain, i.e. before, during and after the holiday. An integrated approach within the tourism industry is, therefore, required in order to ensure the coordination of the various enterprises and individuals involved in the tourist product delivery. SMTE and destinations which fail to serve and facilitate the transformation of tourism demand will be marginalised and suffer significant losses in their market share.

Finally, ITT and CRS pose a potential threat to the SMTE. Go and Welch fear that SMTE can be 'left out in the cold by the rapid advantages in modern hotel technology, especially in the area of reservation systems'. Recent research on the Aegean islands demonstrated clearly that SMTE are unable to follow the ITT developments and capitalise on potentials, owing to lack of know-how and capital. As most entrepreneurs or experienced managers have little education or training they tend to ignore the opportunities just because they cannot control it. They often feel that computer programmers will be 'external controllers' in their property. Consequently, they marginalise themselves, believing that ITT can be utilised only by larger organisations which have more divisions, funds and know-how. In this way, both their market shares and profit margins are jeopardised.

Perhaps, complicated CRS *developments* are the most influential of all ITT applications on tourism, changing the best business practices worldwide. CRS facilitate the distribution of tourism products and assist transportation /hospitality/entertainment enterprises to handle their inventory efficiently and profitably. CRS offer the opportunity for instant update as well as the ability to provide information and support for the request/ reservation/confirmation/purchase processes for a combination of tourist products worldwide. It is estimated that 95% of US travel agencies are linked to at least one CRS and 88% of all airline tickets are issued through a CRS. There are several types of CRS serving different enterprises, namely: airlines, hotels, rent-a-car organisations, tour operator and regional CRS.

Airlines were pioneers in CRS development and have benefited vastly since the 1970s. The growth of schedules and tariffs as well as the frequent alterations, forced by deregulation in the USA, made airlines' planning and operation unbearable without CRS. Most airlines developed their own systems, while the need for networking forced them to upgrade their systems to global distribution systems (GDS). All airline services, several hotels, major car hire companies and ancillary services such as entertainment worldwide are coming under the same 'umbrella' system which facilitates the distribution of a wide range of these products.

Furthermore, hotels installed hotel information systems or property management systems in order to facilitate management of their inventory. Maximising profits requires a maximisation of both occupancy rates and tariffs. Hotel CRS can contribute to this task, in both property and corporate levels, by improving capacity and operational efficiency, controlling inventory centrally, providing last room availability, producing extensive marketing and operational reports, supporting pricing decisions, promoting to certain segments and organising distribution channels effectively. Several types of hotel CRS can be identified: *in-house CRS* operating for a single property, *hotel chain CRS*, integrating the rooms of an entire chain, *independent hotel reservation agents CRS* facilitating bookings in a wide range of interconnected hotels, and finally *hotel representation and consortium CRS*, promoting subscribed hotels. Similar CRS have been developed by rent-a-car firms, ferry and railway companies and every tourism product which needs to be booked in advance. Moreover, tour operators have introduced CRS, where tourism products are held in a form of bundles, distributed to the travel retailers through videotex networks, and monitor the availability of 'holiday packages'.

Finally, global distribution systems (GDS) have emerged through the integration of most of the abovementioned systems with the most powerful airline CRS. Consequently, GDS can offer access to major hospitality and tourism firms worldwide, while they can provide one-stop travel shopping opportunity. In this sense they can be characterised as 'travel distribution supermarkets'. The competition of GDS has forced them to consolidate and experts believe that 'we are now seeing the development of a global framework or maybe three global distribution networks based upon SABRE, AMADEUS/WORLDSPAN and GALILEO'. Pelletier suggests that 'the signs are that it will prove very hard to prevent the large and powerful players in the business most of whom will have their own or shared systems from gaining advantages over the non-vendors'.

The brief analysis of the existing CRS illustrates that there is a great complexity in the market. Inter-connections between CRS, loosely finalised procedures, and little understanding of CRS operation led SMTE, to misunderstandings and little utilisation of the potential provided by CRS. Hitherto, CRS and GDS have targeted the business traveller market and consequently incorporate exclusively scheduled airlines, hotels which belong to chains or consortia and multinational rent-a-car firms. The product standardisation and the existence of their own CRS, has established these firms' existence within the GDS. Consequently, the budget-oriented and flexible leisure market is only being served by the tour operators' systems and has attracted little attention from other CRS or GDS. Thus, both the growing independent leisure market and the SMTE are inadequately served and suffer from isolation.

Page proposes that 'to function in the knowledge economy, small businesses need straightforward access to information-market intelligence as well as databases of market opportunities prospective customers and clients, supplies, possible distributors, agents and partners'. SMTE are often lost in a competitive and tricky CRS jungle where every system is marketed as the solution to their distributional problems. Lack of computer literacy, in most SMTE, in combination with little understanding of potential use of these networks 'place SMTE at a severe disadvantage, effectively barring them from the main stream of business'. Go and Welch suggest that SMTE are 'the weakest and most vulnerable part of the hotel industry',

> while the Economist Intelligence Unit warns that while the independent property paradoxically may continue to offer the levels of personal services, they may at the same time find it much more difficult to remain in contact with their markets. If it becomes increasingly normal to use computerised systems to reserve and even pay for hotel space, there is the possibility that the small properties will be left out in the cold.

Small and independent hotels need to enhance their distribution channels without losing their distinct character and their ability to provide uniquely delivered services. Perhaps Go and Welch express this threat clearly, 'Romantic, distinctive and charming as the private country hotel may be in almost any country in Europe, all that will count for little if there are no customers. All hotels must ensure that they are put before their market in the most effective way'. As, on the one hand, the vast network of family-run properties in Europe need to ensure !heir presence in the GDS systems and, on the other, they cannot afford to have individual membership, CRS stand as an opportunity for SMTE to initiate the desperately needed cooperation.

From computer reservation systems (CRS) to destination management systems (DMS) to regional integrated computer information reservation systems (RICIRMS)

> The airline-owned CRS of the North are generally biased in favour of origins, airlines and transnational travel companies and against destinations, non-airline land service companies, and small and medium sized national companies which cannot afford the price of entry and transaction costs of the international airline CRS network.

As CRS and GDS have a business traveller orientation and offer chain-multinational corporations, homogeneous, expensive, standardised products, they effectively marginalise SMTE. Hurst proposes that

> we must focus on creating a system which meets the needs of a whole accommodations industry both for the lesser known locations, the small to medium sized properties, Catering to the leisure market, as well as city centre hotels catering to the business traveller. It is these properties, more so in some ways than the large business city centre hotels already well served by the CRS, which require the support of a destination database system.

In this sense, several destinations initiated a slow process of developing destination-oriented information and reservation systems for the local tourism enterprises and (2) their attractions.

Destination management systems (DMS) primarily offer leisure and sensibly priced products, with heterogeneous and customised attributes, primarily served by independent SMTE. Several names have been attributed to these systems namely: destination information systems; destination management systems; destination databases.

There is hardly any adequate definition describing the concept or the existing DMS but 'a destination database is, in its simplest form, a collection of information, probably computerised and interactively accessible, about a destination'. Vlitos-Rowe quotes Haines's definition:

> A new breed of information technology that attempts to combine information and reservation by using artificial intelligence to link the two and, at the same time, derive a powerful marketing database with detailed customer preferences. These systems combine destinations information and produce databases with enquiries or client databases and offer a combined information retrieval and reservation capability.

Furthermore, Vlitos-Rowe suggests that 'DMS is intended to provide complete and up-to-date information on a particular destination. These complete data ensure that smaller establishments, as opposed to international hotel chains and other land services associated with travel are included'. Several DMS case studies are described in various documents. Most of these systems can be divided into several categories according to:

(1) *Services they provide: information only,* where only information for certain products can be retrieved; reservation only, where only availability can be

checked and reservations can be made; *information and reservations*, where both the above functions are available; and, finally, *multiple services systems*, which undertake an integrated role of information technology requirements for both tourism supply and demand

(2) *Sectors they serve: hospitality systems*, which undertake hotel reservations only; *transportation only systems*, which provide timetables, availability, fares and ticketing for either aeroplanes, ferries, trains or coaches; *attraction systems*, offering information and ticketing facilities for specific attractions in a certain area; and, finally, *integrated systems*, which offer the opportunity to retrieve information and make reservations in all services which can possibly be used by tourists at the destination.

(3) *Vendor of system*: systems developed by or under the support of the public sector dominated the existing systems; however, private enterprises have been set up as well; while cooperation between public, private sectors and local professional associations is another form of development.

(4) *Automation and technology utilised: semi-manual* systems utilise traditional ITT such as telephones, telex, fax, while computerised networks provide the opportunity for online response to any requests. These networks can utilise simple text or multimedia interfaces, enabling the user to retrieve a range of texts, music, video, computer animation, photographs, maps, etc.

The DMS concept can be taken a step forward to RICIRMS, by proposing a very wide range of services for both tourism enterprises and consumers. Acting at a regional level the system should incorporate and coordinate the entire population of tourist services providers. Both individual products, such as hotels, restaurants, transportation and 'packages' created by principals, travel agencies, tour operators and other companies should be displayed. Failure to do so would remove the completeness of the system and would jeopardise the confidence that the system can provide the 'best available deal'. Moreover, the system should be *multi-integrated,* i.e. utilise all available ITT to coordinate SMTE and integrate with the local economy. Although several DMS are not computerised, it is suggested that full benefits can only be gained when the system is utilising latest ITT. *Computerisation,* and networking of the entire population of enterprises at the destination would be essential for establishing an online network. The consistent reduction in ITT prices will make basic equipment affordable even to tiny organisations, and, consequently, it is unlikely that they will be disadvantaged unless they choose to be so by ignoring these developments. Several authors have emphasised that RICIRMS should provide information, about everything in relation to the destination. Information can be classified in a '5A' framework: Accommodation-Accessibility Attractions-Activities-Ancillary services. *Reservations* and purchasing of tourism products through an RICIRMS should also be encouraged. It is vital that all required tourist products display their updated availability and price and can be purchased via the system. Tourists could either use self-service terminals and borne computers to make reservations or they could ask booking agents or travel agencies to make the reservations for them. When no agencies are involved a fraction of their normal commission should be passed to individual customers as special discount. Bookings should be guaranteed against adequate deposit and a cancellation policy should clarify the obligations of both tourists and suppliers.

The system should also have a *Management* function for both the SMTE and the entire destination. Destination-wise, the maximisation of tourists' facilities usage and the maximisation of tourists' expenditure per capita is important for the local economy as it generates public and private income, employment, multiplier effects and foreign currency. Thus, RICIRMS can be utilised in order to promote the destination, announce specific events, make tourists aware of attractions, activities and local festivities and stimulate their spending in order to maximise the economic benefits of the tourism activity. Equally important, destinations should inspire tourists' sensible behaviour and exchange of sociocultural experiences. RICIRMS can diffuse information on the host society, local culture, history, customs, codes of behaviour or dressing, and everything that would bring the host community and tourists towards a closer relationship and mutual understanding. Furthermore, destination management techniques can be introduced through an RICIRMS.

Visitor management techniques could be incorporated and proper distribution of tourists within the destination should be attempted. Warnings of overbookings, overcrowded areas, sold-out facilities, events or attractions, as well as traffic jams, should he displayed on the system. Alternative routes or services should be then proposed, by the system, in order to save customers' dissatisfaction and destination deterioration. The major impact of RICIRMS on SMTE is the efficient management of the SMTE inventory and the opportunity they provide for SMTE marketing. As the most important objective of every tourist enterprise is to maximise occupancy and average expenditure, RICIRMS can help by providing a comprehensive and up-to-date availability plan as well as by rationalising the pricing process. Yield management can be utilised, while marketing techniques such as direct mail, guest histories and frequent customer databases can increase the income of both the SMTE and the destination. The development of an alternative distribution channel will effectively reduce the tour operators' monopolistic buying power and will offer SMTE fair profit margins. The latter point is made consistently by researchers in the Mediterranean destinations.

The diffusion of off-season attractions, combined with sensible pricing would stimulate demand for the 'low season' and thus would increase SMTE profitability. In addition, the system should provide managerial assistance for the SMTEs' functions. RICIRMS have the capacity to incorporate various databases or networks which could assist entrepreneurs such as purchasing networks, where not only can data for raw material suppliers be kept but also an online purchasing system could be in place, providing the, opportunity to access directly and effectively the best producer. In addition, the system can provide the essential network for telebanking and thus reduce waiting time in banks as well as provide flexible banking hours. Moreover, RICIRMS can facilitate the centralisation of several SMTE functions such as accounting, marketing and recruitment to external contractors who would develop an expertise in the needs of these enterprises and split the cost between subscribed members. Teleconsulting might also be facilitated, where SMTE could place an enquiry and a specialist consultant would provide an appropriate answer within hours. The benefit of having experts managing several functions of geographically spread SMTE, especially for island destinations such as the Aegean archipelagos, at an affordable cost is tremendous. Finally, a wide range of information such as tourist statistics, new legislations, incentive policies, grant opportunities and special requests for cooperation would be enormously helpful.

These business services can enhance the management expertise of SMTE, as well as reduce telecommunications costs, the need for entrepreneurs to travel and the unproductive time radically. Most of these services can attract public or European Union funding.

In recent field research on the Aegean islands' SMTE the vast majority suggested that a RICIRMS should be developed. They concentrated its benefits in provision of information to prospective tourists and the travel trade worldwide, reduction of dependency on tour operators, promotion of tourist products abroad, attraction of better 'quality' and wealthier tourists, coordination of destinations SMTE, and reduction of islands' isolation. Most of them were interested in getting reservations through a similar system. Furthermore, a considerable portion was willing to cofinance the development of a RICIRMS, depending on the cost and size of the SMTE, while a commission was readily offered for every reservation coming through the system. Unfortunately, they were unable to predict the benefits of networking and value added chains formulated by RICIRMS.

From *the consumer point of view,* destination information is a vital element of the consumer decision-making process, while it is a critical component of the destination's marketing mix. Murray suggests that 'the greater the degree of perceived risk in a pre-purchased context, the greater the consumer propensity to seek information about the product'. This is particularly the case for 'destination naive tourists' and especially for the infamous or new resorts where little public knowledge exists. Moreover, individuals seek travel information in order to make judgements regarding the possible payoff of a product purchase, given perceived risks as well as to remove some of the intangibility in the tourism product by getting more information on aesthetic, affective and imaginative aspects of the product. In addition, tourists use information in order to facilitate their travel planning and maximise their experience 'efficiency' while at destination. Stanton suggests that 'current market trends such as increasing volatility, fragmentation and customer sophistication, imply an ever-increasing need for destination database developments to take place in order to properly meet customer demands and preferences'.

RICIRMS is the most suitable tool to provide tourist information to the new/sophisticated/experienced/ demanding tourist who is travelling independently and requires more information to be available. In the current hectic business environment consumers tend to be equally time and cost-conscious. Consumers want better returns on the time they spend as well as better value for money. As the market for shorter but more frequent holidays is growing rapidly, consumers will consistently need more flexibility and last-minute arrangements. This trend would require a vast amount of information to be instantly accessible as well as an opportunity to cheek availability and make reservations from one point of sale. Convenient payment methods, through global financial institutions such as credit card corporations, would be basic prerequisites for purchasing any product. Of course, a 'user-adoring' interface (rather than just 'friendly') would need to be in place. Vogel concludes that there is a great demand for 'easy access to transparent and easy to compare information on a wide variety of choices of destinations, holiday packages, travel, lodging and leisure services, the actual prices and availability of such services. Customers also want immediate confirmation and speedy documentation of their reservations'.

RICIRMS can serve tourists in the pre-trip decision period as well as during their trip. A wide range of information should be on display such as transportation schedules, facilities, accommodation-catering-entertainment establishments, last scat/bed availability, description of resorts and enterprises, weather reports, travel regulations, exchange rates. The data should be displayed in a flexible way, where users can set their priorities and preferences for their specific needs. Moreover, users with different expertise should be able to customise the system to their pace. In order to acquire consumers' confidence this data should be up-to-date, unbiased, precise, complete and accurate, and they need to offer the 'best available deal' for the consumer. Furthermore, expert systems technology can be incorporated in order to propose specialised tourist product bundles, based on key parameters or preferences set by the user, or his/her past consumer behaviour. Users should be able to acquire a printed copy of all relevant information and material they need for their trip. Furthermore, a consumer database can be incorporated in order to work as a marketing tool for both destinations and SMTE. Advanced segmentation, direct mail and customised marketing techniques can be utilised. Once at the destination, consumers can utilise RICIRMS's massive computing facilities for other purposes, such as communications and file transfer with their working environments, forwarded electronic mail address, teleworking, electronic bulletin boards discussing issues and experiences about the destination.

Locally, intelligent tourist kiosks with self-service multimedia and interactive capabilities can be conveniently located in hotel lobbies, and at key tourist locations, providing 24-hour information and reservation services for tourists searching for suitable accommodation, transportation or activities. Moreover, the system can be within local SMTE and regional tourist information offices computer systems.

The ultimate aim should be that every single SMTE should have a computerised system which would be able to access the RICIRMS and acquire a wide variety of services for both tourists and entrepreneurs. SMTE who cannot afford to install a computer system or who lack capable personnel should be able to communicate via conventional media, such as telephone, fax or telex through a dedicated operator, or should be given incentives to acquire a terminal. Access to banking systems is of equal importance in order to facilitate payments by credit card. Perhaps the most important function of RICIRMS would be to distribute information and enable reservations at prospective *tourists' place of origin*. In this function it will stimulate and administrate demand for the destination and the SMTE. The system can be distributed through a national node in the most important countries of origin. This node can be hosted by a specific enterprise distributing the RICIRMS, the flag airline's offices of the destination country or the national tourist organisation office in this market. RICIRMS should encourage access by both individual and institutional customers, namely travel agencies and tour operators. The system should ensure that both computer and videotex interfaces can be connected. In addition, a dedicated operator should be available to deal with requests emerging through conventional telecommunication media.

Undoubtedly, airlines lead the technology diffusion in the tourism industry. CRS and GDS can host RICIRMS in order to provide the opportunity for consumers and travel agencies to have access to destination-related comprehensive information. GDS would benefit by selling airline tickets and perhaps getting a fair commission on other reservations through RICIRMS. Jones suggests that 'the emphasis is not on the question of the storage of the destination's full product in the airline CRS but on enabling that CRS to draw on the product the destination has to offer, when the situation arises'. GDS can also gain a significant competitive advantage by becoming a one-stop point of sale, promoting any type of tourist products worldwide. Since technology, expertise and networking are in place, GDS need comparably minor investments to enhance their potentials. An expansion into the 'low margins-high volumes' leisure market would be inevitable. GDS would eventually become a platform for travel information and reservation for both business and leisure markets. It is evident that GDS are getting more involved in various RICIRMS pilot projects while GDS speculate the most appropriate direction.

The most significant problem RICIRMS distribution has to overcome is compatibility. Several CRS, GDS and DMS operate already, utilising different software and working processes, creating unnecessary overheads at all levels. Some of these systems are incompatible deliberately in order to discourage users to swap between systems. Thus, 'information technology islands' are formulated, trapping the 'best deal' within the borders of the 'island'. This will be intolerable to both customers and industry in the near future. The days of capitalising on consumer lack of information and knowledge are definitely limited. CRS and RICIRMS interface standards should be established and thus, a global compatibility between systems should eventually be reached. Industry should be able to use the very same equipment to access various systems. User-friendly interfaces would reduce the need for specific training and make it easier for everybody to benefit from the system. Experienced and educated users will be able to operate various systems and therefore benefit from its potentials. In conclusion, systems and vendors should open their accessibility and consistently compete on the value they can offer, rather than restricting users to limited options.

The organisational framework of an RICIRMS is

very significant for its success. Since public sector and national tourist organisations are normally responsible for the marketing and the strategy of a destination they are often regarded as most appropriate to undertake the development and maintenance of RICIRMS. Sheldon suggests that similar systems can be nationally centralised, regionally centralised or regionally networked. Hitherto, the public sector has dominated the development and operations of DMS, mainly because SMTE, cannot afford to develop an RICIRMS for themselves. Massive investments in equipment, data collection, engineering, artwork and maintenance are required. Moreover, SMTE lack the expertise and the experienced personnel to oversee such a project. Research in the Aegean islands suggested that RICIRMS should be driven by nonprofit cooperation schemes, such as the local hoteliers and travel agencies associations and should be backed by public sources such as national tourist organisations. Other local tourist enterprises can contribute while universities and research institutes might be able to assist in both ITT and tourism marketing sides.

Several interviews with SMTE suggested that an individual vendor could develop an RICIRMS. Apart from the fact that development costs are prohibitive, it is strongly believed that an RICIRMS should be a nonprofit organisation, which, however, should be able to break even. The existence of an individual vendor who would be interested in maximising his return on investment or perhaps influencing prospective tourists towards certain more commissionable or profitable products would be disastrous for an RICIRMS. In this sense no advertising should be permitted in an RICIRMS. An index form representation, equal for all participants, should be adapted. In order to avoid discrimination, tourism products should not be listed alphabetically. Instead, a random generator should be utilised to rank the entire population of enterprises meeting customers' criteria. A consumer watchdog should ensure neutrality and fair representation for all participants. Lessons should be learnt by CRS role in the airlines competition and the regulation framework in the USA and the EU. More importantly RICIRMS should be driven by multi-skilled managers who can understand both demand and supply needs, technology and tourists and tourism consumer behaviour. SMTE should build up trust in RICIRMS and support it by allocating it a fraction of their capacity and honouring reservations arising from the system. They might also need to be prepared to sacrifice some of their independence and accept the operation conditions imposed by the system.

The question of who pays for the RICIRMS development and operation is not an easy one. The feasibility of RICIRMS is under scrutiny, especially since the few promising projects collapsed due to lack of funding. Sheldon divides the RICIRMS economics into developing and operating economics. Hitherto, the public sector has played a dominant role in RICIRMS development. A wide range of private sponsors has financed research and RICIRMS pilot research projects. Perhaps a blend of private and public resources should provide the most adequate financial form. However, since RICIRMS should not be profit-making organisations, the private sector cannot have high returns on investments. The involvement of telecommunication companies in RICIRMS (such as Cable and Wireless in CHARMS and BRAVO), demonstrates that there may be fruitful benefits arising from RICIRMS, mainly for supporting services.

On the operation side there is a trade-off between charges made to principals and competence of the system. It is quite apparent that 'a fully comprehensive system can only occur if no listing fees are demanded'. However, a minimal joint fee combined with reasonable commission on bookings is perhaps the most appropriate way. Research at hospitality SMTE on the Aegean islands demonstrated that only a very small fraction refused categorically to pay some money to join an RICIRMS. Several SMTE were willing to cofinance the development and operation of such a system. A few conditions were normally demanded such as a contribution according to hotel size, unbiased representation, the entire population of SMTE at destination be included, and public sector involvement, *inter alia.*

Other considerations, such as the increase of booking volumes, the reservations generated for the low period, the rates achieved through RICIRMS, and the coverage of the international market, would affect entrepreneurs' willingness to pay for RICIRMS services. Interviewees who refused any payment to a RICIRMS often had committed most of their rooms to tour operators or had financial problems and mortgages. Most SMTE viewed RICIRMS as another advertising medium while the major synergies of distribution and operation functions were missing from the picture. Almost the entire population of SMITE interviewed could happily pay commission for bookings made through the system. The level of commission could be greater during low periods but it was stiff in the peak period. Commission levels could reach up to 25% but the 10% norm was usually followed. McGuffre and Go and Welch warn that bookings through CRS can cost, either customer or principal, up to 30% of the product prices, when all commission payments to travel agencies, CRS and credit card companies involved are paid.

However, in bookings where no CRS is used the situation is similar, when two or more travel agencies are involved. Moreover, hoteliers normally have no choice but to offer more than 50% discount /commission to tour operators. Consequently, hoteliers who use RICIRMS should be able to increase their profit margins without increasing the final consumer price. In addition, incoming or handling travel agents, at the destination, were also prepared to pay a joining fee and a commission in order to promote their services, namely local transfers, excursions, and packages at the destination. Tour operators on the other hand who organised trips to destinations could see little benefit from ail RICIRMS, apart from providing a more realistic and appealing destination image for consumers and train travel consultants. Thus, they were reluctant to pay for RICIRMS services. Outgoing travel agencies (OTA) regarded RICIRMS as an information tool for destinations, while the reservation facility was perceived differently by independent and chain OTA. Thus, their willingness to pay was different as well. However, an annual fee, equivalent to the cost of information manuals currently used, was offered unreservedly. In addition, payment according to usage could be in place for information retrieval and bookings.

Finally, consumers could pay a small amount whenever they use the system for information retrieval or bookings. The charge may be incorporated in the product price or may be separated. Litinas and Vourgaridis's research on usage of the AEGEO's pilot projects suggests that only 7% of the individual users were reluctant to pay at all, 55% could pay the equivalent of 3050 pence, 6% around one pound, 22% up to £1.50 and 10% between three and six pounds. That proves that consumers appreciate the services provided by RICIRMS and are willing to pay for their usage. A RICIRMS-literate user could benefit from identifying better product prices and therefore justify the cost of system's usage. Lessons can be learned by examining videotex payment systems in countries like France. In general, pricing of RICIRMS should be based on the examination of different participants' cost and benefits between currently used resources/practices. The more savings on information resources, communication costs, labour costs and training expenses occur, or the more value is added in a product and the greater profit margins that emerge, the more the willingness to pay would increase among the parties involved.

Despite RICIRMS' promising future there is little successful development to date. Several reasons can be posited. RICIRMS represent a very modern approach to destination management, which redefined the best practices in the industry. The immaturity of the industry to capitalise on this change, combined with the opposition of some distribution channel members who benefit more from the existing situation, is also evident. Technology is another factor, as RICIRMS require massive computing, storage and networking capabilities at an affordable cost which have become available only recently. GDS demonstrated effectively that the best practices in the tourism business lie with the multi-integration of ITT and the tourism industry. Consequently, RICIRMS became the next reasonable step.

On the tourism demand side, the sophistication of the customers and their desire for specialised products, which could offer exceptional value, became evident only in the early 1990s. As holidays are becoming a more inelastic product, the price of the package will be less important in the decision making while value added products will dominate. The growth of tourism demand, due to the consistent desire of Westerners to travel and the democratisation or development of other parts of the world such as the Communist bloc, suggests that computerised systems will be required to handle the vast volumes of emerging tourists.

On the supply side, the dominance of the package and the existing distribution channels has made both principals and NTO idle and reluctant to initiate any aggressive marketing strategy. However, changes in consumer preferences combined with the fact that multinational companies aim to please their shareholders, rather than develop sustainable destinations and look after SMTE, initiated a process of identifying strategic tools for destination prosperity. In addition, deregulation in air transportation essentially means that fares in scheduled airlines can be reduced to levels competitive with charter prices. This will enable individual travellers to make their personalised leisure arrangements without paying inflated prices. The ITT training and understanding of THI managers is improving gradually and it provides them with new methods for performing their tasks. THI growth globally means that more information is required by tourists and trade, while new efficient methods to match tourism demand and supply are desperately needed in order to identify the best product for each customer. Finally, concern for SMTE's survival in the contemporary business environment has forced both private and public sectors towards cooperation and utilisation of all potential resources for achieving competitive advantages.

Nevertheless, only a few systems can survive the fierce competition in both THI and CRS industries. Several reasons have been identified for RICIRMS' failures including: lack of adequate finance for development and operation; incomplete representation of enterprises at the destination; incomprehensive presentation of facilities offered; inaccurate pricing and inventory of tourist products; delays in confirmation; lack of easy access and use of system; inconvenient methods of payment; ignorance of international CRS industry standards; unsuccessful cooperation with CRS; lack of involvement, support and coordination with tourist boards; small SMTE interest; limited training; inappropriate technology; limited knowledge of the tourism industry by developers; and conflict with dominant interests.

Information technology (IT) applications greatly affect businesses, including the hospitality industry, and a critical issue concerns the relationship between technology and business. The way of conceiving the business environment (e.g. the firm, the corporation, the competition and so on) becomes the driver of IT applications. The aim of this chapter is to briefly discuss the drivers of IT in the hospitality industry, to pinpoint current problems and sketch the more meaningful trends in the near future. Recent important criticism would suggest broadening our perspective and inserting the hotel business within the context of the service business.

The works of Gamble, Kasavana and Cahill and Moore represent a valuable basis for an outline of the evolution of IT applications in the hospitality industry. Each of these works describes hotel computerisation as a step-by-step process. At the first stage, in the 1960s, IT was interpreted as a powerful tool for the automation of basic hotel functions. Influenced by the experience drawn from other business sectors, particularly industry, the first functions to be automated were concerned with highly structured and repetitive tasks. In the hotel industry these functions included accounting, payroll, reservation and inventory control. The declared aim at this stage of IT application was operational efficiency, primarily timesaving and personnel reduction. At that time the hardware available was not user-friendly and the rare attempts to automate the typical front office operations ended unsuccessfully. The failure of attempts at hotel front office automation at the New York Hilton in Manhattan in 1963 is a symbolic event. On the other hand, computerised hotel reservation systems provided good results.

Later, during the 1970s, the advent of the minicomputer made the use of IT in the hotel industry cheaper and more accessible. IT applications were extended to marketing and control functions. Management, through the detailed and precise recording of front office transactions, were able to draw accurate guest profiles thus making marketing segmentation more effective. Furthermore the quantity of data produced by back office procedures provided timely and analytic control information. In this stage of its evolution the management found IT to be a useful tool for monitoring hotel operations.

At the end of the 1970s and during the 1980s the PMS (property management systems) evolved. Integration became the main requirement: integration within the individual firm and integration between the firm and the outside world (e.g. other corporate firms, CRS, external data sources, etc.). Managers were very sensitive to integration between front office and back office systems. This goal was achieved by integrating front office and back office procedures within a single database. Sometimes a more advanced level of integration was achieved with the concept of CIB (computer intelligent building). This chapter tackles the management of technological equipment such as energy-saving systems, alarm systems, access authorisation and other typical devices. Furthermore the early 1980s saw the definitive achievement of turnkey PMS, off-the-shelf systems produced and marketed by specialised software houses.

The brief history of hotel computerisation we have sketched shows how some guidelines have directed IT applications for the hotel business. First, structured and repetitive operational activities were automated. At a later stage, computer applications were extended to a larger range of operating activities, including front office, but the focus was placed on control, which is the typical function of middle management. Further developments as Gamble argued, are related to the extension of IT to the firm's strategic level, the level of strategic planning executed by top management. Hence the computerisation process has evolved from the lower to the upper hierarchical level of the firm's organisational chart.

Wiseman observes that this perspective of the computerisation process, characterised by various hierarchical levels as we explained, is based on a specific way to view a firm proposed by Anthony in 1965. This approach has not only strongly affected management studies in the late 1960s and most of the 1970s but, Wiseman adds, has also inspired the information system design of the last twenty years. Anthony's view suggested isolating the firm from its environment for a better understanding of planning and control mechanisms. In addition, he considered IT a valuable tool for operational support to management activities. This paradigm became an unspoken assumption accepted by the majority of information system managers—and information systems for the lodging industry have not been an exception. Wiseman called this approach the 'conventional perspective'.

Conventional versus strategic perspective The strategic management studies achieved in the 1980s highlighted many cases where IT played an essential role in the strategic behaviour of the firm and not simply an operational one, A large number of these classic cases are documented. In the early 1980s these experiences, joined to new tools for economic analysis, determined a turning-point in the ways of considering IT within a business, In the light of those changes Wiseman strongly criticised the 'conventional perspective' and proposed an alternative perspective he defined as 'strategic'. The key to understanding the fundamental distinction between the conventional and the strategic perspective is related to the conceptual difference between the function and use of IT. The strategic value of an IT application is not related to the technical functions involved in the application itself but to the manager's use of this technology to tackle a specific competitive issue. For example the hotel financial statement may be considered a boring legal constraint or a powerful tool to carefuliy analyse the cost trends of a business to support the low-cost strategy chosen by hotel management. In the strategic approach IT is not merely evaluated as a tool, but as a fundamental building-block of the strategic structure. In this sense the strategic value of an IT application lies in its positioning inside the strategy of the firm.

Wiseman criticised Anthony's paradigm-based IT applications because the paradigm represents a kind of 'prison' for strategic thought, reducing the range of possible uses to the limits of technical functions. Instead new business can also be generated by a paradoxical use of IT. To synthesise one can say that the user's applicative horizon is broader than the IT system's designers.

To use IT in a strategic perspective, one must recognise the opportunities available in a specific competitive context. The famous IT consultant, James Martin, within his information systems construction methodology known as 'information engineering', dedicated a specific chapter to the so-called 'strategic systems vision'. In order to accomplish this task Porter and Millar suggested two conceptual tools: the information intensity matrix and the value chain. The first tool assesses the high or low information content of the product/service under analysis. The value chain, on the other hand, is a tool to systematically analyse those activities of the firm that are able to give a competitive advantage within the selected basic strategy. In this paper attention is focused on the value chain because recently heavy criticism has been directed towards this.

The value chain configuration enables the firm to improve, in efficiency and effectiveness, the final value to the buyer. Value is measured by the number of clients willing to buy the firm's offerings. In such a way, a firm competes in the competitive arena to reduce costs or to increase value by setting a higher price. The firm's competitive advantage can occur within the chain of value activities in producing goods or performing and delivering services. Value created by the firm increases the competitive margin in the chain. Comparing its value chain with that of its competitors, the firm highlights differences. Differences in the competitive arena are sources of differentiation.

Porter divides value activities into primary activities and support activities. The former, primary activities, are those involved in the physical production of a firm's output. The latter support the primary activities. As Porter states, the firm's value chain is a linkage of interdependent activities. This interdependency can improve the performance of each activity in reducing related costs or enhancing differentiation.

The firm's value chain, within a particular industry, is part of a broader value system. Suppliers create upstream value for the firm and this can eventually create downstream value, through the (distribution) channel value, to the buyer's value chain. Differentiation is the liaison between the firm's value chain and the buyer's value chain. Value, for the buyer is to buy the same perceived 'product' or 'service' at lower price, or to obtain 'uniqueness' at whatever price. In this sense Porter argues: `Quality" is too narrow a view of what makes a firm unique, because it focuses the attention on the product rather the broader array of value activities that impact the buyer'.

Developing the strategic use of IT

The value chain is the basis on which Porter and Millar have designed a specific approach to the strategic use of IT. Of course the strength of this perspective of IT employment is related to the strength of the value chain theory. Porter and Millar observe that in every product or service an information component and a physical component are distinguishable. The same observation is possible for each strategic relevant business activity. When IT can support such information contents then it becomes a strategic weapon for the firm. The main strategic effects of IT are:

- cost reduction;
- a differentiation increase:
- change in the relationship within the competitive arena.

The IT issues are strategic if they support or shape the firm's selected basic strategy for achieving the various targets defined. For example, the first hotel chains equipped with a CRS introduced a strong item of differentiation about the way to make reservations compared to the traditional way based on telex or phone technology. Furthermore, IT can also change the structure of the competitive arena. For instance, a CRS that provides direct booking from the customer by personal computer technology modifies the relationship between service provider and customer, reducing the role played by delivering channels such as travel agencies.

The value chain is a powerful tool for pinpointing all the strategic activities able to create value for the customer or differentiating or decreasing the cost of the product/service.

Porter and Millar assert that the value chain model is applicable to every kind of business and this position is confirmed and specified in Porter. Recently Porter's approach to business strategy has met with strong criticism on the part of Richard Normann who discussed the argument more extensively in Normann and Ramirez. *Harvard Business Review* organised a mini-forum on this issue.

The focal point of Normarn's criticism is the difficulty in designing clear interfaces among the various value activities within the value chain. Normann declares that it is not possible to conceive of service distribution as a linear sequence of separate activities because service distribution is characterised by strong interaction between clients and personnel. This interaction is like a dialogue that is difficult to break down without losing the specific nature of service businesses.

This criticism is more clearly defined and explained in three case histories given by Normann and Ramirez. In this paper the authors argue that the focal point is reinventing value not producing it. More precisely the core business is the promotion of social innovation through the dynamic reconfiguration of the relationships, the roles and the number of business 'players'. No longer then is it a *value chain* but a *value constellation*. On this issue Normann and Ramirez consider the value chain obsolete for every type of business and classify Porter's approach as belonging to the old industrial era as opposed to the value constellation approach belonging to the new post-industrial era.

Normann's thesis undermines the basis of a successful management paradigm and, at the same time, poses an important problem related to IT management. To which reference scheme must we refer in developing effective IT applications in business? If Normann is right, the value chain approach should be refuted as a paradigm to direct IT applications and research towards other directions.

Normann's criticism is well-founded but does not address the basis of the value chain concept. Porter's approach does not simply focus on added value but enlarges the concept to define a firm's activities as the key to get an advantage over competitors. The diagnosis should be made considering all the value activities in the firm's performance as part of a single-industry value system. Reinventing value, as Normann and Ramirez recommend, does not necessarily mean abandoning a strategic tool for the assessment of the firm's current position in the competitive arena. The reinvention of a business could be the result of an analysis of the firm's value chain or of the competitive arena, reconsidering for example new entrants or substitute products/services. There is no 'new logic of value', but only a new starting point, a new positioning of a business. Instead Normann's considerations are very important in adapting the value chain when it must be applied to service businesses such as the hotel industry.

Porter configures all value activities from a manufacturing industry' viewpoint. Even a manufacturing firm which does custom rather than mass production would be difficult to fit into the generic value chain scheme. His suggestions for redefining the value chain, and Normann and Ramirez's criticism have stimulated us to reinterpret Porter's strategic approach in the hotel industry.

Combining the definition of service performance, production and delivery with the nature of service itself, we have attempted to fit Porter's general theory into a specific service industry. In this approach all references are made, in an unambiguous way, to the hotel business.

It is essential to define the value chain or identify value activities in each individual case. since these may differ considerably from industry to industry, and even between two different business units within the same industry. Take, for example, two hotels in the same urban area delivering similar services to business travellers. Hotel service is a bundle of activities, consisting of a core product—a quiet and clean bedroom—plus a set of services. Lovelock proposed a figure that encompasses the core and supplementary services offered to business travellers by a good hotel. If the two hotels do not belong to the same chain, one is not likely to find the same check-in procedures, the same restaurant services, the same personnel policy, the same distribution channels or the same suppliers. These differences in packaging and delivering hotel services could contain the key to gaining competitive advantage over one other.

As Lovelock points out, in managing services, differences between the manufacturing industry and the service industry lie in the 'front office' operations where the customer interfaces with the service operations, and this is particularly true for hotel guests. 'Back office' operations are sealed off from the hotel guests; they are managed in not very dissimilar ways from those of manufacturing firms. Other important features in managing services business, and hotel services in particular, such as the nature of product service, people (staff and customer) as part of the product, the customer involvement in service production and delivery, the importance of the time factor, quality control problems, different distribution channels, simultaneous production and consumption and absence of inventories for services are evidenced by Lovelock and Reid. Though, for the last item, in the hotel industry, Reid emphasises that some elements of the service-product mix are tangible and inventories must be maintained.

From this viewpoint, hotel services are the result of the mix at the setup and delivery phase of physical, organisational and labour activities, interfacing necessarily with hotel guests for the global performance.

In other words, Porter's theory is different from Normann and Ramirez's because each one is a specific answer to a specific problem. Porter poses the problem of understanding how the firm creates value for the buyer. The answer to this question is the identification of those activities that create value permitting the firm to perform its chosen basic strategy. Instead Normann and Ramirez suggest identifying the right offering, e.g. combination of products and services, reinventing new ways to create value for the customer, ways reflecting the complexity of the actual business environment. In a sense Normann and Ramirez focus on the offering while Porter focuses on the process to perform it.

The value chain configuration in hotel businesses

Defining the value chain for the hotel business means identifying value activities that can be potential sources for lowering costs or to enhance differentiations. In our case we have disaggregated a generic hotel firm identifying those activities which can bring a hotel business to gain a certain amount of margin and value in the competitive arena. This arbitrary interpretation is particularly suited to the hotel industry and is related to the characteristics of hotel firms, as capacity constrained firms where guests come for the services. A good outline to identify the strategic activities of hotel business is the hotel guest cycle as described in Kasavana and Cahill. Five primary activities were identified.

Unlike a manufacturing firm, where distribution and sales concern the marketers when the product actually leaves the production line, a hotel firm, which delivers its services to the guest on the premises, is involved in this activity from the moment the marketing plan, to attract people to the property, is formulated. This activity starts a relatively long time earlier, before physical service production and consumption begin. Occasionally, this period becomes shorter when a walk-in customer comes in asking for a bed overnight.

Accessibility, sales systems and procedures, as well as distribution channels, sales personnel and reward systems, form the distribution and sales activity.

Since some elements of the product-service mix are tangible, and inventories of food and beverage items as well as sheets, towels, soap, sanitation products, and general furniture must be maintained, inbound logistics become a fundamental activity in hotel operations. Receiving, checking and stocking goods and raw materials as well as their distribution to department stores are some of the initial steps in preparing the tangible mix of hotel service.

Service setup

This activity concerns the prearrangement of service and front line operations. This activity is carried out mainly by back-of-the-house personnel who do not come into contact with the guest. It includes food preparation, housekeeping operations, maintenance, cleaning and sanitation of common areas, and so forth. What happens backstage is of little interest to the guests, but it is a strategic activity for the hotel as a whole.

Service and front line operations

This activity is 'the moment of truth' for the overall hotel services and operations because it directly involves the physical person of the guest. Service operations can be divided into those relating to the service personnel and those relating to the physical facilities and equipment. This activity allows the firm, through the service personnel, facilities and equipment, to deliver the value service to the guest. Every deed, every action or performance is a potential source to enhance quality. Each point of contact could also be a source of differentiation for the method of delivering services.

Post-service operations

Post-service operations are those activities performed when the guest has checked out, or better yet when he has already left the premises. They are performed by the firm to upgrade the value service and to remind the guest of the hotel 'experience'. This activity is centred in the marketing-oriented hotel organisation and has a tremendous impact on the guest: consider follow-up activities, special programmes for repeaters, birthday or special-event mailings, the rapid restitution of lost or forgotten property, and so forth. These acts complete the marketing cycle, stimulating the guest to repeat reservations or toward positive word-of-mouth promotion.

Primary activities cannot be performed without support activities. These pervade the whole firm and its service performance. We have identified the following support activities.

With increasing competition in the service industry, many authors recommend that firms be marketing-oriented in managing services. In this respect Lovelock states: 'many service firms have developed an effective marketing function to act as a bridge between the organisation and the environment within which it operates'.

Nowadays hotel businesses tend more and more to be marketing-oriented firms, and the marketing function is involved not only with identifying needs and trends within the marketplace but also with the product concept, distribution and pricing strategies, sales activities, the development of communications programmes and monitoring the activities of competitors, as well as control of internal and external operations. On the whole, the marketing function takes part in all hotel operations and acts to support them.

Procurement

This activity concerns the acquisition of all elements, physical and nonphysical, that make hotel services feasible. Procurement is a part of many sub-activities such as linkages with suppliers, raw material control, product and service positioning and image, as well as the monitoring of all personnel and equipment performance in the hotel business, either in backstage activities or in front stage activities. In this view, procurement is spread over many activities performed by the firm and is not limited to the purchasing function.

In every business, sector, or industry, each activity is performed with a heavy dependence on technology. Technology is embedded into the firm's know-how, into production and service procedures, into support facilities and equipment. The technological support is now part of each hotel department and activity: reservation procedures, guest and supplier database maintenance, conservation, cooking and cleaning technology, and so on. Not only is technology itself an integral part of this activity, but every process to improve service and the product line becomes a part of technology development. We also consider research and development part of this activity, because considering R&D strictly as an engineering department is a very narrow view. In the hotel business, technology development includes the search for new food products or new menus at a restaurant, packages or special programmes, new communications systems or new service delivery procedures.

Human resource management concerns staff recruiting and training policies as well as the personnel management function. This activity can no longer be considered a mere handling of wages! High-quality recruiting and training, with related costs, are essential activities in the hotel business because of the high personnel turnover and the related waste. Personnel is a key and irreplaceable element in delivering hotel services and personnel could be a strategic source of competitive advantage for the hotel business. Therefore the role of HRM in identifying and exploiting personnel skills becomes a winning resource to implement the firm's strategy.

Firm infrastructure

This concerns a number of basic activities necessary to run a firm: from general management to budgeting, from general accounting to financial planning and legal aspects, from contacts with regulatory bodies to the monitoring of the firm's overall affairs. It does not deal with any specific activity, but it supports the whole chain. Generally the firm's infrastructure is seen to be above hotel operations, but it can achieve a strategic role in creating a very strong advantage in the competitive arena. Consider the strategic role of general management in creating liaisons with regulatory bodies, state agencies or local boards or in influencing the administrative 'environment'.

In the light of the above statements, it is possible to

reconfigure a new scheme to guide the strategic use of IT. Normann and Ramirez's observations are very useful in analysing the competitive arena and in designing the offering by integrating Porter's concept of the assessment of economic sector attractiveness. The IT impact on the offering can be evaluated by joining Porter and Millar's considerations with Normann and Ramirez's. In this sense it becomes a 'value creation designing'. The value chain model, reconfigured on the basis of each specific business, remains a fundamental tool for designing the business process to achieve the offering. The value chain can be interpreted as 'value creation engineering'. Thus Porter and Millar's considerations about IT support within the value chain continue to be valid.

7

Tourism and the Economy

Many economists approach tourism by measuring its impacts using particular analytical and economic accounting techniques. This is an entirely descriptive approach. The word impact refers essentially to what has happened, not what should have happened. Tourism should first be seen in the context of overall economic Policy and planning. It has to be slotted into a macro-economic view. In attempting to manage an economy many different factors have to be kept in balance.

The study of economics generally divides between:

— the criteria used in developing economic policy, to arrive at objectives and forecasts

— the techniques used to influence economic performance, to achieve these objectives and forecasts

— the techniques used to measure past economic performance.

Economic policy and planning will revolve mainly around certain fundamental objective. The potential contribution of tourism is noted under each of these:

— Balancing the make-up of the economy—sectors and targets

Tourism dominates the economy in some countries, for example, the Baharnas. In others it represents an important way of diversifying the economy often away from commodities, for example, Australia and Indonesia.

Whatever the case, it is important to target tourism's role, and to

Commit resources accordingly.

— Maintaining macro-economic stability

Tourism is assisted by price stability, low inflation and equitable foreign exchange rates. Stability is an essential condition for a successful tourism sector.

— Allocating resources—often scarce resources

Tourism importance must be recognized, for it to be given the resources it needs.

— Achieving economic growth

Tourism's contribution is often significant. Its growth rate may exceed that of other sectors.

— Ensuring the sustainability of economic activities in environmental terms

Tourism has to achieve sustainability if it is to succeed in the long run.

— Achieving the equitable distribution of economic activities by region of the country Tourism is an important way of achieving regional development. For many regions it represents the best economic option.

— Balancing the geographical distribution of the population Connected with regional development, tourism can create jobs where they are needed.

— Achieving an equitable distribution of economic benefits per capita of the population

Many types of tourism, with high multiplier effects, can result in a widespread of economic benefits.

— Minimizing the level of unemployments

Tourism is a major source of employment.

— Maintaining a low and acceptable rate of inflation

Tourism is sometimes developed quickly in formerly underdeveloped regions. Substantial inflows of revenue may occur, ahead of the capacity to fully supply the demand for goods and services. This can create an inflationary effect, and put tourism out of balance with the more traditional sectors of the economy.

— Maintaining the stability of the currency

Inbound tourism as a substantial source of foreign exchange earnings, helps to maintain the stability of the currency.

— Achieving an acceptable balance of trade

Again, inbound tourism is an invisible export and contributes to an acceptable balance of trade,

— Achieving a balance between consumption, saving and investment

Like any other sector tourism can, contribute significantly to this objective.

— Funding a budget to enable the public sector to fulfil its role

Tourism is a good source of government revenues. In addition to normal tax revenues, it may also generate revenue through, for example, bed taxes and airport departure taxes.

Government will set economic policy as it relates to these various areas. However, in some countries the central bank may be an independent branch of government and will undertake responsibility for monetary policy.

Linked to the areas of economic policy and planning, are further objectives of public expenditure and social policy. The economic policies support the social policies and vice versa.

- Generating sufficient government revenues to meet public expenditure
- Providing an adequate educational and vocational training system
- Providing an adequate public health system
- Providing an adequate legal framework from the judicial system to law enforcement
- Providing an adequate network of other essential social services; fire, post office, ambulance etc
- Maintaining an agreed range and level of other social services
- Providing an adequate system of national defence
- Maintaining overseas diplomatic representation
- Ensuring adequate maintenance and expansion of the country's physical infrastructure and public utilities roads, harbours, airports, railways and transportation systems, telecommunications
- Ensuring an adequate supply of produce, goods and services for the consumption of all sections of the population.

All governments, whatever their particular political and ideological beliefs, understand that they must satisfy the above needs. However, it unlikely that they will agree on how to go about it.

The success of any economic system depends on providing people with an acceptable standard of life,

The origin of national development plans

The term 'development plan' is used mainly in the context of macro-economic management. The emphasis of such planning tends to be on public expenditures, where and how they are to be prioritized and allocated, and how government revenues are to be raised to meet them. The economy is analysed sector by sector, and then viewed as a whole. Government decides how to best influence economic performance.

This process takes place in every country in the world, although it may not always take the form of a comprehensive development plan. Sometimes it is associated with national budgeting, the allocation of public expenditures and the corresponding forecasts of overall economic performance.

As long as governments have governed, they have engaged in some form of economic planning to work out how much money they need to spend and how much they need to raise, As a part of this, each government department has to prepare its proposals. Each has to ask for its share of public funds.

Departments compete for funds. The result depends on the influence of each minister of government, on how well the case is argued, and how good the lobbying is. People fight for the biggest share possible. Development plans owe their origin, therefore, to the budgeting process. The need to set up an ostensibly rational basis for setting and funding budgets and establishing a system of priorities. Governments allocate funds to best reflect their policies. Plans gradually become refined to guide the development of the particular sectors, setting out performance targets and ways to achieve them. Since one year does riot allow a long enough period, most plans are developed for four or five years. Such plans contribute to the programme on which governments are elected for their particular term of office. Tourism will usually comprise one part of the plan. All planning should be viewed as a continuous process. Plans should be constantly reviewed, updated and adjusted, according to newly-assessed needs and priorities.

When an ongoing tourism planning process is in place it is easy to make a summary for inclusion in the government's development plan.

Preparing national development plans

A plan normally starts with a review of recent economic performance together with future prospects. It will go on to summarize its main contents, and explain why the chosen government policies are the most appropriate. It will describe in more detail the substance of the plan. It will list the Public expenditure planned under each particular category, e.g., transport, energy, water supply, health, education, and natural resources management and the environment.

It will then deal with the expected role and future development of the private sector. It will generally do this sector by sector: agriculture, forestry, fishing, trade, mining, manufacturing, tourism and other service sectors. The rate of economic development depends more on private sector performance than public sector expenditures. Governments like to help promote (markets and investment) a sector which it views as having potential. It will look at current supply and demand, the marketing opportunities, and the development needs. It may also examine promotional needs for specific markets.

Governments cannot look at one sector alone in an isolated way. Sectors are interdependent, and have to be related to the economy as a whole.

To safeguard against misguided assessments, there should be close consultation with the private sector. Industry leaders can help to judge current conditions and prospects, and to predict likely performance. The main elements to be judged, in formulating an economic development plan, are as follows:

— Identification of development opportunities. Results of surveys, technological and scientific research studies, market studies, and surveys of natural resources.
— Development of appropriate levels of infrastructure, e.g. airports, seaports, inland waterways, roads, railways, water and energy supplies.
— Development of the appropriate legislative framework for economic, activities foreign investment, land tenure, contracts law, commercial law, banking law, etc.
— Development of training facilities and programmes aimed at defined skill standards for the necessary occupations, as well as the, continuing and related levels of general education.
— Promotion of particular types of investment, seeking proposals fro foreign and domestic investors and giving assistance in the formulation of projects.
— Achievement of the best resource-use through land use planning," zoning and planning regulations, and the application of any incentive schemes and tax breaks.
— Achievement of improved savings levels, public and private.
— Development of improved business and financial services, e.g. banking and credit facilities, insurance, commodity markets and security exchanges.

Constraints to growth

The principal constraints to growth are generally:
— skilled manpower
— the necessary natural resources
— finance
— the capacity of the capital goods sector

The need for skilled manpower is obvious. Even

though many tourism and hotel jobs have a relatively low skills base, there is still a need or many highly skilled workers and supervisors. Unless skills training is well developed, its absence represents a major bottleneck. Secondly, the necessary natural resources are obviously a prerequisite for certain types of development. For example, if new land for development is being used up, this represents a major limitation. Some countries may have a shortage of tourism sites for development, for example, in a developed European country. By contrast, others may have an abundance. Indonesia has 17000 islands many of which have tourism potential and are yet to be developed.

Money itself may represent a constraint. An approximate capital output ratio can be 3:1; this is to say that to achieve a 5 per cent growth rate in GDP requires an annual net investment equal to 15 per cent of GDP. This exceeds the savings ratios of most countries. In consequence, development has to fuelled by foreign investment and this is not always easy to attract.

Finally, the capacity of the capital goods market is no less important but is often underestimated, Capital costs in hotel facilities are broken down between construction, and furniture, fittings and equipment. A main constraint in construction may also be lack of skilled workers. It requires at least a year to train general construction workers and longer for more specialized jobs. If the construction sector is already working at full capacity, then this, too, will represent a major constraint. Building materials, if locally produced, may also be short. Items of furniture, fittings and equipment, if locally produced, may also pose a supply problem. This may create a need to import items adding to costs and using foreign exchange.

Foreign investment

If the intention is to attract foreign investment, then the law should obviously be designed to facilitate this objective. Both the law and the procedure in handling development proposals should be helpful. They should not be so ambiguous and slow as to deter potential investors. The two essential criteria are clarity and speed. The law should be cleat', with applications processed in no more than 4 to 6 weeks. Investors should not be pushed from one government agency to another, seeking a variety of *licences and* approvals. An investment board or similar agency should act as a one-stop shop, capable of giving the one comprehensive approval to cover all aspects of the investment.

Investors want a stable investment situation without surprises; transparent and equally applicable to all. It is essential to screen foreign investors thoroughly. One has to ensure that they are serious persons or companies with good financial credentials and a sound business track record.

There may be a need for brokers or promoters to pursue the right kind of foreign investor. If so, they should be chosen by the government on the basis of their established reputation and past proven results.

Among the key provisions which should be included in a foreign investment law, are the following:

— The training of local personnel should be one of the requirements. It is important to ensure the comprehensive transfer of technology. Investors should give details of their proposals.

— Approval should be extended to projects which support the Government's socioeconomic objectives and priorities. Among the criteria may be job creation, regional development, export earnings, income generation, import substitution, environ-mental sustainability and the upgrading of skills.

— Investments may be restricted to particular sectors only, reserving certain kinds of enterprise for local investors.

— Undertakings may be given by the Government not to expropriate or nationalize the enterprise or any of its assets, or take any measures having the same or similar effects. And not to impose price controls on the investor's products or services.

— Permission to purchase foreign currencies and to remit them abroad to meet all obligations associated with the investment; imports of supplies, repayment of principal and interest on international borrowings, reasonable royalties and management fees, dividend remittance, and the repatriation of invested capital.

— Incentives may be extended to projects which

- develop high technology industries
- create a significant number of jobs
- increase exports
- foster regional and/or rural development
- protect and/or conserve the environment
- locate in priority development zones

— Incentives are usually of the following types:

- exemptions from, or reductions in, various kinds of duties and other government levies
- the grant of land or money as a contribution towards a certain type of development, provided that the development meets the agreed conditions and requirements specified
- the provision, at no cost, of the infrastructure required to support a development

- the provision of loan finance at concessionary rates of interest and an extended period for repayment
- the provision, at no cost, of government guarantees, to provide additional security for the necessary loan finance.

An incentive is really a form of government subsidy. But many commentators consider it a pity that incentives are offered at all. They consider it preferable for investment projects to stand or fall on their merits without any form of government intervention, or interference with market forces.

Generally, however, incentives are offered for the following reasons:

— When competition for investment is fierce. One must offer competitive conditions at least comparable and perhaps superior.

— When incentives lessen risk and increase the probability of a good rate of return on the investment. They therefore induce people to invest where and when they might not otherwise invest.

— When the cost to the government of the incentives in question is far outweighed by the economic benefits generated.

There arc three basic principles for governments to follow:

— Do not give away more than necessary.

— Be sure that benefits will exceed the costs.

— Apply incentives fairly and equitably do not negotiate them in an inconsistent and uneven manner the 'horse trading' approach.

In many free market economies there are frequent examples of selective government intervention;

subsidized credit, ceilings on borrowing rates, public investment in selected sectors, protected import substitution, and assistance to export marketing. In tourism, for example, may even go as far as the payment of financial incentives to foreign tour operators who produce a certain volume of inbound tourists. Or sometimes, providing substantial capital grants towards the costs developing hotels in certain areas.

The free market does not always work in attracting investment the best interests of the economy. Incentives are sometimes essential get the kinds of investment needed to achieve certain economic a social objectives.

However, if government money is to be given away (in the form grants or foregone revenue) to encourage private sector investment has to be very well justified. It should only be done as a very resort, and wherever possible it should be avoided.

The development process

Underdeveloped countries are rural by nature. Most people live in rural areas and depend on agriculture for their livelihood.

An efficient agricultural sector is a key to progress. It produces increasing yields per hectare and high productivity per worker. This stimulates development. It creates more prosperous communities and a growing domestic market for manufactured goods. And it creates surplus labour from the farms which is absorbed into new industrial enterprises in the towns.

By 1850 Britain was the only country in the world where the number of agricultural workers had fallen below 50 per cent of the labour force.

A corresponding improvement in access to health and educational services, raises the capacity of people to work effectively. Agriculture becomes mechanized and highly productive, and industry expands. This provides the basis for more infrastructural development.

At the same time, domestic and export markets develop. Prosperity boosts government revenues and this allows for universal health services and education. This is followed by the development of a full range of social services. As people earn more they may save more. Capital markets grow and stimulate more industrial expansion. A country breaks out of underdevelopment.

All this may sound an ingenuous view of the realities of development in the contemporary world. However, many economies have to be restructured. There are many problems: for example, limiting population growth, safeguarding the environment, conserving resources, controlling urban expansion, reforming and deregulating bureaucracies, mobilizing investment, improving education and health, and transforming traditional values.

Tourism is a flexible economic force that responds well to a variety of situations. It can trigger large new resort complexes in hitherto undeveloped regions, or it can equally well create new economic options through small tourism enterprises in undeveloped rural communities. Tourism offers many possibilities.

Clearly tourism should have a favourable economic effect. The tourism multiplier is one way of measuring it. This multiplier analyses the leakages of tourism revenue out of the economy, and the knock-on effects created within the economy.

Just as a note of music may linger on and gradually die away, so a tourist dollar may echo on through the economy.

Within the economy, the front line of people and suppliers providing goods and services benefit from a direct impact. A second line less involved with tourism, benefits from an indirect impact. And finally as expenditure filters on down, there is an induced impact. This multiplier effect can be measured in different ways, for example, the tourist income multiplier; on employment the number of jobs created by tourism revenues; or on the government revenues generated,

To calculate the multiplier effect, data about operational performance and expenditures are analysed together with the characteristics and knock-on effects of transactions. The multipliers are then expressed as ratios, for example, the income multiplier will lie in most cases between 0.4 and 2.0. The number of direct jobs created may be expressed per thousand dollars of revenue, and government revenue as a ratio of total revenue.

For example, Archer and Fletcher show Turkey with a tourist income multiplier at 1.96, Jamaica at 1.23, the Bahamas at 0.79 and Fiji at 0.72., In Jamaica the government revenue multiplier was 0.306—for every US$1000 of tourist expenditure the government received $306. The employment multiplier was 0.000128 an increase of US$7682 in tourist expenditure would create one new job.

Large well diversified economies will be more self-sufficient in meeting tourism's needs, and the income multipliers are the highest. In smaller economies, less diversified and with a narrower base, they will be the lowest. Such small economies will require the importation of many items, resulting in a higher leakage of expenditure abroad.

Comparability of multipliers between countries

For this reason alone, care should be taken in comparing the multipliers between different countries. There are also other reasons why comparisons can be misleading. First, the methodologies employed may differ; the way business activity is sampled, the extent that the indirect and induced benefits are included, and the range and accuracy of the revenue and cost data which are collected may all combine to produce varying results. Also economists sometimes guard the details of their methodology, and it may be impossible to establish the reliability and comparabilily of results.

Large and small hotels

Yet another reason lies in the composition of the hotel sector. Small locally owned hotels usually attract a lower spending market, but have a higher income multiplier. These small operations are generally better integrated into the local economy. Large luxury hotels, by contrast, may attract a higher spending market but import more supplies and generate a lower income multiplier.

Large hotels, because of the above, will for the most part achieve More revenue per visitor than small hotels, and visitors from the upper market segments may also indulge in far more discretionary spending in the destination. As a consequence the net benefits to a destination may be higher, even though the income multiplier is lower. A higher multiplier, however, does tend to indicate a wider distribution of benefits among the society. Small locally owned hotels generate a smaller pot of money, but spread it around more. Large hotels and resort complexes may generate more government revenue as well as more employment.

These are all very broad generalizations. It might be possible to find situations in which some small hotels have very high room rates and revenue, while maintaining close linkages with the local economy. Or where large hotels have low revenues as well as high patterns of leakage.

The need to disaggregate the sector

For this reason, it can be both misleading and of little practical use to calculate only an aggregate multiplier for the sector as a whole. A sector needs to be disaggregated and structured according to its different characteristics, types and size of hotel, and markets. Multipliers can then be calculated according to each sub-sector. This enables policy makers to analyse more effectively the relative strengths and weaknesses of each, and to see where the opportunities for improvement exist. It will also help to indicate the best types of tourism for the future expansion of the sector.

It is important to understand first the types of tourism which it is possible to attract, supply and serve, and second the relative benefits of each. Yet in economic analysis the measurement techniques sometimes come to overshadow the reasons for their application and the use of their results. Multipliers are sometimes calculated, but not understood or related to future improvement and development strategies.

One must not lose sight of the purpose of the technique. The income multiplier is designed to assess how much expenditure stays in an economy, and how it works its way through to provide wide economic benefit. It is easy to see where leakages occur to diminish this effect. And then, very important, to concentrate on eliminating or reducing these leakages.

Tourism professionals should grow accustomed to identifying and thinking about tourism revenues and expenditures, and what leaks out or stays in an economy. They will be able to develop a feel for the economic effects; the cognitive skill of seeing and knowing. Looking at a particular tourism sector, they should be able to formulate a close assessment of its performance. Informed judgement of this kind is not a substitute for more rigorous study, but it helps to keep the economic impact of tourism in constant focus.

The input—output approach

Related to multipliers in the sense of exploring how expenditures repercuss through the economy, is the input-output approach. The mutiplier effects on incomes, employment and government revenues were mentioned previously. A multiplier can also be developed to assess It,(, impact on both sales and output. However, the technique most currently used to measure these latter types or effects is input-output analysis.

Wassily Leontief, a member of the economics faculty at Harvard until 'his retirement in 1975, advanced the development of input-output analysis and was awarded the Nobel Prize for his work.

This type of analysis has some similarity to the tourism multiplier, but is more sophisticated. It measures the overall impact of revenues in a more detailed and comprehensive way. It takes into account the intersectoral structure of an economy. Any economy is locked together a system of interdependent relationships. One sector supplies another the sales from one become an input to another. A model can be developed to simulate how the economy works, reflecting the relationships between inputs and outputs. This is obviously of great assistance in economic forecasting and planning.

Based on detailed study of economic behaviour, a series of input-output coefficients are developed based on different types of transaction. These will enable the model to work in the same way as the economy works. Once the input-output tables have been constructed, the effect of various levels of economic activity can be tracked through the model. This can help to provide answers to the policy makers' questions, for example, what if so many international visitors were received a year, each spending so much money?

A great number of calculations are needed in such analysis, and this technique has been greatly assisted by the development of computer technology. Input-output analysis, as tourism multipliers, is another useful way of monitoring the development and performance of the sector. Tables can be developed specifically to monitor the tourism sector, and included within the scope of a computerized information system designed for this purpose.

Critics of Input-output analysis point to the difficulty in constant way the relationships between sectors. Underlying assumptions, they say, are often too shaky to allow accurate results. However accuracy can be improved as the technique is refined, permitting closer adjustments to be made. The technique is now used not only at the national and regional levels, but also at the global level.

Tourism is not an economic sector in itself but an economic activity which flows into a number of sectors. It does not fit, therefore, into the classifications used for national economic accounting. One has to tinker with various categories, making a range of further assumptions and adjustments, in order to apply the technique to tourism. As time goes by, new approaches will be developed to address the place of tourism in economic accounting, and to refine the economic models used to monitor the sector's performance.

Leakages

The payments outside the country to support international tourism are usually called leakages. As noted, the economic benefits of tourism arise from only those earnings which remain within the economy. It is also more accurate to talk of the import components of tourism in general, since domestic tourism will be affected as well as international tourism.

The items which are imported to support tourism Fall into the following categories:

- construction equipment used to build new hotels and tourism installations
- Construction materials similarly used
- furniture, fixture and equipment used for these new hotels and tourism installations
- operating supplies such as food and beverage, paper supplies, spare parts and engineering supplies, etc.

Some of these represent capital expenditures and some revenue expenditures, either costs towards the creation of the tourism asset, or costs incurred in operating the tourism asset. Apart from items of this nature, capital, services and manpower may also be imported. Capital, both equity and loan finance, may be brought in from outside depending on the legislation governing foreign investment. This will mean the subsequent payment to external sources of dividends and interest.

Services from outside the country may include design and planning work which come to represent a component in the capital costs. They, may also include management fees, if the hotel or installation is to be managed by a foreign company or multinational, and they may also include marketing fees, if monies are to be paid out through advertising agencies, hotel representatives (and overseas representation and sales in general including public relations companies), and fees to purchasing, companies, maintenance companies, training companies, etc.

They may also include foreign personnel, whose particular technical knowledge, skills and experience are needed for the success of the enterprise. Apart from recruitment costs, a proportion of the wages and salaries paid to these personnel is likely to be remitted outside the country.

Leakages of this kind are usually viewed in an entirely negative light since they are a loss to the economy. They do foster international trade, however, and in this sense are positive. Trade is based on concepts of equity and reciprocity, and the balance of trade is a fundamental discussion issue in the development of relations between different countries.

8

Economic and Social Force of Tourism

The receipts from international tourism can provide a valuable source of earnings for many countries both developed as well as developing. Although tourism, is sensitive to the level of economic activity in the tourist generating countries, it provides a more stable earnings than primary products. The income from tourism has tended to increase at a higher rate than merchandise export in a number of countries. There is now almost an assured channel of financial flows from the richer countries to the not so richer, and developing ones, raising the latter's export earnings and rate or economic growth. Tourism is thus a most important source of income for many countries. For instance, there were more visitor arrivals in Spain in 1981 (40 million) according to official Spanish sources than the actual population of the country (36 million). Newly emerging countries in such areas as the Caribbean depend very heavily on tourist income, which often represents the major part of the gross domestic product (G.D.P). Even developed nations like Canada, which derived over 11 per cent of its gross domestic product from international visitors in the year 1975, rely heavily on the income from tourism. Tourism thus forms a very important source of income, especially of foreign exchange for several countries. Although the amount contributed in foreign currency per tourist varies greatly from one place to another, the importance of receipts from tourism in the balance of payments, and of tourist activities in the national avenue, has become considerable for many countries. The major economic benefit in promoting the tourism industry has therefore tended to be the earning of foreign exchange. Income from foreign tourism in the form of foreign exchange earnings adds to the national income and, as an invisible export, may offset a loss on the visible trading account and be of critical importance in the overall financial reckoning. This is more true in case of developing countries. For many developing countries, particularly the small countries, which are mainly dependent upon primary products such as a few basic cash crops, tourism often offers a, more reliable form of income. In the case of some European countries, notably Spain, Portugal, Austria, Yugoslavia and Greece, the invisible earnings from tourism are of a major significance and have a very strong positive effect on the balance of payments. Tourism is thus a very useful means of earning the much needed foreign currency. It is almost without a rival as an earning source for many developed as well as developing countries. These earnings assume a great significance in the balance of payment calculations.

The balance of payments shows the relationship between a country's total payments to all other countries and its total receipts from them. In other words, it may be defined as a statement of income and expenditure on international account. Payments and receipts on international account are of three kinds: (i) the visible balance of trade (relating to tile import and export of goods); (ii) invisible items (relating to the services such as shipping and insurance); (iii) capital transfers. The receipts from foreign tourism form an "Invisible export", similar to other "Invisibles" which come from transportation and shipping, banking and insurance, income on investments, etc. Because most countries from time to time have serious problems with the balance of their international payments, much attention comes to be focused on tourism because of its potentially important contribution to, and also effect upon the balance of payments.

The receipts from international tourism however, are not always net. Sometimes expenditures are involved which must be set against them. Net foreign exchange receipts from tourism are reduced principally by the import cost of goods and services used by visitors foreign exchange costs of capital investment in tourist amenities and promotion and publicity expenditure abroad. Peters has said: "Certain imports associated with tourist expenditure must be deducted.... the importation of material and equipment for constructing hotels and other amenities, and necessary supplies to run them; foreign currency costs of imports for consumption by international tourists; remittances of interests and profits on overseas investment in tourism enterprises, mainly hotel construction; foreign currency costs of conducting a tourism development programme, including marketing expenditure overseas".

Reliance of imports to meet tourist's needs does not however, deny developing countries the opportunity of earning foreign exchange in supplying such goods and services. Imports are, to a large extent, as essential to the operation of the tourist sector as to that of other sectors. The important question is whether the value added domestically on an export good or service is maximized. Maximization of import substitution without due regard to the effect on overall tourism receipts (i.e. demand) may be counter-productive. Secondly, differences in the pattern and level of reliance on imported goods and services, capital equipment and manpower are very wide depending upon the level of development of a country. In some cases this reliance is simply due to a lack of resources that will be transformed into items to be sold to the industry. In others, the industry has not yet drawn on such, supply potential, for which it may be an important stimulus. There is a general need for careful programmes of positive import substitution.

The multiplier effect

It is evident from the above paragraphs that earnings from tourism occupy an important place in the national income of a country. Without taking into account receipts from domestic tourism, international tourism receipts alone contribute a great deal. The flow of money generated by tourist spendings multiplies as it passes through various sections of the economy. In addition to an important source of income, tourism provides a number of other economic benefits, which vary in importance from one country to another and also depending upon the nature and scale of tourism. The benefits from infrastructure investments, justified primarily for tourism--airports, roads, water supply and other public utilities--may be widely shared by the other sectors of the economy. Tourist facilities such as hotels, restaurants, museums, clubs, sports complexes, public transport, national parks are used also by domestic tourists and visitors, businessmen and residents, yet a significant portion of the costs may be borne by international tourists. Tourists also contribute to tax revenue both directly through sales taxes and indirectly through property, profits and income taxes. Tourism provides employment, brings infrastructural improvements and may help regional development. Each of these economic aspects can be dealt with separately, but they are all closely related and are considered together. Let us first look at the income aspect of tourism. Tourism as a source of income is not easy to measure, at least with any degree of accuracy. This is because of the multiplier effect. The flow of money generated by tourist spending multiplies as it passes through various sections of the economy through the operation of the multiplier effect. The multiplier is an income concept. The multiplier theory emerges from the work of Kahn and Keynes. It can be systematically explained as follows: from an initial impulse, such as investment or expenditure, there springs one or more primary effects such as income, savings, etc. These primary effects in their turn, and in the course of a second period, produce secondary effects of the same type as the first. The process is repeated several times in a given lapse of time. The multiplier makes it possible to calculate the sum of the various primary, secondary and tertiary effects of the same type and hence the relation between the total of the effects of the same nature and the primary effect. This relation is represented by the multiplier, which is then applied to the primary effect in order to arrive at the total effect.

The multiplier mechanism has also been applied to tourism and in particular to tourist expenditure. The nature of the tourism multiplier and its effect may be described as follows: The money paid by a tourist in, say, paying his hotel bill will be used by the hotel management to provide for the costs which it had incurred in meeting the demands of the visitor, e.g., such goods and services as food, drink, furnishing, laundering, electricity, and entertainment. The recipients, in turn, use the money they have thus received to meet their financial commitments and so on. In other words, tourist expenditure not only supports the tourist industry directly but helps indirectly to support many other industries which supply goods and services to the tourist industry. In this way money spent by tourists may be said to be used several times and to spread into various sectors of the economy. In sum, the money paid by the tourist, after a long series of transfers over a given period of time, passes through all sectors of the national economy, stimulating each in turn throughout the process.

Every time the money changes bands it provides 'new' income and the continuing series of conversions of the money spent by the tourists form what the economists term the multiplier effect. The more often the conversion occurs, the greater its beneficial effect on the economy of the recipient country. However, this transfer of money is not absolute as there are `leakages' which occur. Such leakages may occur as a result of for instance, by importing foreign goods, paying interest on foreign investments, etc. Any leakages of these kinds will reduce the stream of expenditure which in consequence will limit and reduce the multiplier effect. Income generated by foreign tourist expenditure in countries possessing more advanced economics, which generally are more self-sufficient and less in need of foreign imports, will tend to have higher multipliers than countries which are less self-sufficient and need to support their tourist industries by substantial imports. If the developing countries are to gain maximum economic benefits from tourism, they should control very strictly those imported items for tourist consumption and to keep foreign investment expenditure to a reasonable level. The benefits, otherwise, accruing from tourism will be reduced or even cancelled by the leakages.

The most important leakage would appear to arise from expenditures on importation of agricultural products like food and drink. In a primary macro-economic approach to the prospects opened up by tourism establishment in a developing country, it is regarded as advantageous that a good portion of tourist consumption should consist of food products. It is estimated that the major part of these products can be found in those countries, whose economic structure is largely agricultural in character. In this sense tourist consumption, derived from international flow, can offer an assured outlet to a production which is already active within the country, without raising problems connected with export of such products in the international markets. Home grown products could thus be substituted for imported foodstuffs and a significant saving effected.

Such savings would help to increase the tourism multiplier, which in turn would help the host country to derive maximum economic benefits from its tourist industry. This aspect of the question is all the more important in that the multiplier effect maintains its efficacy as long as no importation takes place. It follows that if the national economy is to derive the maximum benefit from the impact, of international and national tourism, there is an elementary obligation to find all those products needed for tourist consumption. The dynamics of agricultural production in recent years appear to confirm the ability of developing countries to produce the major part of their agricultural products required for tourist consumption without resorting to massive imports. The tourist economy of any country, if it is to remain healthy, must rely upon local agricultural production and this elementary condition seems today to be on the way to realization in the majority of developing countries.

Development of infrastructure

Development and improvement of infrastructure is another important benefit. The benefits from infrastructure investments, justified primarily for tourism airports, roads, water supply and other public utilities--may be widely shared by the other sectors of the economy. In addition to development of new infrastructure, the improvements in the existing infrastructure which are undertaken in order to attract tourists is also of crucial importance. These improvements may confer benefits upon the resident population by providing them with amenities which, hitherto, they had not enjoyed. Furthermore, the provision of infrastructure may provide the basis or serve as an encouragement for greater economic diversification. A variety of secondary industries may be promoted which may not serve the needs of tourism. Thus, indirectly, tourist expenditure may be responsible for stimulating other economic activities.

One of the characteristics of underdevelopment is that of deficiencies in the basic infrastructures, which lie at the root of a series of serious problems related to the development of tourism. Construction of primary infrastructures represents the foundation of any future economic growth even though they are not directly productive. The tourist industry illustrates the elementary need for basic infrastructures. It has today the important benefit of being able to profit from the existing infrastructures and thus to make a decisive contribution to the growth of the national economy. The traffic arising from international and national, tourism, moreover, represents a reward for the capital invested and can now contribute to the financial efforts required for maintenance. The satisfactory degree of development achieved in this specific sector now permits major tourist progress, while giving further proof of the complementary character of tourism in relation to other economic sectors. Creation of basic infrastructures for tourist usage will also be of service to the other sectors of the economy like industry and agriculture. The outcome of this is better equilibrium of general economic growth.

Regional development

Another important domestic effect relates to the regional aspects of tourist expenditure. Such expenditure is of special significance in marginal areas, which are relatively isolated, economically underdeveloped, and have unemployment problems. The United Nations Conference on International Travel and Tourism held in Rome in 963 noted that tourism was important not as a source of foreign exchange, but also as a factor in the location of industry and in the development of less developed regions. It further stated that in some cases the development of tourism may be the only means of promoting the economic advancement of less-developed areas lacking in other resources.

The underdeveloped regions of the country can greatly benefit from tourism development. Many of the economically backward regions contain areas of high scenic beauty and of cultural attractions. These areas if developed for use by tourists can bring a lot of prosperity to the local people. Tourism development in these regions may become a significant factor in redressing regional imbalances in employment and income. Tourist expenditure at a particular tourist area greatly helps the development of the areas around it. Many countries both developed as well as developing have realized this aspect of tourism development and are creating and developing tourist facilities in underdeveloped regions with a view to bringing prosperity there.

Khajuraho in India which is now an internationally famous tourist spot is an example of one such region. To illustrate, Khajuraho, a remote and unknown small village about twenty years ago, is now on the world tourist map attracting thousands of tourists both domestic as well as international. Today, Indian Airlines (domestic carrier) flies a jet plane between capital city of New Delhi and Khajuraho and seats are not easy to come by. Thousands of tourists visit the place by air, rail and road transport every month to see the architectural beauty of temples and erotic sculptures whose creators were the Chandela kings, who held sway in North India from the 9th to the 13th centuries. Today 22 glorious temples remain, with perhaps the most classic Indian architecture, wreathed in seemingly living sculpture. Together they represent the finest expression of the art of medieval India.

The area around Khajuraho is now pulsating with life. The place has provided employment to hundreds of local people in hotels and shops. There is already a thriving clay model industry devoted to making replicas of the famous temple sculptures. A number of shops dealing with items of presentation, handlooms and handicrafts have created jobs for many. As a result of this, local people are recipients of additional income which has resulted in their increased prosperity. The subsequent development of areas around Khajuraho will provide additional employment opportunities resulting in general prosperity of the people.

But for the development of tourism in the area, Khajuraho, would have remained a remote unknown village. Many such areas of tourist interest where industrial development is out of question because of distance from markets, lack of raw materials and transportation facilities, scarcity of power, water etc., can greatly benefit if developed properly. These areas if developed for tourism can provide lot of prosperity in the region and can provide jobs for a large number of unskilled workers. It can generate work for the construction industry and a wide range of other supporting industries. What is more, it can be a source of prosperity to the local population.

There is no dearth of areas which could after they are developed for tourism become great assets to the region in particular and to the country as a whole. French government has created a series of new resorts particularly to bring prosperity to the areas which traditionally have been underdeveloped. The Italian government is likewise attempting to develop tourism in Southern Italy in order to help redress the economic imbalances which have long existed between the north and the south. Tourism is to be regarded not as an area of peripheral investment but as one of primary investment whose benefits will help in creating employment opportunities and in the regeneration of backward regions.

Effects on employment

Another major direct economic effect of tourism relates to employment. The problems of unemployment and underemployment are more acute in the developing countries. Why, then, do the developing countries not concentrate their major efforts on a tertiary economic activity such as tourism, which calls for manpower on a large scale? The problems which the industrialized countries face in recruiting manpower for the tourist industry confirm that, in any productive process consisting of services, human labour remains the basic need. None of the technological progress achieved has succeeded in rendering the human factor less indispensable in this sector, and this is true to an absolutely indisputable extent if we draw a comparison with other productive sectors. The high social impact of the tourist industry is well known, for it has repercussions in every other national economic sector through the multiplier effect, which is particularly marked in those services that are complementary to the tourist accommodation industry.

The tourist industry is a highly labour intensive service industry and hence is a valuable source of employment. It employs large number of people and provides a wide range of jobs which extend from the unskilled to the highly specialised. In addition to those involved in management there are a large number of specialist personnel required to work as accountants, housekeepers, waiters, cooks and entertainers, who in turn need large number of semiskilled workers such as porters, chambermaids, kitchen staff, gardeners, etc. In addition, it should be emphasised that tourism is also responsible for creating employment outside the industry in its more narrowly defined sense and in this respect those who supply goods and services to those directly involved in tourism equally are beneficiaries from tourism. Such indirect employment includes, for example, those involved in the furnishing and equipment industries, souvenir industries and farming and food supply.

Construction industry is another very big source of employment. The basic infrastructure--roads, airports, water supply and other public utilities and also construction of hotels and other accommodation units create jobs for thousands of workers both unskilled and skilled. The entire important sector of basic infrastructures represents appreciable source of employment of manpower. In many of the developing countries, where chronic unemployment often exists, the promotion of tourism can be a great encouragement to economic development and, especially, employment. When discussing about employment, it is necessary to consider the seasonal nature of the tourism industry. Where general diversification alternatives are scarce, a combination of heavy dependence on tourism and highly marked seasonality calls for measures to develop off-season traffic.

Tourism and economic value of cultural resources

It may appear strange to discuss cultural tourism in this era of mass tourism. As an example of this conception of tourism a statement by J. Fourastie may be quoted here: "It is necessary for us to learn to look, to behold, to meditate, to question--actions virtually unknown if we are to judge by the bands of tourists who are content with a brief glance which will allow them to affix the mention 'seen' to the greatest number of countries or monuments. We can then hear them say 11 have done Italy, Greece, Mexico'--as if it were sufficient to pass through a place to know it. A man who has seen ten Cathedrals once has not seen a single one, a man who has seen the same Cathedral fen times may perhaps have seen something".

Nevertheless, the first appearance of tourism in the world had a cultural motivation, and tourism has always stood as a unique vehicle for the cultural propagation that is necessary to a deeper understanding of peoples. Tourism, with its basic element of movement, stands for the possibility of communication between differing civilizations and it has served in this sense since its first emergence. Tourism has always been an essential medium for broadening the limits of human know ledge. From the very early times, a mainspring of the urge to travel has been that based on the cultural interest. Even today we can witness large masses of people travelling to foreign countries to become acquainted with the usages and customs, to visit the museums and to admire works of art. As Medlik says: "When the tourist comes in contact with the place he visits and its population, a social exchange takes place. His social background affects the social structure and mode of life of his destination; he is in turn affected by it and sometimes carries back home with him new habits and ways of life". Every type of civilization, from the most sophisticated and advanced to the most primitive, is a source of attraction and curiosity for mankind.

Tourism remains basically a cultural phenomenon. One way of hastening the beneficial effects resulting from tourism is to bring the cultural heritage into the economic circuit, thus justifying the investments made at the cost of the national community for its preservation. Taking a strictly economic view of the cultural heritage of a nation may not be altogether justified, considering that the preservation of its culture is one of the basic responsibilities of any community. But considering the financial obstacles especially for the developing countries, this may appear to be a rational approach. Hence mass tourism can contribute unique benefits to the exploiting of the cultural heritage of a nation and can serve indirectly to improve the individual cultural level of both nationals and foreigners, while at the same time developing into national wealth. The circle thus closes: cultural and tourist economy, instead of standing in opposition, derive reciprocal advantage from one another.

An Italian illustrated review, the Milan *'Tempo'*, sometime back published a full-page advertising display featuring a middle-aged lady of unmistakably foreign origin, wearing a flowered hat, sunglasses and gloves and laden with an assortment of parcels. The caption in the advertising display reads: "A foreign tourist stands admiringly before a work of art. She came to Italy for this purpose. She bought six pairs of shoes in Milan, nine tablecloths in Florence and seven dresses in Rome. Our artistic heritage is an inexhaustible source of culture and wealth. Let us protect it!" There is an affirmation in the above publicity slogan as to how cultural resources are brought into the economic circuit of the country.

Cultural resources have another specific characteristic which can act as a positive element in the developing countries. Those developing countries that possess an ancient civilization or an original culture can benefit greatly from tourism as many people would like to experience the exotic. Thee will be a great urge on the part of the tourist to visit and become acquainted with the ancient civilization. The greater part, if not the totality, of the developing countries possesses clearly determined and original characteristics capable of attracting flows of tourists from industrialized countries who are in quest of novel human knowledge. The main justification for cultural tourism is in fact not solely the cultural heritage alone. It also means the prospect of contact with other civilizations, their original and varied customs and tradition with their distinct characteristics. The entire process creates a powerful lever on motivation towards travel. A factor favourable to the developing countries is the unequalled and characteristic novelty of the different civilizations, ancient or recent, so revealed, which can only add a further and decisive motivation for undertaking the journey.

A two-way exchange is thus achieved between the industrialized and the developing countries. This two-way exchange is expressed in the following terms by Boyer: "We can say that the tourist process provides or should provide for exchanges between economic values (from the countries which send out tourists) and cultural values (from the countries that receive tourists)". It may be added that Boyer is clearly referring to the industrialized countries as generators of tourists, and to the developing countries as receivers of tourists. The characteristic benefit resulting from cultural tourism for the national economies and the balance of payments of the developing countries are quite significant.

Tourism and international understanding

Improving international understanding is another major area where tourism can play and has played a major role. Tourism can be a vehicle for international understanding by way of bringing diverse people face to face. It has been cited as a major contributor to international goodwill and as a prime means of developing social and cultural understanding among all peoples of the world. The interaction of a large number of people with the local population of the country visited results in making friends and goes among way in increasing friendships. Tourism can greatly enrich and promote friendship and goodwill. People belonging to different countries, practising different life-styles and speaking different languages come together to make friends. There is a mingling of cultures which has positive, effects. Tourism helps to break down prejudices, barriers and suspicions that exist between nations. The very best way of getting to know another country is to go there, and when vast numbers travel, the narrow, rigid boundaries that keep people in compartments naturally tend to shrink and a positive move towards better international understanding begins to operate.

Tourism thus is not only an economic activity of importance inasmuch as it earns a country the foreign exchange. It is an important medium of social and cultural development and also of promoting lasting goodwill and friendship among the nations of the world. It also helps in the regional development of the country and acts as a means of social education and better understanding among the peoples in different regions of the country. In the long run the, most important contribution of tourism is developing understanding among varied cultures and life-styles.

The world Tourism conference which was held at Manila, Philippines in October, 1980 considered the nature of tourism phenomenon in all its aspects and the role tourism is bound to play in a dynamic and vastly changing world. Convened by the World Tourism

Organisation the conference also considered the responsibility of various states for the development and enhancement as more than a purely economic activity of nations and peoples. The significance of tourism to developing countries came up for detailed discussion during the conference. The participants in the World Tourism Conference attached particular importance to its effects on the developing countries. The Conference from the beginning pronounced, itself on this subject. It stated its conviction "that the world tourism can contribute to the establishment of a new international economic order that will help to eliminate the widening economic gap between developed and developing countries and ensure the steady acceleration of economic and social development and progress, in particular of the developing countries."

Manila Declaration on World Tourism considered almost all the aspects of the tourism phenomenon. Besides the economic aspects, social, cultural, spiritual aspects also were considered. The conference was also convinced that world tourism can be a vital force for world peace and can provide the moral and intellectual basis for international understanding and interdependence.

The declaration states:

(1) Tourism is considered an activity essential to the life of nations because of its direct effects on the social, cultural, educational and economic sectors of national societies and their international relations. Its development is linked to the social and economic development of nations and can only be possible if man has access to creative rest and holidays and enjoys the freedom to travel, within the framework of free time and leisure whose profoundly human character it underlines. Its very existence and

development depend entirely on the existence of a state of lasting peace, to which tourism itself is required to contribute.

(2) On the threshold of the Twenty-first century and in view of the problems facing mankind, it seems timely and necessary to analyse the phenomenon of tourism, in relation fundamentally to the dimensions it has assumed since the granting to workers of the right to annual paid holidays moved tourism from a restricted elitist activity to a wider activity integrated into social and economic life.

(3) As a result of people's aspirations to tourism, the initiatives taken by States regarding legislation and institutions, the permanent activities of voluntary bodies representing the various strata of the population and the technical contribution made by specialized professionals, modern tourism has come to play an important role within the range of human activities. States have recognized this fact and the great majority of them have entrusted the World Tourism organization with the task of ensuring the harmonious and sustained development of tourism, in cooperation, in appropriate cases, with the Specialized Agencies of the United Nations and the other international organizations concerned.

(4) The right to use of leisure, and in particular the right to access to holidays and to freedom of travel and tourism, a natural consequence of the right to work, is recognized as an aspect of the fulfilment of the human needs by the Universal Declaration of Human Rights as well as by the legislation of many States. It entails for society the duty of providing for its citizens the best practical, effective and nondiscriminatory access to this type of activity. Such an effort must be in harmony with the

priorities, institutions and traditions of each individual country.

(5) There are many constraints on the development of tourism, nation and groups of nations should determine and study those constraints, and adopt measures aimed at attenuating their negative influence.

(6) The share tourism represents in national economies and in international trade makes it a significant factor in world development. Its consistent major role in national economic activity, in international transactions and in securing balance of payments equilibrium makes it one of the main activities of the world economy.

(7) Within each country, domestic tourism contributes to an improved balance of the national economy through a redistribution of the national income. Domestic tourism also hightens the awareness of common interest and contributes to the development of activities favourable to the general economy of the country. Thus, the development of tourism from abroad should be accompanied by a similar effort to expand domestic tourism,

(8) The economic returns of tourism, however real and significant they may be, do not and cannot constitute the only criterion for the decision by States to encourage this activity. The right to holidays, the opportunity for the citizen to get to know his own environment, a deeper awareness of his national identity and of the solidarity that links him to his compatriots and the sense of belonging to a culture and to a people are all major reasons for stimulating the individual's participation in domestic and international tourism through access to holidays and travel.

(9) The importance that millions of our contemporaries attach to tourism in the use of their free time and in their concept of the quality of life makes it a need that governments should take into account and support.

(10) Social tourism is an objective which society must pursue in the interest of those citizens who are least privileged in the exercise of their rights to rest.

(11) Through its effects on the physical and mental health of individuals practising) it, tourism is a factor that favours social stability, improves the working capacity of communities and promotes individual as well as collective well-being.

(12) Through the wide range of services needed to satisfy its requirements, tourism creates new activities of considerable importance which are a source of new employment. In this respect, tourism constitutes a positive element for social development in all the countries where it is practised irrespective of their level of development. .

(13) With respect to international relations and the search for peace, based on justice and respect of individual and national aspirations, tourism stands out as a positive and ever-present factor in promoting mutual knowledge and understanding and as a basis for reaching a greater level of respect and confidence among all the peoples of the world '

(14) Modern tourism results from the adoption of a social policy which led to the workers gaining annual paid holidays and represents the recognition of a fundamental right of the human being to rest and leisure. It has become a factor contributing to social stability, mutual understanding among individuals and peoples and individual betterment. In addition

to its well-known economic aspects, it has acquired a cultural and moral dimension which must be fostered and protected against the harmful distortions which can be brought about by economic factors. Public authorities and the travel trade should accordingly participate in development of tourism by formulating guidelines aimed at encouraging appropriate investments.

(15) Youth tourism requires the most active attention since young people have less adequate income than others for travelling or taking holidays. A positive policy should provide youth with the utmost encouragement and facilities. The same attention should be provided for the elderly and handicapped.

(16) In the universal efforts to establish a new international economic order, tourism can under appropriate conditions, play a positive role in furthering equilibrium, cooperation, mutual understanding and solidarity among all countries.

(17) Nations should promote improved conditions of employment for workers engaged in tourism and confirm and protect their right to establish professional trade unions and collective bargaining.

(18) Tourism resources available in various countries consist at the same time of space, facilities and values. These are resources whose use cannot be left uncontrolled without running the risk of their deterioration, or even their destruction. The satisfaction of tourism requirements must not be prejudicial to the social and economic interests of the population in tourist areas, to the environment or, above all to natural resources, which are the fundamental attraction of tourism, and historical and cultural sites. All tourism resources are part of the heritage of mankind. National communities and the

entire international community must take the necessary steps to ensure their preservation. The conservation of historical, cultural and religious sites represents at all times, and notably in time of conflict, one of the fundamental responsibilities of states.

(19) International cooperation in the field of tourism is an endeavour in which the characteristics of peoples and basic interests of individual states must be respected. In this field, the central and decisive role of the World Tourism Organization as a concept-utilizing and harmonizing body is obvious.

(20) Bilateral and multilateral technical and financial cooperation cannot be looked upon as an act of assistance since it constitutes the pooling of the means necessary for the utilization of resources for the benefit of all parties.

(21) In the practice of tourism, spiritual elements must take precedence over technical and material elements. The spiritual elements are essentially as follows:

(a) the total fulfilment of the human being;

(b) a constantly increasing contribution to education;

(e) equality of destiny of nations;

(d) the liberation of man in a spirit of respect for his identity and dignity;

(e) the affirmation of the originality of cultures and respect for the moral heritage of peoples.

(22) Preparation for tourism should be integrated with the training of the citizen for his civic responsibilities. In this respect, governments should mobilize the means of education and information at their disposal

and should facilitate the work of individuals and bodies involved in this endeavour. Preparation for tourism, for holidays and for travel could usefully form part of the process of youth education and training. For these reasons, the integration of tourism into youth education constitutes a basic element favourable to the permanent strengthening of peace.

(23) Any long-term analysis of mankind's social, cultural and economic development should take due account of national and international tourist and recreational activities. These activities now form an integral part of the life of modem national and international societies. Bearing in mind the acknowledged values of tourism which are inseparable from it, the authorities will have to give more increased attention to the development of national and international tourist and recreational activity, based on an ever-wider participation of peoples in holidays and travel as well as the movement of persons for numerous other purposes, with a view to ensuring the orderly growth of tourism in a manner consistent with the other basic needs of society.

(24) The States and other participants in the Conference, together with the World Tourism Organisation, are strongly urged to take into account the guidelines, viewpoints and recommendations emanating from the Conference so that they can contribute, on the basis of their experience and in the context of their day-to-day activities, to the practical implementation of the objectives set with a view a to broadening the process of development of world tourism and breathing new life into it.

(25) The Conference urges the World Tourism Organization to take all necessary measures, through its own inter machinery and, where appropriate, in

cooperation with other international, inter-government and nongovernmental bodies, so as to permit the global implementation of the principles, concepts and guidelines contained in this final document.

Tourism promotion is one of the important elements of the marketing mix as well as an important tool for marketing. As applied to the tourism industry, the most important function of marketing is to bring about an awareness of the product in the minds of existing as well as prospective consumers in the overall market areas. This awareness about a particular product or a service is to be brought about through a medium and the medium in this case is the 'message'. Through an appropriate message the detailed information about the product is passed on to the consumers.

The message about a product, however, is to reach a consumer. It is to be communicated. There are several channels through which the message is to be communicated. These include both print as well as electronic media, direct mail and persuasion, sales support and public relations.

All the above activity form a part of overall tourism promotion. The term promotion is interpreted and defined in several ways. Basically, the purpose of promotion is to inform, to persuade, to encourage or more specifically to influence the potential customers or trade intermediaries like travel agents, tour operators, reservation services, hotel and charter brokers, through communication channels to think and act in a certain manner.

Systematic communication both with the actual and potential customers as well as with trade intermediaries is very essential with a view to bridging the gap between the producer of goods and services on the one hand and the customer on the other. This is necessary as like in any other industry, successful marketing in tourism cannot rely only on a product of the right kind, or a market related pricing policy or reliable and effective distribution network alone.

The basic function of all tourism promotional activities is to have an effective and meaningful communication with the consumer and the trade intermediaries. How is this awareness to be brought about in the minds of consumers and intermediaries in the market areas? This is possible through certain identifiable methods which are being practised by all the marketing organisations. The awareness is brought about through certain methods/marketing tools. These are as follows:

A. Advertising

B. Sales support activities

C. Public Relations

All the above tools are, however, complementary to each other. It is the proper and judicious blend of these which is essential for the successful promotion of a programme or a product.

Advertising

Advertising is a non-personal communication of a sales message to actual or potential purchasers of a product by a person or an organisation selling a product or a service. The sales message is delivered through a paid medium for the purpose of influencing the buying behaviour of those purchasers. The term may be defined as "any activity designed to spread information with a view to promoting the sales of marketable goods and services." As such, it operates in two ways: firstly, by spreading information among consumers, about the possibilities of consumption, and secondly, by seeking to influence their judgement in favour of the particular goods which are the subject of the advertisement. Use of certain paid media space is, however, a prerequisite.

Advertisement can, therefore, also be defined as "a paid public message designed to describe or praise a product." Unless a communication has as its purpose a sale of a product or service, it is not properly considered to be advertising. For example, the publication of a message in a newspaper by a philanthropic organisation soliciting funds is not an advertising activity. It is only a public announcement as there is, no sale of a product involved.

Origin of advertising

The history of advertising is quite *ancient and* interesting. The original advertisements, perhaps, were announcements written on public walls several thousands of years before the birth of Christ, offering various commodities for sale. As economic forces expanded with the rapid growth of population and the discovery of new worlds, so did the advertising activity prosper. Since the effect of advertising is directly proportionate to the strength of the channel of *communication or* medium carrying the message to prospective purchasers, it was not until the late seventeenth century that the subject took on any great importance. Printing process from movable type had been in existence, for about 200 years, and primitive 'newspapers' were beginning to flourish.

As the various media were being developed particularly newspapers and magazines, merchants were able to offer their products to larger group of consumers, and expenditures for advertising increased correspondingly. Thereafter, the advances made in the sphere of photography, photoengraving, and printing served to bring advertising into focus as a major economic force. Finally, the spurt in mass media magazines and newspapers with circulation in several millions, radio broadcasting facilities capable of influencing millions of people simultaneously have raised the business of advertising to a major importance in the world's economy. Added to all this the introduction of television gave a real boost to advertising in recent times.

Setting objectives

Setting objectives of advertising by an organisation is very important. An advertising objective is a clear and concise description of exactly what the advertising programme is intended to accomplish in a given period of time. Very often the management is not sure exactly why it is spending money and time on advertising without realising what it expects to achieve from this in return.

Advertising is an investment and like all investments it should produce measurable results. Measuring results vis-a-vis inputs put in terms of investment is, therefore, very important and a crucial aspect which each *organisation needs* take care of. The first and the foremost reason for setting advertising objectives is, therefore, to measure the return on one's advertising investment.

The second reason is that with the availability of so many alternative methods for marketing products available and with both consumers and customers becoming more and more value-conscious every day, organisations must seek the most efficient way of marketing the goods and services if they are to remain competitive. There is another important reason for setting objectives. An advertising campaign is the product of the combined work of an entire team of specialists. The team consists not only of top management marketing, advertising and product managers, but also of agency copywriters, media personnel, art directors, TV producers, etc. It is, therefore, important that all these people are concentrating on a single product and putting their concerted efforts in the same direction. Without written and concise objectives all this would be difficult to achieve. Objectives, therefore, serve the purpose of coordinating, and integrating marketing and advertising efforts.

Professor Robert Buzzell of the Harvard Business School, in a written submission to the Federal Trade Commission during hearings on modem advertising practices in July 1971, gives the following example of possible advertising objectives for a manufacturer's consumer product advertising:

To increase sales directly by:

(i) encouraging potential purchasers to visit dealers or distributors;

(ii) announcing special sales, contests or other promotions;

(iii) securing new dealers or distributors,

(iv) inducing professional persons e.g. to recommend a product;

(v) distributing coupons to be redeemed on purchases;

To create awareness and interest in the company's product by:

(i) informing potential buyers about product features;

(ii) announcing the availability of new products;

(iii) demonstrating the benefits of a produces use;

(iv) comparing a product with competing product;

(v) showing how a product should be used;

(vi) informing potential buyers about the company's technical skills, production facilities, technical services, etc;

(vii) informing purchasers about where products can be obtained;

(viii) announcing changes in prices, packages, labels, etc.;

(x) publicising a new brand name or symbol.

The above advertising objectives for manufacturer's consumer product advertising can be applied for the tourism product advertising to achieve best possible results. The broad objectives in tourism advertising include making the tourist product as widely known as possible and to make it as attractive as possible for the prospective consumers.

Advantages

There are several inherent advantages in this method. The biggest advantage is its *wide coverage.* Advertising is especially appropriate for communication with a large number of perspective purchasers of a commodity or a service. A uniform sales message is directed towards all prospective purchasers. An advertisement can be placed before a large number of prospective customers as compared with the efforts of a salesman. *Frequency* is another advantage. It can make its appeal frequently, whereas the calls of salesmen are usually not so frequent. Another advantage is its accessibility. It may reach prospects whom salesmen would find difficult to interview, owing to lack of interest, or inaccessibility to salesmen. Advertisement may reach such prospects through many types of media and under a variety of circumstances, and may thus attract their attention and arouse their interest. Lower cost is another major advantage. Large numbers can be reached economically, Le, at a lower cost per contact than in any other technique available.

Advertising may be used to do a variety of selling tasks. A great deal of advertising attempts to win acceptance for the product. Such advertising may produce few specific demands for the advertised brands, yet when retailers display or show advertised goods they sell more readily than non-advertised ones. Therefore, retailers often hesitate to handle non-advertised goods unless they are obtainable at low prices. Advertising thus directly stimulates sales to retailers. Advertising may at times be used to make the complete sale. Some direct mail and periodical advertising attempts to make sales by requesting readers to forward orders accompanied by the necessary payment. When the number of potential buyers is small and when they are widely scattered it could be extremely costly to reach them through salesmen. Advertising then becomes the most economic means of doing the entire sales job.

Planning the advertising

While planning the advertising, the agency must give careful consideration to the actual make-up of the advertisement. The headline copy, illustrations, colour scheme, size, layout, and method of printing or reproducing the advertisement must be planned very carefully, This is necessary in order to gain attention of the customer, maintain his interest in the message, question of periodicity of advertisement. How frequently to advertise? For instance, is it better to use a full-page advertisement once a month or a quarter-page weekly? A frequently presented thought is likely to force itself into our consciousness. People are inclined to believe statements they hear or see repeatedly and hence the logic of frequent repetition of advertisements. In starting a special campaign the advertisements should not be spaced regularly. Early in the campaign they should be used close together, while later on they can be issued at much longer intervals. This is desirable because consumers forget rapidly at first and much more slowly later on. After the facts are retained by the prospects, the advertisements can be presented at much longer intervals.

Media selection

The advertiser should give careful attention in planning to the selection of the medium or media especially adopted to his needs. The selection will depend upon the factors like the area to be covered, the type of audience to be reached, the appeals to be made and upon the services and facilities of the particular medium in relation to costs. The important factors which, influence the media selection are: (i) media habits of the target audience, 00 product characteristics: for example, TV may be the appropriate media for those products which may require a demonstration of their operation for effective impact on the target audience; and (iii) cost of the media.

Message selection

The massage selected for use in the advertisement should be such that it retains the interest in the minds of the customers about the product. The customer must maintain his interest in the message, and secure the action desired by the seller of the product. The objective is to present the advertiser's message in such a way that the illustration may lead the reader to favourable considerations of the advertisement, The important characteristics of an effective message are:

(i) *Information: it* should be adequate for a decision,

(ii) *Interest: it* should be able to catch the attention of the largest audience.

(iii) *Authenticity: it* should avoid exaggerated claims,

(iv) *Persuasion:* it should be capable of creating a favourable conviction in the target audience, and

(v) Memory value: it should have something in it which can help the target audience to remember it.

Cost

agency must relate the estimated cost of the objectives planned and the contribution expected from advertising. Can the advertiser carry on a campaign large enough to make it effective? Are the funds available or will they become available through the sale of the product. How much does the agency spend for the advertising? The various methods commonly used are:

(i) *Affordable method: here,* the advertising budget is set on the basis of what the agency can afford;

(ii) *Percentage of sales method:* in this case, the agency sets the advertising budget on the basis of specific percentage of sales,

(iii) *Competitive parity method:* here the company sets its budget to match those of its major competitors;

(iv) *Objective and task method:* in this the advertising budget represents the outlay required to perform the various tasks which are necessary to achieve the properly defined advertising objectives of the company. This method is considered the most rational.

Determining advertising effectiveness

In today's world, advertisement through any media has become extremely expensive. In view of this it becomes very important for the agency to ensure that the money spent on it does bring returns by way of increased sales. This could be done by way of evaluating or testing the effectiveness of advertising. Testing methods may be used to evaluate the results of an advertising campaign. By evaluating and analysing the effectiveness of advertisements that have been used, future advertisements may be improved. In addition, tests may be applied before advertisement has been run. Pretesting of an advertisement prevents expenditure that would not be profitable and leads to expenditures that give the best results. In determining advertising effectiveness the commonly used methods are given below:

(i) *Inquiries:* Answer back coupons, with some inducement, are incorporated in many advertisements, The amount of response is an indication of the effectiveness of the concerned advertisement.

(ii) *Recall tests:* Here the respondents are shown the magazine cover or any other media vehicle in which the concerned advertisement had appeared. They are then asked to tell which advertisements in that publication they remember.

(iii) *Recognition tests*: Here the respondents are shown the advertisement and asked if they have read them.

(iv) *Sales tests*: Here, the actual sales results before and after the concerned advertising are examined. The sales results in the selected 'test markets' are also compared to those in some chosen 'control markets', i.e., the markets where the concerned advertising is not done. This is done to eliminate certain factors, other than advertising, which may also have influenced the sales.

Advertising the powerful instrument of modern marketing has only recently come to be used extensively for promotion of tourism. This is a far cry from the era when colourful folders and posters were the only apparent form of travel promotion. In the field of tourism advertising is mainly used to create initial awareness and interest in the tourist service or destination to be promoted and motivates potential tourists to decide to make further equities about costs, bookings, facilities, etc. It implies indirect communication with selected target groups the potential tourists through paid messages designed to praise a particular destination or an area. For a country which is trying to attract tourists, there can be two principal forms of advertising. (i) consumer advertising, and (ii) trade advertising. To reach a wide a number of consumers, such media as newspaper advertisements, radio spots, TV prime time advertising are used. However, this form of advertisement is very expensive. For a developing nation it is extremely difficult to afford such a type of advertisement because of financial constraints. Trade advertising on the other hand which is an indirect form of advertising is a very economic method.

The trend today is towards group travel. A tourist for various reasons chooses to travel as a member of a group, as opposed to travelling individually. The result, therefore, has been that a number of very large tour operators have established their offices in such market areas. While the tour operator puts together inclusive tour packages, the tourist merely pays one package price for all services and is assured of a holiday. Such packages are then sold in retail by numerous smaller travel agents located in various market areas and the result is that a group is formed. For a country which is trying to market its product, the area towards which these efforts are aimed is thus narrowed down to the important tour operators/wholesalers The media used to achieve this is large scale advertising in travel trade journals and newspapers of international repute having travel sections.

Advertising plays a crucial role in marketing a tourist product. If the tight combination of conditions is present the effect of advertising would be to increase the demand for the particular country's tourist product. Among the factors favourable to the successful use of advertising are the rising trend of demand in the particular product and an opportunity to stimulate selective demand, i.e., preference for the particular product. This is most likely where there is a possibility of product differentials, and where consumer satisfaction depends largely on hidden qualities that cannot easily be judged at the time of purchase, or where strong emotional buying motive exists as in the case of tourism.

Steps in planning an advertising campaign

There are several stages through which any advertising campaign must evolve. It may be explained here that term product in the larger sense includes not only products such as soaps and cigarettes but also service 'products' such as tourism, insurance, etc. The following are the various stages:

Defining the product

Before one can develop any communication of advertising for a product it is essential to know what is that the product offers to consumers. This is very important. When you advertise a soap you are not advertising a cake of compound of alkali and oil in an attractive printed pack but you may be advertising beauty or deodorant protection or youthfulness and so on.

To assess, therefore, what the product means to the prospective users we have to first ascertain the benefits that the users will derive from the product. Here are a few examples of this kind of benefit derivation:

Car tyre can offer confidence;
security or safety;
Household cleaning can offer convenience, pride or hygenic conditions;
Cosmetics can offer romance,
self confidence or glamour;
Cigarettes can offer
social status, confidence;
Travel can offer rest, relaxation glamour,
confidence or status.

From these examples one can see that in most cases the user benefit is not always apparent as a product feature. But it must be remembered that people buy things for the benefits they derive when using them. We must look at the product through the mind and eyes of the user. To do this it is sometimes necessary to conduct research amongst users or prospective users to find out what it is that they get from particular products. One can at the same time assess their knowledge, attitude, and usage of competitive or substitute products so that the strengths and weaknesses of one's product are known.

This study of consumer assessment is important as in any system of communication the idea existing in the mind of the receiver will effect the interpretation of the message being received. In some cases it may prevent the message from either being noticed or perceived, let alone being received or understood.

Once we have arrived at this product benefit definition we must then study this in relation to other factors.

First, the relative importance to the consumer of the several product benefits the more important the benefit the greater its motivating values. Second, the relative position of one's own brand and substitute brands in regard to these product benefits to create a unique and memorable message, the main ideas or benefits should be as distinctive and different from others as possible.

Let us now assume that we have studied our product and its users and potential users attitude towards the product and have arrived at a definition of product benefits which we feel are most important. We have by this stage got our proposition. We now proceed to the next stage in our planning.

Defining the market segments

We have a product, we know what users expect or want from it Now we must assess how many users we have and where they are located. Most of this information will have been collected through various sources and supplied by the organisation marketing the product. The kind of information that should be available will relate to the following:

(a) *Consumer information*

(i) Type of consumer-number, sex, age, socioeconomic profile;

(ii) Location of the consumer—whether they will be found in cities, small towns or rural areas or in all areas and in what proportion in each;

(iii) Geographic distribution—whether there are any regional variations in the market spread and if so, why;

(v) Shopping habits—the amount or size of individual purchases, the frequency or number of times a product is bought during a month or a year, whether bought on regular planned basis or through an impulse decision at point of sale;

(v) Decision making—often the person who actually buys the product does not always make the decision and buy or select the particular brand. It, therefore, becomes important to find out who it is who makes the decision and also the extent of the actual buyer's role in changing or influencing this decision. The reason for finding this out is to get an idea as to whom the advertising message should be directed. The person who decides is very important and in the case of joint decisions it may well be necessary to direct the advertising to two or more decision-makers.

(b) *Distribution Information:* Types of outlets, number of such outlets and the importance of each type; the location of these outlets in different cities, towns and rural markets, the dealer's part in the selling activity.

(c) *Sales Information:* The trends over the years and any significant shifts that may have occurred in different geographic areas and the reasons for these changes is a very important information. Seasonal variations that may be related to weather, festivals and other local and national reasons are also very important. In giving us all this information the manufacturer will not merely be giving us information about his product but also of competitive and substitute product against which his product will compete.

This information will provide us with a knowledge of the dimension of the market so that we will be in a position to assess which particular markets are of greater importance. This will also assist in creating the media plan to reach each market and also in creating relevant messages for each. In terms of media selection, the statistical information that will be supplied will enable to plan a campaign using media which will provide cover, reach and frequency related to the market definition.

(d) *Attitude segmentation:* This relates to segmenting the market by user motivation. For example, it has been shown that certain type of people use certain products in larger quantities and more regularly than others. In the same way some people travel more often than others. These groups are termed the heavy user group. And, in most cases it is not usual socioeconomic categorisation that distinguishes them. This may be termed as attitude segmentation or separation. The problem in such segmenting or separating into two groups is that unlike socioeconomic segmentation it is difficult to physically isolate the group. This can, however, be achieved through segmenting as it were the advertising message. It is important to note, however, that this sort of segmentation should not be overdone. Social appeals or segmented campaigns should only be developed if it is found that there are large enough groups of consumers who have attitude which would respond to such appeals. Often, however, it is not only the advertising that is segmented but the product itself is separately produced for each of the segments.

At this stage we will have progressed from product definition to a knowledge of the market, its size, location and, different segmentation patterns.

Interpreting the marketing objectives

What we have been discussing until now is information of the environment in which the advertising campaign will have to work. As we have discussed earlier, since advertising is only the communication aspect of the total marketing function we have to take into account the marketing plans of the manufacturer, both in the long-term and short-term, and relate the advertising to these.

The marketing objectives that are given by the manufacturers will detail the plans that the manufacturer has for his product in the coming year and in some cases for a few years ahead. These plans would cover items such as:

(i) The sales targets for the coming years broken down into regional targets, pack size targets, etc. as the case may be.

(ii) The distribution, merchandising and sales promotion activities planned to support the sales increase;

(iii) The role that advertising is expected to play in creating consumers;

(iv) The inhibiting factors which will work to prevent him from achieving his target, competitive products and their advertising, consumer attitudes, etc.

It is important to note that in any marketing operation the product formulation, packaging and pricing, distribution and availability at point of sale are all of vital importance. All that advertising can do is to bring consumer to the point-of-sale. But if the product is not properly made, packaged or priced or is not well merchandised or promoted at the point-of-sale and, therefore, is not visible, then it is quite possible that the sales effect of the advertising will not fructify. This brings out the importance of integrating these various activities.

Once we have got clearly the marketing objectives of the client and their plans in relation to these objectives we can then see what the advertising has to communicate and to whom with a view to provide the maximum relevant support to the agreed marketing plan.

Planning the advertising campaign

We now know what we have to *sell,* to whom we have to sell, where the prospective consumers are located and also how the product will be made available to them. Our object now is to create an advertising campaign Which will reach target audience and motivate them to come to ask for and buy the product.

Let us now go to the concept of the proposition in the narrow funnel. We have not processed all the facts that the manufacturer has given us and we have perhaps had a dialogue with the consumer, through research, to ascertain his knowledge, attitude and usage of the product and its competitors. As a result we have found out the proposition that we feel would be most motivating. We have also found out where the consumer is located, how and when he buys the product. We are now in a position to get down to work on the two aspects which make up an advertising plan: (1) the Creative Strategy and (2) the Media plan.

The creative strategy: Creativity in advertising has to work within the discipline of our 'funnel'. Let us see how this happens. We have at the one end the proposition. We now have to transform the proposition into the idea which is to be communicated. In converting the proposition into the idea we have to use creativity. But this is an important point, you will notice that this is where the funnel narrows. This narrowing of the funnel is significant inasmuch as it is no use being creative without direction and relevance. For bright ideas to be useful there must also be the right ideas. It is this idea that we now have to communicate to our target group. In order to communicate it we have to bring to bear what may be called the skilled craftsmanship of advertising. Media people, production people and creative people will be involved in this area. But the most vital creative work is what is done in the narrow section of the funnel in creating an idea from the proposition.

In terms of this craft aspect of the agency's activities we will have to channelise the idea into various material that will be required for the advertising campaign. This can range from press advertisements to film commercials, to radio spots, to posters and other point-of-sale material, TV spots, etc. All these items will be creative interpretation of the idea.

The Media Plan: While creativity is perhaps most closely related in an agency with the development of an idea and its interpretation into advertising material, it also plays a role in the development of a media plan. Let us know briefly the way in which an agency constructs a media plan. Media may be defined as vehicles of mass communications which are used to carry advertising messages. Very rarely, except in the case of direct mail advertising& are media developed solely as advertising communication vehicles.

One may broadly classify media into two groups:

(a) Media which are read, seen or heard by the consumer for their 'editorial 'work. These are the newspapers, magazines, the radio programmes, cinema shows, TV programmes which are read or tuned into or watched by the consumer for the editorial' material which they offer. The advertising benefits from the editorial climate of this media.

(b) Media, usually more 'reminder' type of media such as outdoor media, hoarding, transportation signs, posters, kiosks, neon signs, etc., which are noticed in passing only. They obtain consumer exposure due to the fact that the consumer's living habits cause him to pass by them. For instance, commuters in trains and buses, motorists and pedestrians on roads are all exposed to such media.

Point of sale items also fall within the same group. In preparing media plans one has to study the behaviour and exposure of consumer groups with regard to both kinds of media. We have to study both kinds of media. We have to study what media our target consumer looks at for 'editorial' pleasure and when he does so and in what frame of mind. By studying his living habits and his pattern of movement we can assess which of the second group of media he will be exposed to as a general rule. In the more advanced countries it is possible to get detailed statistics on the kind of audience that each medium has. In advanced countries this information is very detailed indeed and permits one to prepare very accurate media plans. In other countries, however, this information is still very scanty and apart from basic circulation information it is rare that one gets much else. However, through experience one gradually builds up a fund of knowledge which enables one to select appropriate media for appropriate markets. Here, apart from the circulation information a study of the quality of the medium in terms of editorial content and style is a very useful method of evaluating reader types.

Media planners have to create what is known as the media mix consisting of various types of mix comprising of various types of media. The selection of these media will depend on:

(a) The target audience that is to be reached: its reading or media exposure habit and its location and movement and shopping habits. This information will permit us in selecting such media as will reach target consumers most effectively;

(b) The product to be promoted and its use by the target audience.

For instance, if one were selling holiday travel to a businessman and one were also selling machinery to the same businessman, it would be perhaps inappropriate to release the former advertising in technical magazines though they might provide adequate coverage of this particular businessman. It would be equally inappropriate to release the latter advertising in a leisure magazine reaching the target audience.

(c) The nature of the message—whether it is a persuasive long copy story, or whether it requires demonstration of the product in action or presentation of the product in colour. All these factors would influence the media planner. Magazine would allow long copy stories, film or TV commercials, project demonstration and poster and colour press advertising would present the product in colour for easy identification.

The term mix suggests that a number of different types of media are frequently required to provide total coverage for any campaign. For example, while one might use press or TV to put across the main informative story of a product it may be necessary to utilise some outdoor and point of sale media in order to effectively remind the consumer of the product on his way to the market or at the time of buying. This interlinking of different media brings into focus the importance of designing creative material with a unified theme so that the reminder media material can bring back to mind the advertising message conveyed earlier by the informative media.

(d) Competitive activity: it is considered good media tactics to design a media plan that will let the advertising dominate competitive activity. Often, when the budget is smaller than that of the competitor the media planner recommends heavier use of fewer media so as to achieve this dominance.

(e) Budget restraint. The media planner has to assess carefully the different buys he can make within the budget and then recommend what he feels will give the best impact value for the particular campaign.

At the end of the exercise the media planner will have worked out a list of media detailing the audience that each media offers,, the number of insertions or spots to be released in each, the number of times the target audience will be reached and a cost-analysis for each media.

In order to relate this plan specifically with the targeted sales, separate analysis can also be prepared indicating the amount of coverage or number of contacts that will be exposed to advertising in each of the sales territories.

We have now a media plan which takes into account the target consumer, the creative requirement, market location and budget limitations. The Creative Strategy and Media Plan are then presented to the client. This is what is called an Advertising Presentation. At this presentation the agency relates their plans to the total marketing effort and indicates how it will fit in.

Implementing the campaign: Once the advertising campaign has been approved in terms of the creative strategy and the media plan, the agency next has to apply different 'crafts' in order to implement the campaign in the manner in which it was planned. 'These range from the preparation of press advertisement material to the production of IN and film commercials, recording of radio spots and production of point 0 sale material, etc. On the other hand *the* media buyer and scheduler has to implement the media in terms of preparing estimates, schedules and release orders for press, cinema, radio and other media. The agency takes on for the advertiser the responsibility of seeing the right time so that the total plan, as envisaged, becomes operative. Once the Campaign has beer released it becomes necessary to assess its impact. This brings us not only to the final stage of activity on a campaign but also brings us to the first stage of the next campaign.

Assessing the Impact and Value of a Campaign: It is not possible always to evaluate the effect of an advertising campaign in terms of sales as too many other factors are involved. This is particularly so in service advertising. Therefore, the result of a campaign cannot only be shown by way of sales. But there must be some way of measuring the value of the campaign. In answer to this question it is felt that the impact of an advertising campaign should be assessed by the extent to which it results in changing the attitude of the selected target consumers, Therefore, having planned, prepared and released our campaign we start after a suitable interval to compile information on its impact value.

This study will provide information on the following:

1. *Awareness:* the extent of shift in the degree of awareness of an agency or product is highly relevant as unless people are aware of something they can neither have an attitude towards it not act in regard to it.
2. *Attitude dimensions* are also important. It is necessary to measure to what extent the right attitudes have been communicated and accepted. We will have to find out at the time of formulating the proposition what these right attitudes should be.
3. *Purchase of* the product is very important as merely having a favourable attitude towards the product is not enough. It must be one that is motivating enough to cause usage. The measure of users that are created due to the shift in attitude *therefore becomes* very important.
4. *Repurchase of* the product. It is said that advertising can result in a first sale but it is for the product itself to perform and earn the second sale. By 'perform' of course one does not only mean preference in visible terms but in satisfaction terms as well in this case, the amount of satisfaction a traveller has derived from a visit, etc. In other words the product must live up to the expectation which the advertising has created.

Pre-testing advertising

Pretesting of advertisements is yet another technique of advertising testing. This attempts to assess the communication value of an advertisement whether press advertisement, or TV or radio spot in advance of the actual release or screening. In this way it is possible to develop advertising material which most effectively conveys the proposition idea. This pretesting technique can also assist in forecasting the change in attitude, etc. which the campaign can achieve. A set of advertisement commercials, etc., are prepared and these are shown to small groups of representative consumers. The effectiveness of the various approaches in conveying the proposition is then measured. This type of testing assists the agency to judge whether the idea created is in fact correctly communicating the motivating proposition to the target consumer. In this way we are back again at the first stage of the next campaign and the cycle begins once again.

Advertising agency

An advertising agency may be explained as an organisation consisting of one or more persons, the function of which is to provide advertising, merchandising, and other services and counsel relating to the sale of a client's goods and services. The compensation for the services is generally derived from commissions rendered by the various media, the facilities of which are purchased by the agency on behalf of the client. The major difference which distinguishes the agency from other service organisations such as publicity and public relations firms arises from the fact that the greater portion of the income of the agency is represented by commissions received not from the customer of the agency, called the 'client, but from newspapers, magazines, television and radio stations and other media from which the agency purchased time and space for the client.

The advertising agency is a service organisation which undertakes the planning and preparation of advertising, The agency service consists of interpreting to the public, or to that part of it which it is desired to reach, the advantages of a product or service. Originally agencies were media owners, service departments and not independent organisations as they are today. In the early days of advertising, agencies acted as representatives of newspapers and sold space in them to advertisers. At first, the agencies bought space in bulk, and made their profit by selling it in smaller units for as much as they could get. Later, agencies started to sell space on a commission basis, and a commission system is still the current basis for agency remuneration, agencies taking their profit from commissions granted by media owners rather than from advertisers.

Later on the agencies started a copywriting service and soon afterwards design and art services were added to their functions. By this time agencies were really working more for the advertisers than for the newspaper proprietors, and before long they became full fledged service organisations giving their clients a complete range of advertising services.

The agencies also became independent, and bought space in whichever newspaper and other advertising media they thought best served their clients interests.

Today the term agency no longer applies in the legal sense, since the agency makes contracts in its own right with its clients on the one hand and with media owners on the other. It remains a party to the advertisement contract, which it would not were it an agency in the legal sense of the word. Agencies are thus liable in law for debts to media, even though they made the booking on their client's behalf.

Selecting an agency

Selection of a suitable advertising agency is a major factor which determines the success or failure of a promotional work of an organisation. The choice of an advertising agency will depend on the size of a promotional budget, the range of services required *and above all the objective assessment of the professional* qualities of the agency.

Most of the national tourist organisations and major tourist enterprises have *appointed their own* advertising agencies. The advertising campaigns of these organisations are run through the *agencies. The national tourist offices usually hire the services of* the specialised advertising agencies in various tourist generating markets to help them in market research, audience information gathering, designing messages and getting advertising schedules in wells-elected media.

Agency procedure

When an organisation appoints an agency, the first task of the agency personnel is to find out about their clients activities and Problems. The agency would spend considerable time making a *thorough* investigation until the advertiser's problems have been properly identified and defined. The size of the appropriation and the period to be covered are also important to the agency. Normally the client will give the agency all *the* information it needs when *he gives his* advertising 'brief. The quality of work produced by the agency to a large extent depends *on the* client's Aft in giving *his* agency all the relevant information it needs in order to prepare advertising proposals on his *behalf.*

Once the agency is confident that it has a correct understanding of the situation, it can start the vital work of preparing an advertising campaign, to help the client achieve his marketing objectives.

Once the problem is clearly defined, the agency staff will start to solve it. Here the accounts executive' plays a very important role. He may start by calling, a meeting of 'Plans Board' on which there will be representatives of all the important agency departments present to consider the theme to be featured in the advertising. The media department will advise on media to be used. The 'Plans Board" discusses the clients overall marketing problem from every angle and finally agrees on a basic solution.

Each major advertising agency has various departments whose area of work are well defined. The following are the major departments of an agency and their scope of work:

(i) *The Research Department*: When the agency staff attempts to define their clients marketing problems *they may* decide that they lack sufficient information to reach a sound judgement and will take the assistance of the Research Department. A good amount of information is readily available in published form. Before any field research is undertaken there is always desk research which involves checking through existing sources of information. As soon as information collected has been checked, there are further meetings of the 'Plans Board' to consider the advertising and marketing campaign. Once this is done, the individual departments set to work to crystalise their ideas and to produce detailed proposals in accordance with the agreed broad plan.

(ii) *The Media Department:* Once the general strategy is agreed, it is now up to the media department to get down to detailed planning with the aim of spending the client funds in such a way that his advertising message Teaches prospective buyers as effectively and economically as possible. The media department then evaluates the media and selects the most suitable one in the light of clients requirements.

(iii) *The Creative Department:* The Creative Department takes i work to a more advance level. Copy is written for press advertisements or printed material and layouts prepare For posters or display material, roughs and dummies a made and storyboards drawn up for TV or cinema commercials.

(iv) *Review of Proposals:* As soon as detailed media and creative proposals are ready, the Plans Board meets again to review the progress of the work. The purpose is to check the proposals point by point to be submitted to the client b ensure that there are no discrepancies in the work of the individual departments.

(v) *Presentation of Proposals:* Once the detailed proposals have been approved by the review board, they are made read for presentation to the client. The media schedule is typed out in its final form as is the advertisement copy. The finished versions of designs are prepared by the creative staff. These are then presented to the client. Creative and media proposals are presented together. Where the presentation is on the major campaign, the agency may call on all those concerned to make a "dry run' beforehand, amounting almost to a rehearsal. Some agencies even put the entire presentation on film or video tape and screen this to the client rather than risk the possibility of error that is always present in the 'live' presentation.

(vi) *Execution of the Proposal:* Before giving an agency a 'go ahead' or a formal approval to proceed, the client checks the proposals to ensure that they are sound and that they dovetail with his company's marketing objectives. Once the agency has the client's agreement, the advertising proposals are put into effect.

Index